THE COMPLETE WORLD ENCYCLOPEDIA OF
APPLES

THE COMPLETE WORLD ENCYCLOPEDIA OF
APPLES

A COMPREHENSIVE IDENTIFICATION GUIDE TO OVER 400 VARIETIES ACCOMPANIED BY 90 SCRUMPTIOUS RECIPES

ANDREW MIKOLAJSKI

With photography by Peter Anderson

HERMES
HOUSE

This edition is published by Hermes House,
an imprint of Anness Publishing Ltd, Blaby Road,
Wigston, Leicestershire LE18 4SE; info@anness.com

www.hermeshouse.com; www.annesspublishing.com

If you like the images in this book and would like to investigate
using them for publishing, promotions or advertising, please visit
our website www.practicalpictures.com for more information.

© Anness Publishing Ltd 2012

Publisher: Joanna Lorenz
Editorial Director: Helen Sudell
Project Editor: Melanie Hibbert
Designer: Nigel Partridge
Production Controller: Wendy Lawson
Illustrator: Maj Jackson-Carter
Photographer: Peter Anderson

A CIP catalogue record for this book is available from the
British Library.

PUBLISHER'S NOTE
Although the advice and information in this book are believed
to be accurate and true at the time of going to press, neither
the authors nor the publisher can accept any legal responsibility
or liability for any errors or omissions that may have been made
nor for any inaccuracies nor for any loss, harm or injury that
comes about from following instructions or advice in this book.

ACKNOWLEDGEMENTS
Th publishers would like to thank the following for their
contribution to this project: Jim Arbury at RHS Garden Wisley,
Surrey, UK, and Brogdale Collections, Kent, England.
Photographers: Peter Anderson, Martin Brigdale, Nicki Dowey,
Jake Eastham, Gus Filgate, Ian Garlick, Amanda Heywood,
David Jordan, Dave King, William Lingwood, Charlie Richards,
Craig Robertson, Simon Smith, Sam Stowell, Debi Treloar and
Jon Whitaker.
Picture credits: Corbis: 12–13, 14tr; Alamy: 15tm;
GAP Photos: 19t, 20tl, 23b, 26tm.

CONTENTS

INTRODUCTION

The apple has long been one of the most popular – if not the most popular – of all fruits and much time and energy have been devoted to its development. Prized for its taste and keeping qualities, the humble apple is now the most widely cultivated tree fruit, both in commerce and in gardens.

No one knows exactly when apples were first discovered and eaten, but they are believed to have originated in Turkey. The fruit would have been taken via ancient trade routes to virtually every part of the huge land mass that comprises Eurasia. In more modern times, trees have been introduced into the Americas, southern Africa and Australasia. Nowadays they are grown throughout temperate parts of the globe and have become of great significance to the economies of many countries as an exportable commodity. Such is the adaptability of the apple, that it is only in tropical, desert and extremely cold regions that trees cannot be relied on to produce good crops.

Due to their ease of cultivation and their tolerance of changeable climates, apples have never been considered a luxury food. Historically, they were an essential element in the diet of many peoples from all strata of society.

A fruit for health and fitness

The apple has often been seen as a symbol of youth, fertility and longevity. It is frequently offered as a love token between men and women who are of marriageable age.

'An apple a day keeps the doctor away' is an old proverb and recent research suggests that there may well be more than a grain of truth in this. The fruit contains natural substances that studies indicate may be able to play a significant part in strengthening bones and lowering cholesterol as well as providing some protection against certain cancers, Alzheimer's disease, asthma and other respiratory diseases. This is aside from their natural vitamin content and the dietary fibre they provide, both essential in a balanced diet. Apples are the ultimate convenience food, small enough to slip into a lunch box (or even your pocket) and providing an ideal snack when you are on the move and hunger strikes.

A versatile fruit

Down the centuries, apples have been bred for improved size and flavour and, very importantly, for storing for use when fresh fruits and vegetables are in short supply. Not only are the fruits

Above: Apple blossom is a captivating sight in the spring garden. This is the crab apple Malus x schiedeckeri 'Hillieri'.

delicious eaten straight from the tree but, unlike many other fruits, they can be transported over long distances or kept for many months without any adverse effects on their flavour.

Besides the types that are grown for eating raw, the vast range of varieties – running into thousands – includes apples for cooking, for juicing and for cider making. In the kitchen, fruits can be used both for sweet and savoury dishes; the tart, acid flavour of some is a perfect complement to many rich or fatty meats, especially pork and game, while others have a flavour as sweet as strawberries or pineapples.

Nowadays, with international trade and improvements in storage, there is not a single day of the year when a tasty apple cannot be enjoyed. Walk into any supermarket and you will have a choice of several varieties. A farm shop or farmers' market, where locally produced foods are sold, may offer an even wider selection.

Left: Hand picking ripe apples can be enjoyed by all the family.

Easy to grow

Hardy and woody as plants, apples are supremely well adapted to growing in domestic gardens. Unlike many fruit trees, they do not necessarily need a lot of room – though a large, mature apple tree can be a magnificent sight. On dwarfing rootstocks or trained on wires in a potager or on an allotment, apple plants take up very little space but can still produce abundant crops. Many have been bred for disease-resistance and need only the minimum of maintenance once established. Some varieties can even be grown in tubs or large containers, so even if you have only a patio or balcony, you can still have fresh fruit within easy reach.

How to use the directory

The directory section is arranged alphabetically. Details of over 400 apples are given, ranging from old cultivars from major apple growing areas, some now rare in cultivation but found in historic orchards and gardens, alongside more modern cultivars that are found in supermarkets and garden centres. The whole fruits are shown, with, in most cases, the cut fruit along-side, and sometimes with an additional photograph of the fruit on the tree.

Each entry comprises a description of the fruit when ripe: its shape, size, and skin colour, followed by the colour and texture of the flesh and an indication of the flavour.

Shapes of older varieties can vary, some being of very uneven appearance. These varieties are generally less widely grown today but are nevertheless of considerable interest. Sizes of fruits are necessarily approximate. While modern varieties have been bred for uniformity, older varieties in particular can carry fruits of very different sizes that can ripen at the same time. Note also that the taste of a fruit is subjective and to some degree depends on where the apple was grown, the soil type, when it was picked and how long it has been stored.

The information panel indicates the type of apple – dessert, for eating raw, or culinary, for cooking – and its origin: the place where and date when it was first grown. Dates of introduction are often of necessity approximations, even for more modern cultivars which may be extensively trialled before they are available in commerce, so may not always accurately reflect the date the variety was bred. Some are known to have been grown in gardens for many years before being grown commercially. Equally, it is only in more recent times that certain eastern European varieties have become more familiar with the growth of international trade through-out continental Europe.

The parentage of the apple, where known, is given. This can often provide hints as to the flavour of the apple and its performance in gardens.

Conjectural details concerning date, place of origin, and parentage appear with question marks (?) before them.

The flowering season provides an indication of when the flowers will be open – important when choosing compatible cultivars for cross-pollination. However, flowering times may vary from year to year as this can depend on the length and severity of the preceding winter.

Where they exist, other names of the variety are also listed. Some varieties go under different names in different countries. Older apples, bred before the naming of plants was strictly regulated, have often been grown under a number of names.

The note indicates special character-istics, such as resistance to disease, rate of growth, length of time the fruits can be stored, or any other detail of interest. Cultivation is assumed to be broadly similar for all varieties, but where a particular apple is known to do well in certain conditions this is indicated.

Home-cooking

Following the directory is a chapter of apple recipes where you will find 95 enticing dishes, each photographed with clear step-by-step instructions. The selection includes appetizers, salads, sides, mains, desserts, cakes, preserves and drinks, and each recipe is accompanied by nutritional notes.

Right: *The quintessential apple recipe – a deep-filled farmhouse apple pie with cream.*

Above: *An apple tree provides a pretty, tranquil spot for rest and contemplation.*

Identifying varieties

This book aims to bring a greater understanding and appreciation of the huge variety of apples, their cultivation and culinary uses.

While the directory is to some extent intended as a diagnostic tool, it may not be possible to identify an unknown apple through referring to it alone, bearing in mind the vast number of cultivars in existence. Reflecting the popularity of the fruit and the growing interest in historic gardens and home-grown produce, many botanic gardens host special apple days in autumn, when it is possible to have fruits identified by experts.

GROWING APPLES

Apples have been cultivated for hundreds of years, but with modern cultivation methods, you don't need large amounts of space in which to grow your own fruit trees.

It is possible to train trees against walls and fences or use them as garden dividers, and there are even dwarf forms of popular fruits that are small enough to grow in containers. Established fruit trees are able to compete with other plants for moisture and nutrients and so can be accommodated all around the garden. Make sure they are planted in a sunny spot and that there is sufficient access to carry out essential maintenance. If you want to grow a lot of fruit, you should consider allocating a separate area of the garden where the fruit trees are easier to manage and protect.

The following pages will guide you through the satisfying process of growing your own apples, from choosing a tree and planting to pruning, nurturing and after-care.

Above left: These pole apples have been grown as vertical cordons, which are perfect for the kitchen garden where space is limited.
Above right: The shiny, bright red fruit of Malus pumila *'Dartmouth'*.
Left: When apple trees are in full blossom they make a stunning display.

WHAT IS AN APPLE?

Apples belong to the genus Malus, *which comprises some 35 species.* Malus *is a member of the Maloideae subfamily of the family Rosaceae – the rosaceous plants – and apples are thus related to such common garden plants as roses (*Rosa*), cotoneasters and rowans (*Sorbus*) as well as other plants grown for their fruits.*

Nowadays, cultivated apples are all grouped as *Malus domestica*, not a true species but also not a chance hybrid as was previously assumed.

Apples have always been the most widely grown fruit in the temperate zone, with pears a somewhat distant second. Apples are also grown in Mediterranean regions and in cooler areas on higher ground in the tropics.

Geographic origin

While there are a number of trees with apple-like fruits found growing in the wild, the ancestors of the apples we enjoy today are believed to derive from *Malus sieversii*, a species that is found in the mountains of Central Asia in southern Kazakhstan, Kyrgyzstan, Tajikistan and Xingjian, China. This has the largest fruit of any wild apple, up to 7cm (2½in) in diameter. DNA taken from a tree growing in the Ili Valley, at the border of northwest China and Kazakhstan, shows some genetic sequences that are common to *Malus domestica*.

M. sylvestris, a European species found in a range from as far south as Spain, Italy and Greece to Scandinavia and parts of northern Russia, has also contributed to the genome of the cultivated apple, but to a lesser extent than has previously been assumed. *Malus baccata* (found in central Japan and central China) may also have played a part in the development of some varieties.

The plant

An apple plant is a deciduous tree or large shrub. The species from which modern varieties have been bred is a tree of average (though variable) size, at most 15m (50ft) in height. Because of extensive interbreeding, it is difficult to state precisely how big any particular variety can grow. Most are kept artificially small through the use of rootstocks and pruning.

Apple plants begin to bear fruit when they are around four or five years old, and trees have been known to remain productive for more than 200 years.

Flowers

Along with other members of the rose family, apples have single, cup-shaped, five-petalled flowers that open flat to up to 5cm (2in) across. They are usually white, some flowers having pink markings. Some species that are grown as ornamentals, often called crab apples, have deep pink flowers.

Leaves

Apple trees have simple leaves that are arranged alternately along the length of the stem. The leaves are bright to dark green in colour, with toothed margins. The undersides of most apple leaves are greyish-silver in colour and slightly downy. Leaves turn various shades of yellow, orange and red before falling from the tree during the autumn.

Above: Skin colours range from deep red through to golden yellow or dark green. The seed chambers are centred around the core.

Fruits and seeds

The fruit of the apple is classified as a pome. Fruits are round or slightly elongated and narrow slightly towards the blossom end, opposite the stalk.

Ripe fruits have skins that are red, yellow or light green. In red-skinned varieties, the red colour develops only as the fruit ripens, overlaying yellow or yellowish-green. In some varieties, the red almost masks the base colour entirely, while on others it appears as attractive striping or light flecking. Even on ripe fruits that appear evenly red, there will be a trace of green at the core, where the stalk meets the fruit. Apple skins can be waxy, with a slight shine, or show dull, rough patches known as russeting.

Above: The flowers of the apple tree are usually white, sometimes flushed with pink.

Above: The topside of an apple leaf is a deep green colour.

Above: The underside of an apple leaf is a green- or silvery-grey.

Growth cycle

In mid-spring, flower buds emerge simultaneously with the leaves. The unopened flower is encased within five green sepals. These split and curve back to reveal five petals.

In their search for nectar and pollen, bees transfer pollen from the anthers (male) of one flower to the stigmas (female) of another. Pollination occurs when pollen forms a pollen tube that grows downwards to the ovary. In the ovule, a male cell fuses with a female (fertilization).

The petals fall and the style wilts. The ovary grows to become a fruit, covering the fertile seeds within it. Seeds comprise an embryo plant inside a hard outer coat. The seeds mature as the ovary expands to form a ripe fruit.

1 *Flower buds appear.*

2 *Sepals split and curl to reveal five petals.*

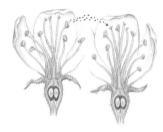

3 *Transfer of pollen from male anthers to female stigmas of another flower.*

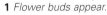

4 *Pollen tube grows downwards to the ovary.*

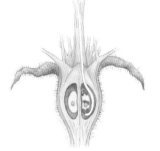

5 *Male cell fuses with a female in the ovule.*

6 *Petals fall, style wilts and ovary grows into a fruit.*

Like other members of Rosaceae, the seeds develop inside a leathery core. Cutting an apple in half crossways reveals a star with five chambers, each containing two seeds. Seeds are dark brown when ripe.

The texture of the flesh is firm, hard when unripe, and mealy in some varieties but usually remaining crisp. It varies in colour from white to pale creamy-yellow. Freshly cut, the exposed flesh rapidly oxidizes, turning yellowish-brown on contact with the air. All parts of the ripe fruit are edible. Other edible pome fruits include pears (*Pyrus communis*) and quince (*Cydonia oblonga*).

Crab apples

A number of *Malus* species are grown mainly as ornamentals. Crab apples make attractive specimens in small gardens, having a generally dainty appearance. They also attract beneficial insects and birds into the garden and can act as pollinators for cultivated apples.

White or pink spring flowers are followed by decorative autumn fruits and, often, good leaf colour. Though the fruit, which is much smaller than cultivated apples, is edible, it usually has to be cooked to make it palatable. Crab apples are popularly used in jellies and jams.

Cross-pollination

When a bee transfers pollen from the stigmas of one flower to those of an open flower on another tree, this is cross-pollination.

Most apples are self-sterile, that is to say that the transfer of pollen from one open flower to another on the same tree will not result in fertilization, and hence fruit. So, for apples to crop successfully, it is necessary to grow two or more trees near to each other that flower at the same time.

The function of fruit

Edible fruit is designed to be attractive to passing animals that eat the fruit, and, in the process, the seed. The indigestible seed is then carried in the animal's gut some distance from the parent plant before being eliminated in its droppings. In favourable conditions, the seed will germinate and grow into a new tree. This ensures that the genetic potential of the parent plant will be spread over an increasingly large area with each succeeding generation.

Depending on their flavour, apples are classed as either dessert (for eating raw) or culinary (for cooking). Culinary apples have a tart flavour that is unpalatable until the flesh is cooked and, usually, sweetened before use. Depending on the variety, culinary apples either retain their shape during cooking, which is good for open tarts, or collapse into a fluffy mass, which is ideal for sauces and purées. Many varieties are multi-purpose and can be eaten raw or used in cooking.

Above: The Egremont Russet is almost covered in yellowish-brown russeting.

APPLES IN HISTORY AND MYTHOLOGY

Mention of apples occurs frequently in many folk tales and early literature. They were prized for their life-giving qualities, supposedly restoring or maintaining youth. This may have something to do with the keeping qualities of the fruits over winter.

Traditionally symbols of plenty, apples have often been used to represent the harvest. In some burial rituals, corpses were interred with a supply of apples, possibly to feed them during the journey to the afterlife.

References to golden apples should not be taken too literally. As texts have been passed down, western translators have frequently used the word 'apple' to stand for almost any fruit, as this would be the one most familiar to their readers. A 'golden apple' may just as likely be a pomegranate or even a citrus such as an orange or lemon.

Classical mythology
Many Greek myths contain references to apples, one of the most famous being the story of Atalanta's race. Though she had many admirers, Atalanta refused to marry. In order to find her a husband, her father persuaded her to marry anybody who could beat her in a foot race. Atalanta agreed, as she could easily outrun all

Below: Greek goddesses Aphrodite, Athena and Hera all lay claim to the golden apple.

her suitors. Hippomenes, also known as Melanion, prayed to Aphrodite, the goddess of love, for help. The goddess gave him three golden apples, with instructions to drop them one at a time to distract Atalanta. Each time she took the lead, he threw an apple in her path, and she paused to pick it up. Thus Hippomenes managed to win the race – and Atalanta's hand.

The fabled Garden of the Hesperides, tended by the goddess Hera, contained a grove of golden apple-bearing trees that bestowed immortality on whoever ate them. One of the labours of Hercules was to steal some of the fruit.

The Judgement of Paris is another famous Greek myth. Three goddesses, Hera, Athena and Aphrodite, all claimed a golden apple labelled 'for the fairest one'. Zeus chose Paris of Troy, the handsomest of men, to arbitrate. Each goddess tried to bribe Paris. Hera offered to make him a king; Athena promised wisdom; Aphrodite said she would give him the most beautiful woman in the world as his wife. Paris chose Aphrodite, and the subsequent

Above: Eating a golden apple from the Garden of the Hesperides gave eternal life.

abduction of Helen of Troy, already married to Menelaus of Sparta, led to the Trojan war.

Norse mythology
In the mythology of the Scandinavian countries, golden apples are also the source of the gods' immortality and perpetual youth. They were cultivated by the goddess Iounn.

In the *Skáldskaparmál*, Iounn was abducted by the giant Pjazi who disguised himself as an eagle. Pjazi had already captured Loki, a trouble-making god, who bargained for his freedom in return for Iounn and her apples. Loki lured Iounn into the forest, telling her he had found some apples that might interest her. Pjazi arrived, again in eagle form, snatched Iounn and took her to his home.

The gods began to grow grey and old at the disappearance of Iounn. They had Loki arrested and threatened him with torture and death. Loki promised to search for Iounn if the goddess Freyja lent him her falcon shape so he could fly north to Pjazi's home. While the giant was out at sea,

Loki turned Iounn into a nut and escaped with her held in his claws. Resuming his eagle form, Pjazi pursued them. Seeing the birds approach, the gods lit a fire. The falcon dropped down but the eagle was unable to stop, caught fire and perished. Thus Iounn was saved.

Apples appear in *Das Rheingold*, the first of the four operas that comprise Richard Wagner's *Ring* cycle, loosely based on Norse sagas. Here, Freya, goddess of fertility, was the custodian of the golden apples that ensured the gods' perpetual youth. She was claimed by the giants Fasolt and Fafner as payment for the building of Valhalla for the god Wotan (or Odin). To redeem Freya, Wotan stole a gold ring from the dwarf Alberich. The ring allowed its wearer to rule the world.

Folklore

Apples appear frequently in folk tales, the most well-known being that of Snow White (*Schneewittchen*), collected by the Brothers Grimm and published in their *Kinder- und Hausmärchen* (Berlin, 1857). Here, the wicked stepmother tempts Snow White with a poisoned apple, a single bite of which is sufficient to cause her apparent death. The piece of apple is only lodged in her throat, however, and she is able to return to life.

Swiss folk hero William Tell had to shoot an apple placed on his son's

Below: Disguised as an eagle, the giant Pjazi abducts the goddess Iounn.

Above: Eve hangs her head in shame after taking a bite of the forbidden fruit.

head as punishment for refusing to bow to country leader Hermann Gessler's hat. Versions of this story appear in several other northern European sagas.

It was believed that if a woman slept with an apple, then offered a bite to the man she liked, he would fall in love with her.

Religion

The 'forbidden fruit' borne by the tree of knowledge of good and evil, while not actually named as an apple in the *Book of Genesis*, has been seen as one throughout the ages.

Apples are sometimes associated with the Virgin Mary, to whom several myths previously surrounding the pagan Venus and Aphrodite were later appropriated. One such is the cult of the Virgin with the Golden Apple at Asenovgrad in Bulgaria, where she is venerated as a patroness of maternity and the family. On the fifth Sunday of Lent, an icon of the Virgin is decorated with a garland of apples, which the priest distributes among women who want to become pregnant. This harks back to a story that a woman once placed an apple as a gift before the icon, begging for a child. The Virgin Mary later appeared to the woman as she slept and gave her a golden apple.

Art and popular culture

Renaissance artists such as Albrecht Dürer commonly depicted Adam and Eve holding apples. This may be as a result of the influence of the golden apples in the story of the Hesperides. There are many famous apple still-lifes by Paul Cézanne, Paul Gauguin and Vincent van Gogh. The Belgian surrealist René Magritte created a famous image of an apple with the caption *Ceci n'est pas une pomme* (This is Not an Apple).

In Chinese art, apples or a still-life including apples represent a wish for peace, and apple blossom is sometimes used as an emblem of female beauty. In 2006 in London, the Chinese artist Gu Dexin created a 'wall' of apples, a slim wire cage containing around 100,000 fruits that were allowed to rot slowly.

References to apples are regularly used in modern culture. New York City is commonly known as the 'Big Apple'. The term was first coined by a journalist in the 1920s, then used more frequently in the 1970s by a New York tourism organization.

Apple Records, with a green apple as its logo, was a record label founded by the Beatles in 1968 as a division of Apple Corps (a pun on 'core'), the name influenced by the famous painting by artist René Magritte.

Perhaps the most well-known logo to date is the apple with a bite taken out of it for Apple Macintosh products.

APPLE BREEDING AND COMMERCE

The cultivation of apples dates back to the time of the Egyptian Pharaohs, when apples were grown along the Nile Delta. By the 7th century BCE, they were known in Greece, and by the first century CE, the ancient Romans had up to 40 varieties, some of which they introduced to the western Empire, including England.

By the first century CE, apples were being grown in every region throughout the Rhine Valley, Germany. The English horticulturist John Parkinson (1567–1650) noted 60 varieties growing in England in 1640. This number had increased to 92 by 1669.

Apple growing in the Americas began in the 16th century, when Spanish invaders took the fruit to Mexico and South America. But when English settlers arrived in North America in the 17th century, they found only native crab apples.

British settler William Blaxton (1595–1675), who arrived in New England, in 1623, is credited with planting the first apple variety on American soil. He developed a nursery in Boston, and bred the first American apple – Blaxton's Yellow Sweeting.

In 1630, newly arrived Puritans took over the orchard. Apple growing spread westward into the Ohio Valley and Great Lakes areas. John Chapman, nicknamed Johnny Appleseed, from Massachusetts, became famous for planting trees throughout Ohio, Indiana and Illinois.

Below: Despite technological advances, picking apples by hand remains the best method.

Johnny Appleseed
Born John Chapman (1774–1845), Johnny Appleseed was an American pioneer nurseryman who introduced apple trees to large parts of Ohio, Indiana and Illinois.

Often depicted in rags, he became famous for his nomadic subsistence lifestyle, often going barefoot and preaching the gospel. In some ways, he was an early environmentalist, as he cared deeply about animals, even insects.

Right: A barefoot Johnny Appleseed cultivates the land before sowing seeds.

Apples were taken to the West Indies in the 18th century. By 1866, 643 different varieties were recorded in Andrew Jackson Downing's *Fruits and Fruit Trees of America*.

Apples have been grown in South Africa since 1652, when the Dutch colonial administrator Jan van Riebeeck, established the first plantings.

Orchards were established in Australia during the 1780s after apples were introduced by British Admiral Arthur Philip (1738–1814). Australia is home to the popular Granny Smith.

Diploids and triploids
Cultivated varieties of apples fall into two groups according to their chromosome count. The majority of apple varieties, along with all other living things that reproduce sexually, are diploids, with 34 chromosomes (17 from each parent). Triploids have 51 chromosomes, 34 supplied by the female and 17 by the male.

Most commercially grown apples are diploids, but there are also a large number of triploid varieties, including the well-known Jonagold and Bramley. The earliest known triploid apple is Gravenstein, grown as early as the 17th century in Denmark.

Triploids are popular because of the the large fruit that they produce and their tendency to contain more vitamin C than diploid varieties. However, triploids set fruit on a relatively small proportion of the flowers and, since they produce very little viable pollen, cannot be relied upon to pollinate other apples. So, if choosing a triploid to grow at home, you will also need to cultivate two diploid plants nearby in order to pollinate both the triploid and each other.

Polyploidy (the possession of more than the usual number of chromosomes) plays an important role in the evolution and breeding of apples.

Nutritional content
Low in calories, apples contain 80–85 per cent water. Raw, unpeeled apples are an excellent source of vitamin C and dietary fibre (both soluble and insoluble). Soluble fibre guards against a build-up of cholesterol in the blood, while insoluble fibre provides bulk in the intestines, holding water that cleanses and moves food quickly through the digestive tract. The fruit's nutritional content is not greatly affected by storage, though there may be some negligible deterioration.

Apples in commerce

While a lot of hybridizing and mutation has occurred naturally, agriculturalists, nurserymen and gardeners have grown numerous cultivars (varieties) through selective breeding programmes. Since these have never been systematically recorded, the parentage of any particular variety remains largely conjectural.

Nowadays, apples are an important commercial crop. China exports the largest number, closely followed by the USA. Turkey, France, Italy and Iran are also among leading exporters.

Repeated crossing and back-crossing has resulted in over 8,000 varieties. Of these, only around 100 are grown commercially, with ten varieties making up 90 per cent of production. A few varieties, such as Delicious and Gala, are grown throughout the world, while others are grown almost exclusively in a single location.

When choosing cultivars, growers look for reliable bearing, good flavour, attractive appearance, pest resistance, volume of crop and hardiness.

If the fruit stores and processes well, and withstands transportation, the value of the variety increases. Waxy-skinned varieties are preferred. Apples that commonly show signs of russeting are seldom grown commercially.

Harvesting

Fruits are harvested from early morning and throughout the day. However, varieties that are prone to bruising, such as Golden Delicious and Pink Lady, are picked from late morning, after the dew has evaporated.

Apples are picked by hand then collected in crates, often lined with plastic to prevent rubbing and abrasions. These crates are transported to a cold store within 24 hours.

Chemical treatments

Apples grown commercially are often treated with a chlorine drench as a phytosanitary measure to reduce the possibility of decay during storage. Golden Delicious, Braeburn and other varieties that are susceptible to diseases such as bitter pit or lenticel spot may be subjected to a calcium drench.

Above: Harvested apples are emptied into large crates to be transported by tractor.

Granny Smith, Pink Lady, Golden Delicious and other apples prone to superficial scald are sometimes treated with diphenylamine (DPA). In some instances, yeast and a fungicide are added to the drench as a means of reducing possible decay during storage.

A synthetic plant growth regulator, 1-Methylcyclopropene, is often also applied to apples after harvesting. This slows down the ripening and maintains the quality of the fruit during extended cold storage and supermarket shelf life.

Storage

Apples can be packed directly from harvest without prior storage, but are first cooled to below 5°C (41°F), and must then be packed within two hours.

All cultivars, except for Granny Smith, must be cooled to -0.5°C (23°F) within five days if they are to be stored, and maintained at this temperature until they are packed.

Early harvested fruits are packed first, followed by post optimum harvested fruit. Apples picked during the optimum harvest window have the highest storage potential and so are maintained either under regular air (RA) or in a controlled atmosphere (CA), with carefully regulated levels of oxygen and carbon dioxide, for packing later. Optimum gas levels vary depending on the variety. Golden Delicious and Red Delicious may be stored for up to nine months under CA, and Granny Smith, Royal Gala and Pink Lady apples ten, seven and six months respectively.

Packing

Apples are graded before packing. Most commercial growers reserve the best quality fruit for export. Fruit that does not make the export grade is either sold on the local market or sent for processing. Apples are usually packed close together to prevent bruising and rub marks. Some pack houses apply an edible coating to the fruit to improve storage quality and extend the shelf life of the fruit.

Inspection

Packed and palleted fruit is checked prior to export to ensure that the quality complies with set standards. Quality checks may include flesh firmness, skin colour, external disorders (including bitter pit), rub marks and bruising, and fruit temperature. The monitoring of pests and diseases, is especially important.

Cooling and export

After inspection, fruit must be forced-air cooled to -0.5°C (23°F) within 72 hours if unbagged or within 96 hours if bagged. Once the correct temperature has been reached, the apples are placed in cooling tunnels to await transportation and distribution.

Below: The highly commercial Braeburn produces attractively marked fruits.

APPLE CULTIVATION AND PLANTING

If apple trees are to do well – growing vigorously and producing abundant crops – they need to be grown in the conditions that best suit them. Take care over planting and new trees will grow away strongly, and you will soon be picking your very own home-grown fruit from them.

Before planting an apple tree it is important to find the right spot to plant it so that it becomes successfully established. Apple trees prefer a position in an open site, although sheltered from strong winds, and in full sun. They will, however, tolerate some shade. You should try to avoid planting trees in positions that may become waterlogged, such as a low-lying part of a predominantly damp garden. Also avoid potential frost pockets, such as low-lying areas where cold air collects.

Soil

Apple trees are tolerant of most soil conditions, but do best in fertile, well-drained soil. They do not do well in very light soils or soils that are prone to waterlogging. However, they tend to grow faster on clay-based soils than on light sandy or chalky soils. The ideal is a crumbly soil with medium fertility and slightly on the acid side. It is not necessary to test the pH level (degree of acidity/alkalinity) of soil when growing apples.

More important is soil structure. To test the soil structure, scrape up a

---

Growing apples organically

It is possible to grow apples successfully without the use of chemicals as fertilizer and to control pests and diseases.

• Choose disease-resistant varieties

• Prepare the ground well before planting, incorporating plenty of organic matter into the soil.

• Clear away all fallen leaves and fruits in autumn that could harbour disease.

• Prune the canopy to improve air circulation among the branches.

• Thin the fruits to two per spur.

• If it is necessary to spray trees, use an organic product.

---

handful of soil, then try rubbing it through your fingers as if making pastry. If it binds into moist crumbs, you have the ideal – a free-draining but fertile loam. If it runs through your fingers easily without binding, the fertility is likely to be low. If you can squeeze it into a solid lump in your hands, you have a heavy clay that will be wet and cold but potentially high in nutrients.

Soil improvement

Adding organic matter to the soil fulfils two functions. It improves the structure of all soil types, binding thin, sandy soils into larger crumbs and opening up heavy clay, allowing water (and nutrients) to pass through freely. Organic matter also raises fertility, promoting vigorous growth and good disease-resistance.

If you have a heavy clay soil, digging in a bucketful of horticultural grit before planting will improve the drainage. The following materials can be used to improve the soil.

Garden compost

The best of all soil improvers is garden compost that is made in a compost heap or bin. The best compost is made from a mix of organic materials: raw vegetable peelings, eggshells, used tea bags, coffee grounds, annual weeds and other leafy material from the garden (including lawn clippings), newspaper, cardboard and old cotton rags.

Leaf mould

Gather up the leaves from deciduous trees in autumn and stack them in black plastic bags. Tie up the bags then pierce a few holes in the sides to allow for air circulation. Store the bags in an out-of-the-way corner. It can take up to two years for the leaves to disintegrate into a crumbly material suitable for garden use.

Above: Create your own compost from organic household and garden waste.

Animal manures

The manure of vegetarian farmyard animals (cows, sheep and horses) can be used as a soil improver provided it is stacked first and allowed to rot down for three to six months – or it can be added to a compost heap as an accelerator. (Note that animal manures often contain weed seeds.)

Bird manures

The manure of chickens and pigeons is often used in gardens, but care should be taken – it is very high in uric acid, which can 'scorch' plants. The material is best treated as an activator and used as an addition to a compost heap.

Spent mushroom compost

Compost used for growing mushrooms is sometimes available. It contains chalk, an alkaline material, so should not be used on soils that are already very alkaline.

Soil improvers

These are sold bagged up like potting compost and are suitable for use by gardeners who are unable to make their own compost. They have the advantage of being weed free.

Buying apple trees

Apple trees are sold usually as either one- or two-year-old plants. A two-year-old tree will produce fruit sooner after planting than a one-year-old. Young trees without lateral branches are often referred to as whips.

Trees are available container-grown or as bare-root plants. Container-grown plants, which are more expensive, are available year-round. Bare-root trees are sold only during the dormant period when they are out of leaf – in late autumn and winter.

Choice of variety depends on several factors. You should consider not only the flavour of the apple, but its pollination requirements, yield and keeping qualities. Some varieties are hardier than others. It is best to buy from a local nursery, who can advise on which varieties will do well in your soil type and on your site. Modern varieties often have higher levels of disease resistance than older ones.

Rootstocks

All apple trees that are sold in nurseries and garden centres are made up of two separate plants that have been grafted together, or attached until they grow together as one plant. The part of the tree that will form the main trunk and

---

Advantages of autumn planting

All hardy trees and shrubs experience a surge in root growth during autumn, even though growth above ground has stopped and the plant appears dormant. An apple tree planted in autumn can thus establish itself in the ground before putting on any new top growth. Growth above ground the following spring will be vigorous.

---

branches is grown from a cutting (the 'scion') that is grafted on to the roots and lower trunk of another (the 'rootstock'). The graft union is clearly identifiable as visible scarring around 25cm (10in) above ground level on a young tree. Rootstocks influence the growth rate and ultimate size of the tree and can also promote disease-resistance. The most widely available are:
• M27 producing a tree 1.5–1.8m (5–6ft) tall
• M9 producing a tree 2.4–3.6m (8–12ft) tall
• M106 producing a tree 3.6–5.4m (12–18ft) tall
Other rootstocks include Budagovsky 9, M26, Mark, Ottawa 3, M7, M2, M4 and MM111.

Family trees

An apple tree that comprises two or three separate varieties grafted on to a single rootstock is called a family tree. They are a good choice if you have room in your garden for only one tree. The varieties on any one tree are all compatible, so the tree is self-fertile and planting a pollinator is unnecessary. However, each variety usually ripens its fruits at different times, thus extending the season.

Family trees are usually grafted on to a dwarfing rootstock and reach around 3m (10ft) in height when mature. These trees can be of ungainly appearance, however, due to the variation in growth rates among the different cultivars.

Right: Apples are not only delicious when they are picked straight from the tree, but they also retain their qualities when stored.

Above: A bare-rooted tree should be planted as soon as possible.

Sourcing unusual varieties

Even larger nurseries carry only a limited range of apple trees – popular varieties that are likely to do well in the majority of situations.

If you wish to grow an old or unusual variety, you may need to contact a grower or orchardist who owns a tree and ask them to graft it for you. Grafting can take place only at certain times of year, and there needs to be a time allowance for the graft to take. Therefore, you may have to wait for up to a year or so before you are able to bring the tree home ready to plant in your garden.

East Malling Research Station

A research station was established at East Malling in Kent, England, in 1913 on the impetus of local fruit growers. An important part of the station's work has been the development and testing of rootstocks. These are now standardized as the 'Malling Series', identifiable through the initial M, as in 'M27'.

Research into and testing of rootstocks is ongoing. The aim is to produce rootstocks that promote resistance to common apple problems such as fireblight, woolly aphid and collar (or crown) rot as well as improved frost resistance, vigour and high yield efficiency (large fruits in quantity).

Planting a bare-root apple tree

1 Before planting, place the tree in a large plastic bucket. Fill with water to cover the root system. Allow the roots to soak for at least an hour.

2 Dig over the soil and remove any large stones and all traces of weeds. Incorporate organic matter to improve the soil, if necessary.

3 Excavate a deep hole that is large enough to contain the tree's root system comfortably. Loosen the soil at the bottom of the hole.

4 Lay a cane across the hole to check the planting depth. The tree must be planted to the same depth as it was in the nursery. Look for the soil mark near the base of the stem for guidance.

5 To ensure the tree grows straight, use a stake to support it. Insert the stake into the ground next to the trunk. Be careful not to damage the root system during the process.

6 Begin to backfill the hole with the excavated soil. As you do so, gently shake the tree periodically to help settle the soil around the roots.

7 Firm the soil around the base of the tree with your hands or your foot. Do not press too hard, or you may compact the surface.

8 Tie the trunk to the stake using a rubber tree tie. Tighten the tie, but make sure it is loose enough around the stem to allow this to thicken.

9 Water the tree well with a watering can fitted with a fine rose. Note that water delivered as a jet from a hose can compact the soil surface.

Planting

Bare-root trees should be planted as soon after purchase as possible. But you may need to delay planting if the ground is frozen or waterlogged. You can store bare-root plants unopened for up to four weeks in a cool but sheltered place, for instance in a garage or shed or other outbuilding.

You should also plant out container-grown trees as soon as is practical, but if this is not possible, stand them in a sheltered but light spot in the garden. Water them frequently if the weather is dry to prevent the compost from drying out. Alternatively, dig a hole in a spare piece of ground and sink the container into it to keep the roots cool.

Heeling in

If you are unable to plant a bare-root plant for several weeks, it is worth considering 'heeling in'.

Dig a shallow trench about 30cm (12in) deep in good soil in a sheltered part of the garden, for instance in a bare vegetable plot. Lay the roots in the trench (angling them if necessary) then lightly cover them with the excavated soil. This will keep the roots cool and moist until you plant the tree.

Planting a container-grown tree

Before planting, prepare the soil as for a bare-root tree. Dig a large hole at

Below: Tree guards help to protect the bark of young trees until it thickens.

Above: An example of a family tree, with Jonagold (left) and Elstar Gray (right) growing from the same trunk.

least twice the depth and width of the container the tree is already in. Fork in organic matter at the base of the hole.

Slide the root ball from the container (it can be beneficial to water the container first, if the compost is dry – it helps consolidate the compost around the roots). Place the tree in the hole. Check the planting depth by laying a cane across the hole. The top surface of the compost should be level with the surrounding soil. (Plant too deep and the base of the trunk can rot where it is in contact with the soil. Plant too shallow and the roots will be exposed to light and air.)

Backfill by sprinkling the excavated soil around the root ball. Lightly firm the plant in with your foot. Water the plant well, using a watering can.

Staking

To protect the newly planted tree from wind-rock, which could disturb the roots, use a short stake. This allows the upper portion of the tree to blow in the wind, which strengthens the trunk in the long term.

Insert the stake as you plant the tree rather than afterwards to be sure of avoiding damage to the roots. When staking a tree, either drive the stake in vertically next to the trunk or at an angle into the prevailing wind. Tie the tree to the stake with a special rubber tree tie. Do not pull this tight around the trunk, but leave a gap to allow the stem to thicken. Loosen the tie as the tree grows. Once the tree is well-established (after two to three years), the stake can be removed.

Tree guards

To prevent damage from mice and rabbits, protect the lower portion of the trunk with a tree guard – a length of plastic (or other synthetic material) that is formed either as a strip that winds round the trunk, which expands as the trunk thickens, or as a loose-fitting sleeve. Once the tree has developed thick bark, the guard can be removed.

GROWING APPLE TREES IN CONTAINERS

Apples can be grown successfully in containers, but they need more care and attention than trees grown in the open garden or in a kitchen garden. It's essential to choose a tree on a dwarfing rootstock. Look for a container-grown tree with evenly spaced top-growth (or crown).

Apple trees should be grown in large containers, ideally 40cm (16in) across and deep or even bigger. When in fruit, the tree will be heavy, so to provide ballast and to prevent it from blowing over, you should choose a container made of a heavy material, such as terracotta or reconstituted stone. If you prefer to use plastic, resin or some other lightweight synthetic material, place large stones or bricks at the base before filling with compost to create stability.

Even so, apple trees in containers should be positioned so that they are sheltered from strong winds. Choose weaker-growing varieties that have been grafted on to dwarfing rootstocks to limit their growth. Spur-bearing types will produce the most fruit.

Below: Choose a tree on a dwarfing rootstock for growing in a container and keep the tree well watered throughout the growing season.

Above: A balcony garden with Malus Klarapfel and Cox Orange growing in pots.

Above: Containers should be positioned where they will receive plenty of sunshine.

Compost

For the best results, use a soil-based compost. John Innes No.3, formulated for trees and shrubs, contains the appropriate levels of nutrients.

Multi-purpose composts can also be used for apples in containers, but you will need to pay more attention to watering, as they are difficult to wet if allowed to dry out.

Garden compost is unsuitable for use in containers. It is not sterile and contains too many micro-organisms and invertebrates. However, if you have a source of leaf mould, this can be added to proprietary compost.

Watering and feeding

Water apple trees in containers regularly, especially during dry weather in spring and summer. It is very important to maintain water levels while the fruit is swelling in summer. Applying a potassium-high fertilizer, such as a rose fertilizer, in spring will boost flower and fruit production. A further dose in autumn helps firm the growth before winter. Alternatively, apply a tomato fertilizer as a root drench when the tree is in vigorous growth in spring and early summer, and again in autumn.

In winter, water just enough to prevent the compost from drying out completely. The aim is to keep the roots just moist. Do not water during freezing weather.

General care

Apple trees in containers will need pollinators just the same as trees in the open garden. If there are no other apple trees in your own garden or one nearby, grow several different ones together or choose a self-fertile variety or family apple tree.

Watch out for pests and diseases and deal with them as soon as you detect any sign of damage. Prune the trees carefully – cutting the stems too hard will result in overly vigorous growth that will not bear fruit successfully the following year.

Although many apple trees can be grown in containers, they should not be viewed as long-term plantings. They are long-lived trees and sooner or later any tree in a container will need planting out in the open if it is to thrive.

Winter care

All plants in containers are susceptible to cold in winter, as the roots are above ground level and liable to freeze. If a hard frost is forecast overnight, either move plants under cover – for instance, into a porch, unheated greenhouse or shed – or wrap a length of horticultural fleece around the container to insulate the roots.

As apples flower relatively late in the season, it is not usually necessary to protect the blossom from frost. But if a hard frost is forecast when the tree is in flower, lightly tent it with horticultural fleece. Remove the fleece during the daytime. You can leave the fleece in position if the temperature remains below freezing during the hours of daylight.

Repotting

When the tree's roots fill the container, it is necessary to repot it.

Tilt the container on its side and carefully slide the plant out. Shake the roots free of compost, washing them under an outside tap to dislodge any that clings on. Scrub the interior of the container. Lightly prune the roots, then return the tree to the container, using fresh compost. If this is not practical, tilt the container and scrape out the uppermost layer of compost with your fingers. Replace this with fresh compost or leaf mould.

Buying an apple tree for a container
It is a myth that you can keep an apple tree small by pruning the roots. You must buy a tree on a dwarfing rootstock. The best one for growing in a container is the Malling rootstock M27.

Planting in a container

1 Line the base of the container with crocks or stones, making sure all holes at the base of the container are covered. This will allow excess water to drain freely while preventing loss of compost through the holes.

2 Begin to fill the container with compost or leaf mould, to a depth of around one-third. Slide the plant from its container. Place it on top of the compost, in the middle of the prepared container.

3 Check the level by placing a cane or straight length of wood across the container. The top of the rootball should be about 2.5cm (1in) below the rim of the container, to allow for watering and maintenance.

4 Fill the gap between the edge of the container and the rootball with more compost. Press fertilizer pellets into the compost, midway between the rim of the container and the rootball.

5 Water the container well using a can fitted with a fine rose or from a hose with the nozzle set to produce a fine spray. This avoids compacting the compost surface.

6 Top-dress the compost surface with small stones to keep the roots cool and prevent excess moisture loss through evaporation. It also makes the pot look tidy and attractive.

TRAINING APPLE TREES

The typical image of a tree is usually a large plant with a solid trunk and a rounded system of branches, but there are also a wide variety of forms into which trees can be trained. Apple trees are trained to produce compact plants that flower and fruit prolifically, and present the crop around eye level.

Most fruit trees can be bought ready trained and this is the most practical option for busy gardeners, but it can be rewarding – and is much cheaper – to train your own. Ready-trained trees will flower and fruit the first season after planting, but if you are training the plant yourself, no crops will be produced until, usually, the third year.

Size

There are several reasons for choosing a particular shape of fruit tree. The first is size. A fully grown apple tree, for example, can take up a lot of space, especially in a small garden, but a dwarf pyramid can be fitted into a limited space, while cordons can be grown along a fence or even as a hedge.

Productivity and quality

Training fruit trees helps to improve productivity and quality. The upper branches of a standard tree can shade the lower branches, and these in turn will shade the ground beneath it, limiting what you can grow there. However, a fan grown against a wall will not only produce a large crop but

Above: In the kitchen garden apple trees can be grown as vertical cordons to save on space.

will supply individual fruits with the maximum amount of light for even ripening. Training trees against walls also provides protection and warmth.

More varieties

When choosing the shape of your tree you should also think about the number of varieties you require. For example, a fan might occupy the whole of one wall, but in the same amount of space you could grow half a dozen cordons or more. These will not necessarily yield more fruit but could provide variety of flavour and availability.

Decorative qualities

Do not overlook the decorative aspect of trained trees. A tall espalier growing against the end of a house can be stunning, as can fans on a smaller scale. Free-standing cordons and espaliers produce excellent screens.

Choosing trees

Before buying a tree consider the above aspects and think about where you are going to plant it and what the best shape is for the space available. It is also worth remembering that basic shapes, such as standards, require far less pruning than more complicated ones. Something to bear in mind, especially if you are not happy on ladders or steps, is that the fruit on larger forms may be out of reach.

The following are some of the fruit tree forms that are most commonly used by amateur gardeners. Basic definitions of the forms are given here, with details on how to create them over several years.

Standard/half-standard

Standard trees are grown on vigorous rootstocks and are usually too large for most gardens. They have a clear trunk of 2–2.1m (6–6½ ft) – 1.35m (4ft) for a half-standard.

To develop the standard (or half-standard), allow a young tree to grow unpruned, clearing the trunk of laterals as for a central leader tree. Once the main stem has achieved the desired height, cut it back, then prune the laterals as for a bush.

Bush

This is an excellent form for any garden where a number of fruit trees are grown, but they must be on dwarfing rootstocks. The aim is to create a bushy plant on a trunk 75–90cm (2½–3ft) tall.

Prune the leader of a young tree or whip to stimulate branching low down. In winter, select the strongest laterals to form the framework and cut back the remainder. Shorten the remaining laterals to outward-facing buds to develop the desired open centre. The following winter, lightly prune these to encourage bushiness.

Central leader tree

This form eventually produces a large tree, suitable for use as a specimen.

Allow a young tree or whip to develop with minimal pruning. Once the tree is established – after three to five years – begin to remove the lower branches to create a clear trunk 1.5–2m (5–6ft) tall. The main upright stem, or the leader, is allowed to continue growing so that the tree achieves its natural dimensions.

If growing apple trees primarily for their fruit, this training method is not recommended. Crops will be small and difficult to harvest as many of the fruits will be borne well above head height.

Above: Training trees as cordons is the perfect way to get several trees into one small garden.

Pyramid

A pyramid is a dainty tree with a strong central leader. Staking is essential, as this tree form is less stable than a bush. The first winter after planting, shorten the leader to 50–75cm (20–30in). Develop lower branches first, cutting back suitably placed laterals to outward-facing buds on the undersides. This encourages a horizontal habit. It is important to remove vigorous shoots on the upper portions of the leader.

As the plant grows, tie in a replacement leader to the stake to develop height, removing all other vigorous upright-growing branches. Prune the upper branches in the same way as the strong laterals towards the base of the plant, cutting to outward-facing buds on the undersides.

Cordon

A cordon is a vigorous upright that has usually been trained at an angle, with stubby side shoots – ideal where space is limited. The aim is to build up a system of short, stubby 'spurs' the length of the stem.

A cordon must be grown against a system of wires. The main stem is tied to a sturdy cane, and this in turn is tied to the wires. To maintain the cordon, remove overcrowded growth in winter and shorten overlong laterals to three or four buds. Shorten the leader, as necessary, in late spring. In summer, cut back any overlong, whippy shoots to the base. A double cordon is similar to a cordon but is upright and has two main stems. Double cordons are obviously more productive than single ones.

Espalier

In this form, lateral branches are trained strictly horizontally, either against a wall or freestanding on wires.

Unless the tree is bought ready trained, plant a whip and cut it back in winter to a strong bud just above the lowest wire. From the new growth, select the strongest as the new leader and tie this to an upright cane lashed to the wires. Select two strong laterals and tie these to canes tied in diagonally to the wires. The next winter, bring these down to the horizontal and attach them to the lowest wire. Cut back the leader just above the second wire and continue this procedure in subsequent years until the espalier is complete.

Fan

A decorative form, also trained on wires, that is useful for varieties that benefit from wall protection. Training is less strict than for an espalier.

Unless bought ready trained, choose a young plant with several strong laterals. On planting, cut all of these back apart from two that are suitably placed for training to the diagonal to either side of the leader. Tie them to

Above: The espaliered tree is decorative and highly productive, capable of producing many tiers of fruit-bearing branches.

canes that can be lashed to the wires. Cut back the leader to just above the upper 'arm'. As suitably placed strong side shoots grow, tie them in to the wires, aiming for an even development to both sides.

Stepover

This is an ideal form to use to edge beds in a kitchen garden. Stepovers are suitable only for apples on a dwarfing rootstock.

Cut back a whip to within 30cm (12in) of the ground. Pull the new leader hard down to the horizontal and train it on a horizontal wire stretched between short uprights.

Below: This stepover Malus 'Red Devil' has been grown on M25 dwarfing rootstock.

PRUNING APPLE TREES

Many gardeners are confused about pruning, but it is not really difficult – the main thing is knowing when to do it, and how much to remove. While failing to prune at all may not cause serious damage, it will not make for the most healthy and productive trees, and they may also become too large.

Apple trees need a regular pruning regime if they are to achieve their optimum cropping. They bear fruit on stems that are in their second year or older. Shoots produced in the current year will flower and fruit in the following year. When pruning, consider the tree's future cropping and aim to produce an equal balance between older shoots and new ones.

When to prune

Apple trees are pruned in mid- to late winter. Trained trees, once established, should also be pruned in summer. Winter pruning invigorates a plant, encouraging it to grow more during the coming season. Summer pruning can inhibit growth, as you are removing a proportion of that year's growth. It helps maintain the form of cordons and espaliers.

Apples trained formally as fans, cordons and espaliers need to be pruned in summer as well as winter. If they are left unpruned, new stems will grow vigorously. Not only will these spoil the tree's form, but they will be relatively unproductive and will cast unwanted shade over fruits developing lower down the stem. The method used for summer pruning of

Above: A pole or pillar apple takes up very little space but can be very productive. It is pruned as for cordons.

trained apples is known as the Lorette system. In late summer, when the lower third of the new growth is starting to firm up, shorten all new shoots. On shoots arising directly from the main stem, count three or five leaves above the basal cluster of leaves, then cut just above the leaf joint. Cut shoots that have grown from existing side shoots back just above one leaf above the basal cluster of leaves.

Summer pruning carries a certain risk as cutting stems encourages new growth, which can be vulnerable to frost damage. Shorten any long, whippy shoots that appear to a growth bud near the base in mid-autumn.

Pruning cuts

Although different fruit trees and styles of training involve different pruning methods, the pruning cuts are the same in all instances. Use sharp secateurs (pruners), loppers or a pruning knife and make sure you are comfortably positioned to make a clean, neat cut. If you need a ladder, either make sure that someone will hold it for you or use one with an integral stabilizer.

Always cut a stem just above a bud and make sure the cut is angled away from the bud. Do not cut too far above the bud, or the stem will die back, possibly allowing disease to enter the tissue. Cutting too close to the bud may damage it, preventing it from growing and encouraging disease.

Branches that are large enough to be cut with a saw are usually cut across at right angles. If the branch is heavy and and likely to split, the sawing is usually done in three stages (see opposite).

Shortening leaders

The leading shoots, or branch leaders, are the main shoots of a tree. You should shorten the previous year's extension growth by up to one-third. Very vigorous shoots on spur-bearers are best left unpruned, as pruning will stimulate even more vigorous growth.

Spur- and tip-bearers

Apples are described as being tip-bearers or spur-bearers, depending on how they carry their fruit. Tip-bearers produce their fruits at or near the tips of branches, while spur-bearers produce their fruits along the branches on short, stubby growths known as spurs.

Above: Cut back all the new, straight growth, which, if allowed to develop, will make crowding and unproductivity worse.

Above: Reduce the number of spurs by pruning a number of the older ones. Leave enough to produce the next autumn's fruit.

Above: When pruning a cordon, any new shoots on existing side shoots should be cut back to one leaf.

The 'June drop'

Apple trees regularly shed a proportion of their fruits in late spring. This is a natural phenomenon and does not indicate that anything is wrong. It is common for a tree to set more fruits than can develop fully, and shedding the excess is a means of ensuring that the remainder will ripen correctly.

Most varieties are spur-bearing, but among these a few are partially tip-bearing. Tip-bearers produce smaller crops than spur-bearers, and should be grown only as standard or half-standard trees or as bushes. Spur-bearers lend themselves to training.

Pruning a spur-bearing apple

The aim in pruning a spur-bearing apple is to produce and maintain the short, stubby growths that will flower and bear fruit.

Shortening side shoots causes them to thicken and produce clusters of flowering shoots. Side shoots fan out from the tree's main shoots. In mid- to late winter, cut these back to five or six growth buds from the base of the shoot. Weak-growing shoots can be pruned harder. Shoots that are already short can be left unpruned.

After around five years, spurs tend to become congested and therefore less productive – they produce too many fruits too close together that cannot grow to full size or ripen evenly.

On each congested spur system, cut out the lower spurs at the base. Thin the remaining upper spurs to leave about three well-spaced spurs. After thinning, each spur system should be capable of bearing four or five good-sized fruits.

Pruning a tip-bearing apple

The aim in pruning a tip-bearing apple is to relieve congestion in the body of the tree and to remove older growth in favour of new wood that will bear future crops.

Shorten old stems that have fruited in previous years. Cut them back either to new shoots that grew during the previous summer (these will flower and fruit during the coming year) or to strong growth buds lower down on the stem (these will shoot during the coming year then fruit and flower the next). You do not need to remove all the old wood in any one year but can leave some stems unpruned. The general aim is to encourage the tree to replace its fruiting wood over a period of years.

Pruning a large tree

Many gardens are home to a large, mature apple tree that is valued as much for its ornamental appearance and home for wildlife as it is as a fruit-bearer. While a systematic pruning regime is not practical, it can be beneficial from time to time to remove older and crossing branches to open up the heart of the tree and rejuvenate it. If you need to reduce the size of a tree drastically (for instance, if it is overhanging a neighbour's garden or is too close to the house), consult a qualified tree surgeon.

Larger branches on mature trees can sometimes be torn off by strong winds, or even by the weight of the crop. It can also sometimes be necessary to remove a large branch to restore the symmetry and balance of a tree, especially on large specimens that have not been strictly pruned. To prevent further damage to the tree, cut away the branch in stages. It is best to carry out this type of pruning in winter, when the tree is dormant.

Below: Carefully cut back congested or crossing branches to the point of origin.

The first cut is made on the underside of the branch, 5cm (2in) out from the final cutting position. The second cut is made slightly further out along the branch, this time from above, by sawing down until the branch splits along to the first cut and is then severed. The final cut can be made straight through from the top because there is no weight to cause splitting.

Fruit thinning

If a tree has set a large amount of fruit during spring, it can be beneficial to thin the fruits out in early summer. This results in fewer apples, but larger and of better quality, and a greater total weight, and helps offset a potential tendency to biennial bearing. Large fruit clusters will also weigh down branches, which can sometimes snap if they are brittle. A further aim of fruit thinning is to expose the developing fruits to the sun, so that they ripen fully and evenly with good skin colour.

The time to thin the fruits is after the 'June drop'. Remove the central fruit from each cluster. Cut out any other fruits that are damaged or mis-shapen. Around two to four weeks later, thin again to leave one fruit per cluster.

PROPAGATING APPLES

Apples are usually propagated by means of grafting. Cuttings taken in the usual way will not produce good plants. The techniques generally used have been developed over the course of many centuries and have proved to be extremely reliable.

It is not possible to increase stocks of named varieties by seed – but seed-raised plants can make attractive ornamentals and may act as pollinators to other apple trees.

Growing from seed

Place a handful of perlite in a clear plastic bag, moisten slightly, add some apple pips and refrigerate. After about six weeks, remove the seeds from the perlite. Fill small containers with multi-purpose or seed compost, water and allow to drain, then press the seeds into the compost surface. Top with a thin layer of horticultural grit or sharp sand. Place the containers in a sheltered space outdoors or in a cool greenhouse.

Once the seed has germinated, keep the seedlings growing strongly by making sure that you water them regularly. Water less from late autumn and water in winter only to prevent the compost from drying out. The following spring, the seedlings should be large enough to pot up individually, using a soil-based compost.

Feed the young plants with a dilute tomato feed. Transfer them to larger pots once the roots fill the existing ones. The young trees should be large enough to plant out after two to three years and should flower and bear decorative fruits from five years.

Grafting

Widely used in the nursery trade as a means of propagating many trees and shrubs, grafting allows new plants of saleable size to be produced quickly from just a small amount of plant material. Fruit trees are nearly always grafted.

Grafting is a technique that involves uniting a cutting or growth bud (known as the scion) with the lower parts (the rootstock) of another. The following techniques are the ones usually used for apples.

Above: Malus scions, successfully grafted under the bark of an old apple tree trunk.

Preparation of the rootstocks

Rootstocks should be well-established at the time of grafting. They are usually sold as dormant plants and should be planted as described for planting a bare-root tree (*see* p.18). They can then be used for chip-budding the following summer and for stem grafting the following late winter.

After planting, remove any side shoots from the lower 30cm (12in) of trunk. Rub out any buds that appear on this part of the rootstock during the growing season. Keep the rootstocks well-watered during spring and summer. This enables you to lift the bark easily when chip-budding.

Below: The sequence of chip budding.

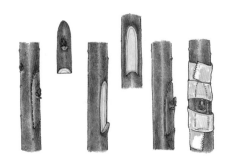

Principles of grafting

For a successful graft, there must be a free flow of sap between the rootstock and scion and the tissues of the two elements should knit together.

Below the bark on a stem is a layer of tissue called the cambium layer which must be aligned so that the stock and scion can fuse together.

Bud-grafting

This method is popular with nurserymen as it is possible to produce a new tree from a single growth bud – hence several new plants can be created from a single stem from the variety you wish to propagate.

Chip-budding

This form of grafting is carried out in mid- to late summer.

Cut well-ripened stems of around pencil thickness from the sunny side of the tree. To prevent moisture loss, strip off the leaves, keeping the leaf stalks intact. Remove any small new leaves that appear at the base of each leaf stalk. To prevent further drying out, wrap the stems in a damp cloth.

Below a healthy, well-developed bud (about 2cm/¾in), make a straight, shallow, downward-angled cut. Starting about 2cm (¾in) above the bud, make a downward cut, cutting behind the bud and down to meet the inner edge of the first cut, removing a 4cm (1½in) sliver of wood.

On the rootstock, locate an area of stem about 23cm (9in) above ground level that is free from buds. Remove a section of wood corresponding in shape and size to the bud. Fit the bud into the rootstock. It should fit exactly, but if the bud is slimmer than the rootstock, line up the bark to one side so that the cambium layers of the scion and rootstock are in contact.

Tie the bud in place with grafting tape. Tie loosely around the bud itself, to allow room for this to grow, but sufficiently tightly to hold it in place.

Aftercare of chip-budding

After about four to six weeks, the wound should start to callus over as the graft takes. Remove the tape. If the graft has been successful, the petiole will be shed in autumn at the same time as the rootstock loses its leaves. The following spring, cut back the rootstock just above the grafted bud. To encourage upright growth, tie the stem to an upright cane inserted into the ground next to the rootstock. For maximum growth in this early stage, remove any flowers that form. Cut back any shoots that appear on the rootstock, but only when they have reached a length of 5–7.5cm (2–3in). The tree can be planted out in its final position in the autumn.

Whip-and-tongue grafting

This grafting method is carried out in late winter to early spring around the time that sap is starting to rise.

The scions are prepared in mid-winter while the tree is fully dormant. Take cuttings of the previous season's growth about 23cm (9in) long. Cut just above a bud on the parent plant.

These cuttings then need to be kept cool and in a state of dormancy until they are grafted a few weeks later. Taking the cuttings in advance means that when you come to do the graft all the fresh sap will be coming from the rootstock. Bundle the cuttings loosely together and bury them to two-thirds of their length in a sheltered part of the garden. Alternatively, seal them in a plastic bag and refrigerate.

When the rootstock starts into growth, cut it back, about 23cm (9in) above ground level, with a downward-sloping cut. Remove any side shoots below the cut. With the cut sloping down away from you, make a second upward cut around 3.5cm (1½in) long to remove a sliver of bark and expose the cambium layer and pith.

About one-third of the way down this second cut, remove a narrow

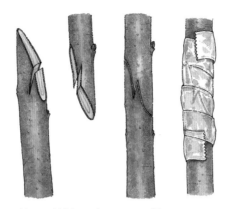

Above: Whip-and-tongue grafting sequence.

V-shaped section of wood to form a 'tongue', into which you will later insert the scion.

To prepare the scion, first trim any soft growth from the tip. Then shorten it at the base to a length of wood that holds three or four buds. Trim the base of the cutting about 3.5cm (1½in) below the lowest bud.

From the base of the cutting, on the same side as the lowest bud, make a slanting cut through to the other side, the same length as the cut on the rootstock. At a point on the cut surface equivalent to the 'tongue' on the rootstock, make a short upward cut. Gently turn the knife to open this, then insert the scion into the rootstock.

Bind the union with grafting tape. The graft should 'take' within four to six weeks, after which the tape can be carefully removed.

Note: When inserting the scion, the cambium layers must line up. If the scion is thinner than the rootstock, place it so that the cambium and outer bark line up to one side.

Aftercare of whip-and-tongue grafting

As the buds on the scion begin to shoot, select the strongest to form the leader of the tree. Shorten the remainder to about 7cm (3in). To encourage upright growth, insert a cane into the ground next to the rootstock and tie the selected shoot to it. Continue to tie it to the cane as it grows. Remove any shoots that appear on the rootstock once they are about 7cm (3in) long. The new tree can be transplanted the following autumn or the spring after that.

Rind grafting

This is a form of grafting over. Instead of using a seed-raised rootstock, scions are grafted on to an established tree, the aim being to test out a new variety or to provide a pollinator compatible with other apple trees growing nearby.

In early spring cut back most of the main branches on the tree to within 60cm (24in) of the main trunk, leaving a few to carry on growing normally. Cut the branches horizontally across.

For the scions, take cuttings of the previous season's growth, each with three growth buds. Trim them just above the uppermost bud with a cut angled away from it. Trim the base of each scion with a sloping cut about 2.5cm (1in) long.

Cutting downwards, make two or three slits in the bark about 2.5cm (1in) long and evenly spaced around each prepared branch of the tree. With the tip of the knife, ease back the bark. Slide each scion into a slit, so that the cut surface at the base of the cutting is in contact with the tree tissue beneath the bark. Bind the union with soft twine and seal with grafting wax.

Remove the binding when the graft has taken and the stems are growing strongly. Cut back the weaker growing stems so that only one remains. It should flower and fruit within three or four years.

It is possible to rind graft several different varieties on to a tree to produce a family apple tree.

Below: The sequence of rind grafting.

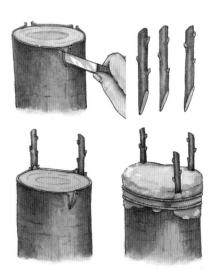

HARVESTING AND STORING APPLES

A principal reason for the enduring popularity of apples is the ease with which the fruit can be stored. Home-grown apples can be enjoyed over a period of many months provided they are harvested carefully, prepared well and stored in appropriate conditions.

Apples are ready to pick when ripe, unblemished fruits start to fall from the tree. The base colour is a clue to ripeness. It should be an even yellow or yellowish-green. On red-skinned varieties, look for this colour around the stem cavity – if it is still mid- or dark green, the fruit is not yet ripe.

Ripe apples should be easy to pick with the stem still attached. Gently roll or twist the apple in your hand so that the stem separates from the branch. The fruits will store best if the stalk is retained.

Over-ripe fruit is not suitable for storing.

Above: Apples should be harvested by hand with a gentle twist of the wrist.

Above: Apples should be well spaced during storage to prevent any rot from spreading.

Storing apples

Apples can be kept for varying lengths of time, depending on the variety. A few seem even to improve during storage, as this allows the flavour to develop fully.

Fruits intended for storage must be unblemished. Ideally, they should be stored at a temperature of 0°C (32°F), to slow down further ripening.

Apples should be individually wrapped so that they do not touch each other while being stored. Otherwise, any rot that develops in an individual fruit will be rapidly passed on to the others.

Place the fruits in open crates or wooden boxes, then keep them in a cool, dry, dark place such as a shed, outbuilding, cellar or garage. Crates for stacking should have slits in the sides or other openings that allow for good air circulation. The storage area should be well ventilated – excessive damp will cause the fruits to rot.

Apples can also be stored in a domestic refrigerator. Fill plastic food bags with firm but ripe, unblemished fruits then seal them. Pierce a few holes in the bags with a wooden skewer to allow free passage of air around the fruits.

Preserving apples

Apples that otherwise do not store well can be preserved by drying or freezing.

Sliced apples can be dried in a low oven for up to eight hours. Allow the apple slices to cool completely before storing them in an airtight container.

Wrapping fruits for storage

1 Cut pieces of silicone paper or baking parchment, about 30cm (12in) square, or less if the fruits are small. Place a fruit in the centre of each.

2 Wrap the paper evenly around the fruit, twisting it at the top to secure it.

What happens during storage?

An apple is not dead at the time of harvest and continues to take in oxygen and give off carbon dioxide and ethylene during storage. But since it is no longer attached to the tree, it has to use up food reserves laid down during its period of growth. Consequently, the sugar, starch and acid content of the apple changes. A stored apple can taste sweeter than one eaten straight from the tree. Concurrently, there can also be a loss of firmness. Eventually, the tissues break down and the apple withers and starts to decay.

Culinary apples can be cut into pieces and frozen before use. However, they may not hold their shape during cooking as well as unfrozen fruits. Frozen apples are suitable for use in fruit pies and crumbles and for sauce making and juicing.

Juicing and cider making

Extracting juice from an apple is a means of preservation, as the juice is usually pasteurized or distilled as part of the process.

For the maximum nutritional content, apples should be juiced unpeeled. If you are using fruit bought from a greengrocer or supermarket, wash it carefully first to remove the wax with which it will have been sprayed.

Cider

An alcoholic drink, cider is made from the fermented juice of apples. It remains particularly popular in traditional apple growing regions, such as south-west England, Ireland, parts of Spain, Germany and northern France. In North America, the term cider is generally used for non-alcoholic drinks, hard cider being the preferred term for alcoholic ones.

Cider can be made from any variety of apple, but in some regions certain cultivars (referred to as cider apples) are preferred. Many varieties have been bred specifically for cider making. Cider can be sweet, medium or dry and varies in colour from pale yellow to brown. Depending on filtration, it can be clear or cloudy (some apple varieties yield a clear cider without filtration). The finished drink can be either still or sparkling.

Cider can also be made from pears, and is usually called pear cider or perry.

Preparing apples for drying

1 Peel each apple with a sharp knife or vegetable peeler and cut out the core, ideally in one piece, using a corer. Try to avoid damaging the whole fruit.

2 Cut each apple into rings of even thickness, around 6mm (¼in). Place them on a non-stick baking tray and dry in a low oven for several hours.

Preparing apples for freezing

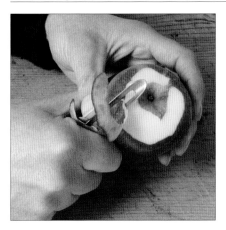

1 Select unblemished apples of even size. Carefully peel each apple with a sharp knife or vegetable peeler.

2 Halve each fruit, then cut into quarters or eighths. Cut out the core and any pips from each segment.

3 Depending on the size of the apple variety, cut each of the segments once more to produce 16 equally sized slices.

4 Bag up the apples in freezer bags, and label each with the date. For the best freezing, suck the air out of the bag before sealing.

APPLE PROBLEMS

Apple trees are subject to a number of problems that can weaken growth, reduce or spoil the crop or occasionally even cause the death of the tree. Problems can be caused by pests and diseases, but sometimes also result from unsuitable growing conditions and sudden adverse changes in the weather.

Identifying a problem is not always easy. Many diseases, for instance, produce symptoms that are similar to those induced by poor growing conditions. However, it is important to deal with any problem as soon as it is noticed. Given appropriate attention, trees usually recover well. It is usually possible to take preventive action so that the problem does not recur.

You can avoid potential difficulties by selecting carefully. Some varieties are known to be resistant to certain diseases, or to perform well in damp soil or in cold areas. A tree that is well-suited to the prevailing conditions will be strong-growing and will recover more quickly than a weak one, should any problem affect it.

Garden hygiene

Practising good garden hygiene can be an important strategy in keeping problems under control. Remove any fallen fruits and leaves from around the tree. They can be a breeding ground for fungi and also shelter invertebrate pests. However, a few windfall apples around a tree will be a valuable food source for birds in winter and beneficial to wasps. Rather than composting these, it is best to burn them. Fungal spores are not killed by the composting process, so you run the risk of returning them to the trees if you use the compost as a mulch around them later on.

Maintaining vigour

Feed and water plants well when they are young to ensure they make rapid progress in the early years. It is also advisable to water established trees during periods of drought in summer, especially if they are bearing heavily. Mulch heavily after watering to conserve soil moisture.

It is often possible to repair any damage to an established tree by judicious pruning.

Above: Adding mulch will improve soil structure and fertility as it breaks down.

Garden pests

Pests range from tiny invertebrates (insects and others) to mammals such as rabbits and deer. Some are active at specific times of the year.

Birds

Although they feed on insect pests, birds can be a pest themselves.
DAMAGE: Birds peck at flower buds and ripe fruits. Pecked fruits attract wasps and other undesirable insects.
CONTROL: Deter birds humanely by hanging old CDs or foil trays from the branches that will flash in the light. Change the positions of these regularly. Netting trees is not recommended as small birds can become trapped.

Rabbits

These small burrowing mammals feed on a range of wild and cultivated plants.
DAMAGE: Rabbits can cause serious damage to trees, as they gnaw at the bark at ground level. This exposes the tissue beneath to disease.
CONTROL: Place tree guards around the base of newly planted trees. To keep rabbits out of gardens, erect a boundary fence at least 1.2m (4ft) high. As a guard against burrowing, sink a length of corrugated plastic or metal into the ground along the fence, to a depth of about 45cm (18in).

Attracting wildlife

You can reduce the incidence of pests by attracting as wide a range of wildlife into the garden as possible.

Below: A bat box under the eaves provides shelter for bats during the day.

• Large apple trees will provide a perch and a potential nesting site for birds that will then feed on insect pests. Berrying plants such as hollies (*Ilex*), pyracanthas and cotoneasters will provide a food source in winter. Carefully sited bird boxes (designed for particular species) will encourage roosting.
• Bats will feed on nocturnal moths. Bat boxes in tall trees and under house eaves will give them a shelter during the daytime.
• A small pile of logs or even a tree stump will be home to a range of invertebrates, including stag beetle larvae. Piles of stones will provide a cool resting place for frogs and toads.
• A garden pond will be a habitat and watering hole for many insects, birds and small mammals.

Above: An otherwise healthy apple has first been pecked by birds and is now attracting wasps.

Deer
Ruminant mammals that are widespread in rural areas.
DAMAGE: Deer browse the branches of trees and bushes.
CONTROL: Erect a fence at least 2m (6ft) high around the perimeter of the garden or plant a tall evergreen hedge to keep them out.

Aphids (greenfly and blackfly)
Sap-sucking insects (Aphidoidea).
SYMPTOMS: The aphids, often clustering on the undersides of leaves, suck the sap, distorting young shoots and leaves. They seldom kill a tree outright, but it may be seriously weakened.
CONTROL: Inspect new growth often for signs of attack, particularly if other related garden plants, such as roses, show signs of damage. Either spray with an insecticide or an insecticidal soap. On a small plant, you can rub off the pests with finger and thumb.

Apple sawfly
Small wasp-like insects (*Hoplocampa testudinea*).
SYMPTOMS: The adult insects first lay their eggs on the blossoms. The eggs then hatch into maggots which tunnel just below the surface of the developing fruit's skin. This causes ribbon-like scars on the outside of the fruit. As the maggots grow, they then tunnel directly into the middle of the fruit, causing it to drop prematurely around mid-summer.
CONTROL: Spray the tree with derris when all the petals have been shed.

Remove and burn all affected fruits that show signs of scarring.
James Grieve and Worcester Pearmain are both susceptible varieties.

Winter moth
A moth (*Operophtera brumata*).
SYMPTOMS: Numerous holes are eaten in leaves. This weakens the tree and leaves it susceptible to other problems. Flightless females climb trees in winter, laying their eggs on branches. The emerging caterpillars feed on the leaves, blossoms and young fruitlets during the spring. The caterpillar weaves a silken thread loosely through the leaves and the small holes made at this stage often go unnoticed. As the leaves develop, the holes enlarge and become noticeable. Caterpillars then drop down to the soil where they pupate into adults – they will emerge from the soil anytime during winter.
CONTROL: Tie sticky grease bands around trunks in winter to prevent the females from ascending into the topgrowth. Remove and burn this in spring. (Bands should also be wrapped around any supporting stakes.)

Codling moth
A moth (*Cydia pomonella*).
SYMPTOMS: Maggots are found in fruits. The adult lays its eggs on the surface of the developing fruit in late spring. The larvae then tunnel into the centre. The caterpillar is fully fed around late summer, so it eats its way out of the fruit and spends the winter in loose flakes of bark on the tree trunk.
CONTROL: You can control numbers by hanging sticky pheromone traps in trees. These mimic the scent of

sexually mature females. Males are attracted by the scent then are caught in the traps. These traps not only reduce numbers but also indicate the presence of the pest in a garden. Spraying with an insecticide in early summer can control the caterpillars. The pest can also be controlled through the use of a pathogenic nematode (*Steinernema carpocapsae*), which enters the caterpillars and infects them with a bacterial disease. Spray the nematode on the trunk and branches, and also the soil under the branches, in early autumn, after the caterpillars have left the fruit. Note this treatment gives no protection against female codling moths flying in from nearby gardens to lay their eggs the following year.

Woolly aphid
Sucking insects (*Erisoma lanigerum*).
SYMPTOMS: Fluffy white areas appear on bark. The pest is often mistaken for a fungus or mould. The aphid appears in the spring on the bark of some fruit trees – it is common around bark which has not been cleanly pruned. If you rub your finger over them, the aphids will be crushed and wet, which is the proof that the infestation is not mould. The waxy coating makes them difficult to treat with sprays. In severe cases, the bark will develop lumps that may split in frosty periods, leaving the tree open to apple canker.
CONTROL: If the aphids are noticed early, simply paint them with methylated spirits, or scrape them off individually. If larger areas are infected, spray with derris. Failing this, cut the resulting lumps out from the bark.

Below: These apples have the tell-tale scars caused by apple sawfly maggots.

Below: This apple damage is caused by a tunnelling codling moth caterpillar.

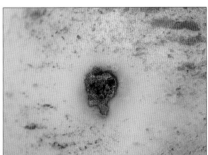

Diseases

Bacteria, viruses or fungi are the main causes of diseases in apples, often entering plants through the flowers or wounds.

Canker

A serious fungal disease (*Nectria galligena*) of apples and related fruits.
SYMPTOMS: Sunken, discoloured patches are seen on bark. The canker is first noticeable in autumn as a swelling of the bark – often at the site of a pruning wound or damaged bud. The central part of the swelling begins to die back and the bark flakes off leaving a sunken discoloured area. In summer, white fungus grows on the diseased bark, turning to a red fungus-like growth in winter.
CONTROL: Diseased patches should be cut back to healthy wood, using a knife or chisel. Burn the diseased wood. The exposed healthy wood can be painted with a canker paint. If canker is a major problem, spray with a copper-based fungicide in late summer to early autumn. Three consecutive sprayings are needed.

Mildew (powdery and downy mildew)

A fungal disease caused by a number of different pathogens.
SYMPTOMS: Light grey powdery patches appear on leaves, shoots and flowers, normally in spring. The flowers turn a creamy yellow colour and will not develop correctly. Powdery mildew remains on the surface of the plant. Downy mildew penetrates the plant, eventually killing it. Both types of

mildew are prevalent in cool and over-damp conditions.
CONTROL: All infected growth should be removed and burnt – do not put it on the compost heap. If the problem persists, spray with copper fungicide. Avoid over-watering and prune to improve air circulation within the crown of the tree. Reduce the amount of fertilizer being applied.

Brown rot

A fungus (*Monilinia fructigena* and *M. laxa*) that enters fruits through wounds made by wasps, caterpillars and birds.
SYMPTOMS: Entire fruits rot and turn brown. The fruit becomes soft and grey spots of fungus grow on the browned fruit. Eventually the fruit will shrivel and fall off.
CONTROL: The disease is spread by contact, so all infected fruit, whether on the tree or on the ground, should be removed and burnt as soon as possible. If the disease has reached fruits in storage, these should also be removed and burnt and the storage area thoroughly cleaned with a disinfectant. Annual cleaning of the storage area with soda and warm water is a good preventive measure. Keep the soil and grass around the tree clear, removing leaves and other debris regularly. No chemical control is available.

Scab

A fungus (*Venturia inequalis* and *V. pirina*) that attacks apples as well as other related fruits.

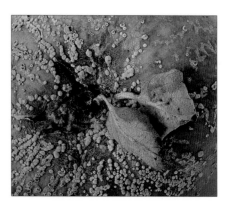

Above: This apple has turned brown and is covered with buff fungal spores of brown rot.

SYMPTOMS: Olive green or brown blotches appear on the leaves. The blotches turn browner in time and brown scabs appear on the fruit. The diseased leaves will fall early and the fruit will become increasingly covered in scabs – eventually the fruit skin will crack.
CONTROL: Remove and burn diseased fruit and leaves (including shed leaves) as soon as possible. Spores can over-winter in the fallen leaves, so clear and burn all leaves which fall in the autumn and winter. When planting new trees, avoid low-lying areas where air movement is restricted. Plant the trees in the open where they will benefit from good air circulation, avoiding damp conditions.

Granny Smith and Delicious are particularly susceptible.

Botrytis (grey mould)

A common fungal disease (*Botrytis* spp.) that can affect nearly all plants.
SYMPTOMS: Botrytis is first noticeable as brown spots, which are followed by a furry grey mould. The cause of the disease is too much dampness in cool conditions – growing plants in over-fertile conditions encourages botrytis.
CONTROL: All infected growth should be removed and burnt – do not put it on the compost heap. If the problem persists, spray with copper fungicide (Bordeaux mixture). To prevent further occurrences, improve growing conditions. Avoid over-watering and prune to improve air circulation within the crown of the tree. Reduce the amount of fertilizer being applied.

Below: The fungal spores of apple canker surround the sunken patches on this branch.

Below: The light grey powdery patches on these apple leaves are caused by mildew.

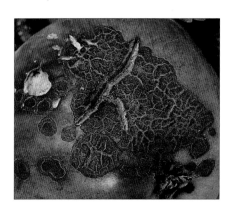

Above: Apple scab is a fungal disease that is spread by wind and rain.

Fireblight
A bacterial disease (*Erwinia amylovora*).
SYMPTOMS: Leaves turn brown and wither without being shed by the plant. Shoots can die back. Flowers wilt and young shoots wither and die. Cankers appear around the base of dead shoots in autumn. In severe cases, trees can die.
CONTROL: Cut back affected growth, cutting at least 60cm (2ft) behind the diseased material. Plant disease-resistant varieties. Spray trees when in flower with copper fungicide.

Silver leaf
A fungus (*Chondrostereum purpureum*) that enters plants through recent wounds, such a snapped branch, or often as a result of pruning during or just before a period of wet weather.
SYMPTOMS: Leaves turn silver then brown. The silver sheen is due to a poison which the fungus releases that causes the outer cells on the leaf to separate. Branches die back. Mauve fruiting bodies (brackets) appear on dead wood. The extent to which the disease has penetrated the tree can be determined by cutting off a branch (at least 2.5cm/1in in diameter) and wetting the cut surface. Affected tissue shows as a purple or brown stain.
CONTROL: Cut back all affected growth to about 15cm (6in) beyond the point where the brown or purple staining ceases. Sterilize all tools before and after use. Feed, water and mulch plants well to promote recovery. If fruiting bodies have appeared on the main trunk, dig up the tree and destroy it.

To minimize risk of infection, carry out all pruning during settled, warm weather in early summer and paint all pruning wounds with a wound paint.

Physiological problems
Inappropriate growing conditions are often the source of problems. Irregular water supplies can lead to cracking of the fruits and uneven growth. Water trees well during periods of drought while the fruits are ripening. Apply a deep annual mulch around the base of trees in spring to conserve soil moisture and maintain even growth.

Bitter pit
Caused by a chemical imbalance in the tree, bitter pit indicates either a shortage of calcium or too much potassium or magnesium. This is often due to a shortage of water at a crucial time in the development of the fruits.
SYMPTOMS: Several small brown sunken pits on the surface of the apple. The flesh below the pits is also browned and tastes bitter. The number of affected areas will rise considerably during storage. Fruits showing signs of bitter pit should not be stored.
CONTROL: There is no reliable treatment once the problem has been noticed. To avoid recurrence, the following season mulch around the tree with well-rotted compost to conserve water, especially in dry periods. Do not over-fertilize.

Biennial bearing
Producing irregular crops is a common problem of apples, particularly of some

Below: The dark blotches on these apple leaves are caused by silverleaf.

varieties. It can be caused by a number of factors.
SYMPTOMS: Trees crop heavily one year then produce hardly any the following year. The habit can be set in the year after a particularly hard winter that has wiped out all the flowers so no fruit is set during the season following. The tree then bears heavily as if to compensate, thus exhausting its capacity to flower and fruit the year after that. Heavy attack by pests and diseases at flowering time can also lead to biennial bearing in the same way.
CONTROL: If a tree has cropped poorly, reduce the number of flowers in the following spring, pinching out up to nine out of ten clusters (leaving the surrounding leaves intact). This leads to a moderate crop that year, and the tree should crop normally the year after, thus breaking the pattern.

Replant disease
This disorder occurs where a plant is replaced with one of the same type that then fails to thrive.
SYMPTOMS: Plants establish poorly and roots fail to grow. The plant may die.
CONTROL: If the new plant is still alive, dig it up and transfer it to a site where apples have not already been grown. Alternatively, dig it up, then excavate a fresh hole in the same place, 60cm (2ft) across and 30cm (1ft) deep. Wash the roots under running water, then replant the tree, backfilling with fresh soil taken from another part of the garden. Use of mycorrhizal fungi when planting is believed by some gardeners to reduce the risk of replant disease.

Below: The various brown sunken pits on this apple indicate a chemical imbalance.

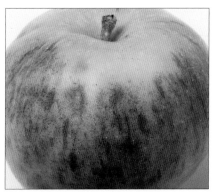

A DIRECTORY OF APPLES

With more than 7,500 apple cultivars known to exist world wide, it is not surprising that this well-loved fruit comes in such a diverse range of shapes and sizes.

The apples on the following directory pages are listed alphabetically, from Acme to Zoete Ermgaard, for easy reference. The selection provides an overview of as varied and as international a selection of apples as possible.

Each directory entry gives a detailed description of the shape, size, flavour, colour and texture of the fruit. The cultivars are illustrated photographically from the top, the bottom and cut in half. Some fruits are shown growing on the tree. Entries are accompanied by notes and a text panel provides information on the type, origin, parentage, flowering season and other names of each variety.

Above left: Rossie Pippin. *Above right*: Winston.
Left: A flourishing crop of attractive rosy-red fruit weighs down the branches of this apple tree.

Acme

The rounded fruits, around 6cm (2¼in) across, are yellowish green, heavily flushed with crimson. The flesh is firm and creamy with a rich and fruity flavour.

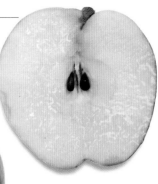

Right: *Fruits develop red striping as they ripen.*

Note: This variety is self-sterile so a compatible pollination partner must be grown nearby to ensure fruiting.

Type: Dessert.
Origin: Boreham, Essex, UK, 1944.
Parentage: Worcester Pearmain x ?Rival (female) x Cox's Orange Pippin (male).
Flowering: Mid-season.

Adam's Pearmain

This old variety produces conical fruits, around 5cm (2in) across or more, that are citrus yellow striped with red, with regular russeting. The flesh is creamy yellowish white, firm-textured, juicy and with a nutty flavour similar to Egremont Russet. This was a popular variety in the 19th century.

Type: Dessert.
Origin: Herefordshire, UK, 1826.
Parentage: Unknown.
Flowering: Mid-season.
Other names: Adamsapfel, Hanging Pearmain, Lady's Finger, Matchless, Moriker, Norfolk Pippin, Norfolk Russet, Pearmain d'Adam, Rough Pippin, Rousse du Norfolk, Russet aus Norfolk and Winter Striper Pearmain.

Note: Adam's Pearmain shows some resistance to scab. Young trees bear freely.

Alfriston

This traditional old variety has slightly knobbly, bright yellow-green fruits, often more than 7cm (2¾in) across, with a sharp, acid flavour. They are soft and coarse in texture. Fruits can be stored for several months and cook well.

Type: Culinary.
Origin: Uckfield, Sussex, UK, late 1700s; renamed Alfriston 1819.
Parentage: Unknown.
Flowering: Mid-season.
Other names: Alfreston, Freen Grove, Green Goose, Lord Gwydyr's Newton Pippin, Oldaker's New, Shepherd's Pippin and Shepherd's Seedling Pippin.

Note: Canker can be a problem on heavy soils. Trees bear heavily.

Allen's Everlasting

Type: Dessert.
Origin: Ireland, before 1864.
Parentage: Possibly a seedling of Sturmer Pippin.
Flowering: Mid-season.
Other names: Allen's Dauerapfel, Eternelle d'Allen and Harvey's Everlasting.

Slightly flattened in shape, the fruits, around 6cm (2¼in) across, are rough-skinned and greenish yellow, touched with red as they ripen and russeted over the whole surface. The flesh is firm, juicy and pale yellow with a rich flavour.

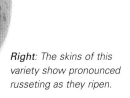

Note: Trees are not particularly vigorous. The apples store well.

Right: The skins of this variety show pronounced russeting as they ripen.

Allington Pippin

Type: Dessert.
Origin: Lincolnshire, UK, before 1844, originally as Brown's South Lincoln Beauty; renamed 1894 and introduced 1896.
Parentage: King of the Pippins (female) x Cox's Orange Pippin (male).
Flowering: Mid-season.
Other names: Allington, Allingtoner Pepping, Brown's South Lincoln Beauty, Pepin d'Allington, South Lincoln Beauty and South Lincoln Pippin.

The conical fruits, around 7cm (2¾in) across, are dull green or yellow with a red flush or red striping. The flesh is creamy white. The flavour is distinct, strong and sharp, with a bitter-sweet quality.

Note: Unripe fruits are also suitable for cooking, keeping their shape well.

Amanishiki

Type: Dessert.
Origin: Amori Apple Experiment Station, Japan, 1936, renamed 1948.
Parentage: Ralls Janet (female) x Indo (male).
Flowering: Mid-season.

The fruits, around 5cm (2in) across, are rounded and yellowish green with a red flush. The creamy white flesh is sweet in flavour but inclined to be insipid. Fruits ripen best in areas with reliably warm summers.

Note: Its female parent is an old variety from Virginia – evidence of the importance of maintaining old varieties for breeding purposes.

Ananas Reinette

This variety produces bright golden yellow, almost cylindrical, yellow green fruits, up to 6cm (2¼in) across, with russet freckling. The flesh is white-yellow, crisp and juicy, with an intense flavour that is reminiscent of pineapples when they are ripe. The skins can turn almost orange in the sun.

Type: Dessert.
Origin: Believed to be the Netherlands, recorded 1821.
Parentage: Unknown.
Flowering: Mid-season.
Other names: Ananas, Ananasii, Ananasova reneta, Ananasrennett, Ananasz renet, d'Ananas, Reinette Ananas and Renetta Ananas.

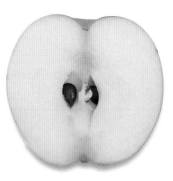  

Note: Trees are suitable for training in all forms, making this a useful apple for small gardens. This is a popular apple in northern Europe.

Angyal Dezso

The fruits, of slightly irregular shape, are around 7cm (2¾in) across. They are greenish yellow with some light brown russeting. The flesh is crisp and coarse with a sweet to subacid and nutty flavour.

  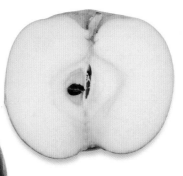

Note: Trees are moderately vigorous. They are self-sterile so need a suitable pollinator.

Type: Dessert.
Origin: Believed to be Hungary, c.1900.
Parentage: Unknown.
Flowering: Late.

Annie Elizabeth

This variety is unusual among cultivated apples in having maroon flowers. The large, irregular (prominently ribbed or angular), flattened fruits, to 8cm (3in) across, are bright yellow-green, flushed with red. The flesh is white. Its sweet flavour makes it one of the best apples for stewing and baking.

Type: Culinary.
Origin: Knighton, Leicester, UK, c.1857 (introduced c.1898).
Parentage: ?Blenheim Orange (female) x Unknown.
Flowering: Late.
Other names: Carter's Seedling, Sloto, Slotoaeble, Slotrable, Slotraeble, Sussex Pippin and The George.

Note: Trees show some disease resistance and are tolerant of mild, damp climates. The fruits store well.

Annurca

Type: Dessert.
Origin: Italy, 1973.
Parentage: Unknown.
Flowering: Mid-season.
Other names: Annurca
Bella del Sud and Annurca
Rossa del Sud.

The rounded fruits, to 5cm (2in) across, are bright yellow-green with a red flush. The creamy white flesh is sweet, crisp and juicy. This variety is of great commercial importance in Italy, and is grown almost exclusively in Campania.

Note: In 2001, Annurca was recognized as a typical regional product by the European Union and awarded GPI (protected geographical indication) status under the name Melannurca Campana.

Right: This variety is well-known in its native Italy.

Antonovka

Type: Culinary and dessert.
Origin: A Russian variety that arose in Kursk, first recorded in 1826.
Parentage: Unknown.
Flowering: Early.
Other names: Antenovka, Antoni, Antonifka, Antonovka obyknovennaya, Antonovka prostaya, Antonovskoe yabloko, Antonowka, Antony, Bergamot, Cinnamon, Dukhovoe, German Calville, King of the Steppe, Nalivia, Possart's Nalivia, Russian Gravenstein and Vargul.

The irregular fruits, often larger than 7cm (2¾in) across, are bright yellowish green with some russeting and spotting. The creamy white flesh is crisp and juicy with an acid flavour. The fruits cook well.

Note: Trees are vigorous and hardy. The fruits cook well. This variety is sometimes used as a rootstock because of its resistance to cold.

Apez Zagarra

Type: Dessert.
Origin: France, 1973.
Parentage: Unknown.
Flowering: Late.
Other name: Apez Sagarra.

The fruits, somewhat irregular in shape and around 6cm (2¼in) across, are dull green and heavily russeted. The creamy white flesh has a fairly distinct aniseed flavour.

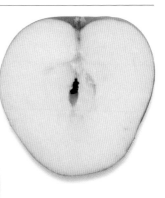

Note: This variety is local to the Basque region of France. Trees are moderately vigorous.

Ashmead's Kernel

The bright green-yellow fruits, slightly flattened and irregular in shape, are around 7cm (2¾ in) across. They are flushed orange with light cinnamon brown russeting and the yellowish flesh is firm and juicy. The flavour is sweet, slightly acid and richly aromatic.

Note: This is one of the best of the old varieties. It was crossed with an unknown male to produce Improved Ashmead's Kernel, first recorded in 1883.

Type: Dessert.
Origin: Gloucester, UK, *c.*1700.
Parentage: Possibly a seedling of Nonpareil.
Flowering: Mid-season.
Other names: Aschmead's Saemling, Ashmead's Samling, Ashmead's Seedling, Dr Ashmead's Kernel, Samling von Ashmead, Semis d'Ashmead and Seyanets Ashmida.

Baldwin

This triploid variety produces uniformly large, rounded fruits, around 7cm (2¾ in) across. The skins are tough, smooth, light yellow or greenish, blushed and mottled with bright red and indistinctly striped with deep carmine. Russeting is sometimes found towards the base. The yellowish flesh is coarse-textured and juicy but lacking in flavour.

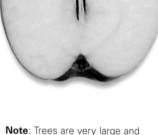

Note: Trees are very large and vigorous but biennial bearing can be a problem. This variety was formerly commercially important in the USA.

Type: Dessert.
Origin: Wilmington, MA, USA, *c.*1740, as a chance seedling (introduced *c.*1780).
Parentage: Unknown.
Flowering: Mid-season.
Other names: American Baldwin, Baldwin Rosenapfel, Baldwin's Rother Pippin, Beldvin, Butter's, Butter's Woodpecker, Butters' Red Baldwin, Calville Butter, Felch, Late Baldwin, Pecker, Pepin Rouge de Baldwin, Red Baldwin's Pippin, Steele's Red Winter and Woodpecker.

Ballarat Seedling

Note: Trees are vigorous. Fruits store well and can also be used in cooking. This variety was found in the garden of a Mrs Stewart and is sometimes informally called the Stewart apple.

The fruits are large, slightly irregular and around 8cm (3in) across. Skins are green with a red flush. The flavour is subacid and the fruits need a long hot summer to ripen fully. The flesh is coarse and hard.

Type: Dessert.
Origin: Ballarat, Victoria, Australia, early 1900s but possibly older.
Parentage: ?Dunn's Seedling (female) x Unknown.
Flowering: Mid-season.
Other names: Ballarat, Stewart's, Stewart's Ballarat Seedling and Stewart's Seedling.

Ball's Pippin

Type: Dessert.
Origin: Langley, Buckinghamshire, UK, 1923.
Parentage: Cox's Orange Pippin (female) x Sturmer Pippin (male).
Flowering: Mid-season.
Other name: Lane's Oakland Seedling.

The fruits, around 7cm (2¾in) across, are round and flattened in shape with yellowish green and russeted skin tones. The flesh is crisp and sweet in flavour.

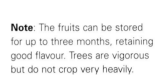

Note: The fruits can be stored for up to three months, retaining good flavour. Trees are vigorous but do not crop very heavily.

Barnack Beauty

Type: Dessert.
Origin: Barnack, Northamptonshire, UK, c.1840, introduced c.1870.
Parentage: Unknown.
Flowering: Mid-season.
Other names: Barnack, Beckford Beauty and Piekna z Barnaku.

The flushed fruits, rounded to slightly conical in shape and 5cm (2in) across or larger, are sweet, crisp and juicy with a good flavour. They are also suitable for cooking. The spring blossom is particularly attractive.

Above: The attractive Barnack Beauty has a sharp flavour and is frequently found in old orchards in the east of England.

Note: This variety may not crop well in all areas.

Barnack Orange

Type: Dessert.
Origin: Belvoir Castle, Leicestershire, UK, 1904.
Parentage: Barnack Beauty (female) x Cox's Orange Pippin (male).
Flowering: Mid-season.

The flattened fruits, to 6cm (2¼in) across, are yellow-green with a pronounced red flush. The creamy white flesh has an aromatic flavour somewhat reminiscent of Cox. The flesh is firm and rather coarse in texture.

Note: Fruits can be stored for up to five months. They are similar to those of Barnack Beauty (above) but are sweeter and ripen earlier.

Bascombe Mystery

The knobbly, green fruits, around 6cm (2¼in) across, turn more yellowish as they ripen. The white flesh is firm, fine and tinged with green, with a sweet to subacid flavour.

Type: Dessert.
Origin: First recorded 1831.
Parentage: Unknown.
Flowering: Late.
Other names: Bascomb Mystery and Bascombe's Mystery.

Note: Trees are moderately vigorous with an upright to spreading habit. This variety was popular in Victorian times.

Bassard

The fruits are irregularly rounded in shape and around 6cm (2¼in) across. They are bright yellow-green with some russeting. The greenish-white flesh is firm and coarse with a rather acid flavour.

Note: Late flowering makes this a suitable variety for frost-prone areas. It is resistant to leaf spot diseases. Fruits can be stored for four to five months.

Type: Culinary.
Origin: France, first described 1948.
Parentage: Unknown.
Flowering: Late.

Baumann's Reinette

The fruits, flattened and around 7cm (2¾in) across, are greenish yellow with a brilliant red flush. The creamy white flesh is crisp and rather coarse textured and fairly juicy. The flavour is a little acid and faintly aromatic.

Type: Dessert and culinary
Origin: Belgium, 1811.
Parentage: Unknown.
Flowering: Mid-season.
Other names: Baumana, Baumanova reneta, Couronne des Dames d'Enghien, Krasnyi renet, Red Winter Reinette, Reinette de Bollwiller, Reinette rouge d'hiver de Baumann, Renet Baumann, Roter Reinette and Rothe Winter.

Note: Trees are moderately vigorous. The attractive fruits can be stored for four to five months.

Baxter's Pearmain

Type: Dessert and culinary.
Origin: Norfolk, UK, 1821.
Parentage: Unknown.
Flowering: Mid-season.

Note: Trees are hardy and vigorous. They bear fruit abundantly even in years when other apple varieties are cropping poorly.

The texture of the slightly irregular fruits, around 7cm (2¾in) across, is rather coarse and dry. The skins are yellow-green with a red flush or red streaks. The creamy white flesh is slightly acid in flavour and reminiscent of Blenheim.

Beauty of Bath

Type: Dessert.
Origin: Bailbrook, Bath, UK, introduced c.1864.
Parentage: Unknown.
Flowering: Early.
Other names: Batskaya krasavitsa, Cooling's Beauty of Bath, Frumos de Bath, Krasivoe iz Bata, Schöner von Bath and Schönheit von Bath.

The slightly flattened, somewhat irregular fruits, around 6cm (2¼in) across, are bright green with a strong dark red flush and some streaking. The creamy white flesh is soft, juicy, sweet and somewhat acid with a distinctive flavour.

Note: This is usually one of the first apples to ripen. Trees crop heavily and show good disease resistance. Fruits do not store well and are best eaten straight from the tree. A commercially important variety in the 19th century.

Beauty of Kent

Type: Culinary.
Origin: ?England, c.1820.
Parentage: Unknown.
Flowering: Mid-season
Other names: Beauté de Kent, Bellezza di Kent, Countess of Warwick, Gadd's Seedling, Kentish Beauty, Kentish Broading, Kentskaya krasavitsa, Pippin Kent, Reinette Grosse d'Angleterre, Schöner aus Kent and Worling's Favourite.

The fruits, conical and irregular in shape, are around 6cm (2¼in) across and often larger. They are deep yellow, tinged with green, and show faint red patches or striping. Though edible raw, they are better cooked. The flesh, coarse in texture, is white and juicy with a sharp, subacid, though pleasant, flavour.

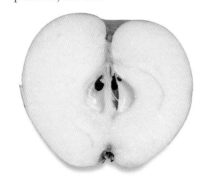

Note: This variety is suitable for growing in all areas. Canker can be a problem on heavy soils.

Beauty of Stoke

The green fruits, flushed red, are rounded and around 6cm (2¼in) across. They have a sweet flavour, unusually for a cooking apple, though the creamy white flesh is coarse and dry.

Type: Culinary.
Origin: Rufford Abbey, Nottinghamshire, UK, recorded 1889.
Parentage: Unknown.
Flowering: Mid-season.

Note: Trees are moderately vigorous. The fruits cook to a bright lemon-yellow purée.

Bedfordshire Foundling

This yellow-skinned variety has a sweet, sharp flavour. The flesh is firm, juicy and somewhat coarse-textured. The fruits, large and angular in shape, around 7cm (2¾in) across or more, cook well.

Note: Trees are moderately vigorous. The fruits can be stored for four to five months.

Type: Culinary.
Origin: ?England, c.1800.
Parentage: Unknown.
Flowering: Mid-season.
Other names:
Bedfordshirskii Naidyonysh, Cambridge Pippin, Findling aus Bedfordshire, Mignon de Bedford, Trouvé dans le comté de Bedford and Trovatello de Bedfordshire.

Belle de Boskoop

Above: Belle de Boskoop is a versatile apple that has retained its popularity.

The fruits are lumpy, around 6cm (2¼in) across and flushed yellow-red with fawn areas. They have firm, dense, coarse-textured, white-green flesh with a pleasant, aromatic flavour and cook well. They keep well, with the flavour becoming progressively sweeter during storage.

Note: Trees are vigorous and resistant to scab. They can be slow to bear but crop well once mature. This triploid variety is very popular in continental Europe. It is vulnerable to frosts and does not do well in dry soils. Clones include Boskoop Jaune, Boskoop Rouge and Boskoop Verte.

Type: Dessert and culinary.
Origin: Boskoop, the Netherlands, c.1865.
Parentage: Probably a chance seedling or possibly a sport of Rechette de Montfort.
Flowering: Early.
Other names: Apfel der Zukunft, Boskoopskaya krasavitsa, Frumos de Boskoop, Gold Reinette, Piekna z Boskoop, Reinette de Montfort, Reinette Monstrueuse, Renetta di Montfort and Schoner von Boskoop.

Belle de Magny

Type: Dessert.
Origin: France,
recorded 1888.
Parentage: Unknown.
Flowering: Late.
Other names:
Bell de Mani,
Belle de Magni
and Krasavitsa
iz Mani.

The fruits, irregular in shape and around 5cm (2in) across, are pale yellow-green with a pinkish red flush. They have fine, softish, creamy white flesh with a rich and subacid flavour.

Note: This variety, grown in Louis XIV's orchards, is self-fertile. It is susceptible to aphids and scab.

Belle de Tours

Type: Culinary.
Origin: France (Indre and Loire), 1947.
Parentage: Unknown.
Flowering: Late.
Other name: Lambron.

Fruits have crisp, juicy, white flesh with an acid flavour. Skins are bright green to whitish yellow, sometimes with a reddish blush. They are roughly conical and irregular.

Note: This variety is increasingly rare in culivation, though old specimens are still being found in its place of origin. It is usually grown as a free-standing tree rather than being trained into a particular form.

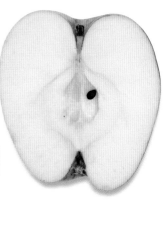

Belledge Pippin

Type: Dessert.
Origin: Derbyshire, UK, first recorded 1818.
Parentage: Unknown.
Flowering: Mid-season.

The small, rounded, regularly shaped fruits, to 5cm (2in) across, are bright yellow-green in colour (turning yellow as they ripen) with some darker spotting. Russeting can appear as grey dots. They have coarse, soft, whitish to greenish-yellow flesh with an acid flavour.

Note: Fruits are also suitable for cooking.

Ben's Red

The flattened fruits, around 6cm (2¼in) across, are bright yellow-green with a strong pinkish to dark-red flush and some flecking and striping. The creamy white flesh is crisp, dry and coarse with a sweet strawberry-like flavour.

Type: Dessert.
Origin: Trannack, Cornwall, UK, *c.*1830.
Parentage: ?Devonshire Quarrenden (female) x Farleigh Pippin (male).
Flowering: Early.

Note: The fruits are good for juicing.

Beregi Sóvari

The somewhat flattened fruits, around 5cm (2in) across, are bright yellowish green with some spotting and russeting. The creamy white flesh is firm and fine with a sweet flavour. This variety is believed to be a sport of Nemes Sovari Alma.

Type: Dessert.
Origin: Hungary, recorded 1900.
Parentage: Unknown.
Flowering: Mid-season.

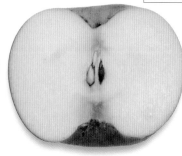

Note: Trials in Hungary have indicated susceptibility to fireblight, making this an unsuitable variety for breeding programmes.

Bess Pool

The rounded, slightly irregular fruits, around 6cm (2¼in) across or more, are yellowish green with a red, sometimes striped, flush. They have a rather dry, slightly coarse-textured, white flesh with a sweet and pleasant flavour. There is sometimes a red staining just under the skin.

Type: Dessert.
Origin: Nottinghamshire, UK, first recorded 1824.
Parentage: Unknown.
Flowering: Late.
Other names:
Black Blenheim, Muskierte gelbe Reinette, Red Rice, Ronald's Besspool, Stradbroke Pippin and Walsgrove Blenheim.

Note: Late flowering makes this variety useful in areas prone to spring frosts.

Bismarck

Type: Culinary.
Origin: Variously reported as Bismarck, Tasmania; Carisbrooke, Australia; and Canterbury, New Zealand; before 1887.
Parentage: Unknown.
Flowering: Mid-season.
Other names: Bismarckapfel, Bismarckapfel aus Neuseeland, Bismarckovo, Fürst Bismarck, Pomme Bismarck and Prince Bismarck.

The fruits are around 6cm (2¼in) across and often larger on young or regularly pruned trees. Skins are yellow-green with a strong red flush and some striping. Fruits have firm, fine-textured, juicy flesh with an acid flavour.

Note: This variety, named after Prince Bismarck, a German politician, is a useful general-purpose cooker. The flesh collapses on cooking. Trees are large and crop well.

Blaxtayman

Type: Dessert.
Origin: Wenatchee, Washington, USA, 1926 (introduced 1930).
Parentage: Winesap (female) x Unknown.
Flowering: Mid-season.
Other names: Nured Stayman and Stayman's Winesap.

The attractive fruits, around 6cm (2¼in) across, are yellow-green with a generally even, solid red flush. They have a very juicy, softish, yellowish flesh with a sweet flavour.

Note: This variety is a sport of Stayman Winesap, the skins of the fruits having a more even and solid flush.

Blenheim Orange

Type: Dessert and culinary.
Origin: Woodstock, Oxfordshire, UK, c.1740.
Parentage: Unknown.
Flowering: Mid-season.
Other names: Beauty of Dumbleton, Belle d'Angers, Blenhaimska zlatna reneta, Königin Victoria, Lucius Apfel, Northampton, Prince de Galles, Prince of Wales, Reinette dorée de Blenheim, Renet Zolotoi Blengeimskii, Ward's Pippin, Woodstock and Zlota reneta Blenheimska

This classic variety has attractive, flattened, yellow fruits, around 7cm (2¾in) across, flushed red with fine russeting. Carried in abundance, they have a very distinctive, rich, nutty flavour. They have yellowish white, somewhat fine-textured and rather dry flesh which rapidly becomes mealy.

Note: Fruits cook well to a stiff purée. Trees, which are very vigorous, are prone to biennial bearing.

Blue Pearmain

The slightly conical, red fruits, around 6cm (2¼in) across, have a distinct bluish bloom and/or purplish red striping – hence the name. The flavour is mild, sweet, rich and aromatic. The texture is soft, rather dry and coarse.

Note: Fruits can shrivel in storage but retain good flavour. This variety was widely grown in New England in the 19th century.

Type: Dessert.
Origin: ?USA, early 1800s.
Parentage: Unknown.
Flowering: Mid-season.

Bohnapfel

The rounded fruits, around 5cm (2in) across, are light green with an orange-brown flush and striping. The skin can be tough. They have firm, coarse, yellowish white flesh with a subacid to slightly sweet flavour.

Note: This variety, a triploid, is suitable for juicing. Trees grow well at high altitudes and show good resistance to wind and frosts. There are numerous clones.

Type: Dessert and culinary.
Origin: Rhineland, Germany, late 1700s.
Parentage: Unknown.
Flowering: Mid-season.
Other names: Anhalter, Bobovoe bolsoe, Ferro rosso, Grochowka, Gros Bohnapfel, Grosser Rheinischer Bohnapfel, Jackerle, Nagy Bohn alma, Pomme Bohn, Pomme Haricot, Reinskoe bobovoe, Salzhauser Rheinischer, Strymka, Wax Apple and Weisser Bohnapfel.

Boïken

The fruits, which are around 6cm (2¼in) across, have firm, fine-textured, juicy, acid flesh but with very little flavour. The smooth skins are yellowish, marked with pinkish red. The variety is named after Dikewarden Boïke.

Note: Trees are vigorous and show good resistance to frost but biennial bearing may be a problem. Young trees fruit well. The fruits store successfully.

Type: Dessert.
Origin: Bremen, Germany, known since 1828.
Parentage: Unknown.
Flowering: Mid-season.
Other names: Beuken, Birkin, Boiken Apfel, Bolken, Jablko Boikovo, Pomme Boiken and Zlotka Boikena.

Bolero

Type: Dessert.
Origin: Kent, UK, 1976.
Parentage: Developed from Wijcik, a sport of McIntosh.
Flowering: Mid-season.
Other name: Tuscan.

The rounded fruits, around 6cm (2¼in) across, are green with a yellow blush. The flesh is crisp and juicy with a sweet flavour. The flesh is similar to that of Granny Smith.

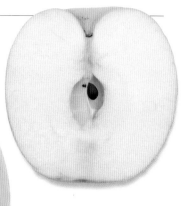

Note: This variety naturally grows as a column rather than spreading, so is useful in confined spaces. Trees show some signs of self-fertility.

Bonne Hotture

Type: Dessert.
Origin: ?Maine-et-Loire, France, recorded 1867.
Parentage: Unknown.
Flowering: Mid-season
Other names: Bonne Auture, Bonne Hoture, Bonne-Auture and de Bonne-Hotture.

The slightly flattened fruits, to 5cm (2in) across, are bright green with amber markings and conspicuous spotting. The flesh is crisp, creamy green and sweet and nutty in flavour, with a texture similar to that of a pear.

Note: Trees develop a broad crown with dense foliage. Fruits can be stored for five months or more.

Bonnet Carré

Type: Dessert.
Origin: France, recorded 1948, though believed to be much older.
Parentage: Unknown.
Flowering: Late.
Other names: Admirable blanche, Belle Dunoise, Blanche de Zürich, Calville Blanche, Calvine, Cotogna, Fraise d'Hiver, Framboise d'Hiver, Glace, Melonne, Niger, Reinette Côtelée, Taponelle and Weiss Zürich.

The fruits, angular and somewhat irregular in shape, are around 6cm (2¼in) across. They have soft, yellowish white flesh, with a sweet, perfumed flavour.

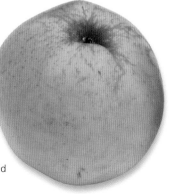

Note: This variety is best trained as an espalier. Fruits keep well.

Braddick Nonpareil

The rounded fruits, somewhat flattened, are around 6cm (2¼in) across. The skins are bright green with a strong red flush and some russeting. The firm, creamy white flesh is sugary and has a sweet-sharp flavour.

Type: Dessert.
Origin: Thames Ditton, Surrey, UK, before 1818.
Parentage: Unknown.
Flowering: Mid-season.
Other names: Braddicks Sondergleichen, Ditton Nonpareil, Ditton Pippin, Lincolnshire Reinette and Nonpareille de Braddick.

Note: The fruits store well, the flavour becoming somewhat sweeter. Trees, which crop freely, are suitable for esaplier training.

Bramley's Seedling

More commonly referred to as just Bramley, this classic English triploid variety has waxy-skinned, sometimes flattened, irregular, green fruits, up to 8cm (3in) across or more. They have an acid flavour. The flesh collapses on cooking.

Type: Culinary.
Origin: Southwell, Nottinghamshire, UK, between 1809 and 1813 (introduced 1865).
Parentage: Unknown.
Flowering: Mid-season.
Other names: Bramley and Bramleys Samling.

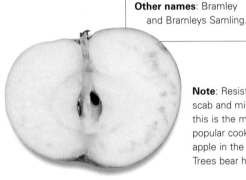

Note: Resistant to scab and mildew, this is the most popular cooking apple in the UK. Trees bear heavily.

Brenchley Pippin

This variety produces rounded, greenish yellow-skinned fruits that are around 6cm (2¼in) across. They can show areas of brownish orange strewed with russet dots. They have a sweet, aromatic, fruity flavour. The yellowish flesh, tinged green, is tender in texture, juicy and sweet.

Type: Dessert.
Origin: Brenchley, Kent, UK, 1884.
Parentage: Unknown.
Flowering: Mid-season.

Note: The fruits store well over a long period. This apple has been widely cultivated in Kent, England.

Brownlees' Russet

Type: Dessert
Origin: Hemel Hempstead, Hertfordshire, UK, *c*.1848.
Parentage: Unknown.
Flowering: Mid-season.
Other names: Brownlee Russet, Brownlees, Brownlees graue Reinette, Brownlees-Reinette, Brownley's Russet, Reinette grise de Brownlees and Renet seryi Braunlis.

The slightly irregular fruits of this apple, around 6cm (2¼ in) across, are heavily russeted with brown-green. They are juicy and have a somewhat acid, sweet-sharp but pleasantly nutty flavour. The flesh is fine-grained, crisp and greenish white.

Note: This variety is also suitable for cooking. Trees are compact with attractive deep pink flowers. Fruits store well but tend to shrivel.

Burr Knot

Type: Culinary.
Origin: UK, first recorded 1818.
Parentage: Unknown.
Flowering: Mid-season.
Other name: Bute's Walking-stick.

The skins of this variety are lemon yellow with a red blush and a few russet dots. The fruits, somewhat irregular in shape and around 6cm (2¼ in) across, are of no particular merit. They have soft, coarse-textured, rather dry flesh with an acid flavour.

Note: Trees are grown for their botanical and historic interests: the stems produce numerous burrs and cuttings taken from these root freely.

Cagarlaou

Type: Dessert.
Origin: Lozère, France, 1947.
Parentage: Unknown.
Flowering: Late.

The slightly conical fruits, around 6cm (2¼ in) across, are bright yellowish green with a strong red flush. The creamy white flesh has a sweet, perfumed flavour.

Note: This variety, which is very hardy, is normally grown as a free-standing tree rather than being trained. The fruits store well.

Calville Blanc d'Hiver

The fruits are knobbly and of irregular shape and around 6cm (2¼in) across. They are dull yellowish green, becoming brighter as they ripen, with some darker spotting. The creamy white flesh is soft, fine-textured and juicy with a sweet, aromatic flavour.

Note: Fruits may fail to ripen fully in cold areas unless trees are trained against a warm wall. They store well over winter and keep their shape when cooked.

Type: Dessert and culinary.
Origin: Europe, probably France or Germany, recorded 1598.
Parentage: Unknown.
Flowering: Mid-season.
Other names: a Frire, Admirable Blanche, Blanche de Zurich, Calville Acoute, Calville de Gascogne, Calville de Paris, Cotogna, Eggerling, Framboise d'Hiver, Melonne, Niger, Ostenapfel, Paris Apple, Pomme de Fraise, Pomme de Glace, Reinette a Cotes, Sternreinette, Tapounelle, Vit Vinterkalvill and Winter White Calville.

Calville de Maussion

The knobbly, uneven fruits are yellowish green with darker spotting and around 7cm (2¾in) across. The whitish flesh is sweet, subacid and aromatic in flavour.

Note: Trees are extremely vigorous. This variety is an excellent winter apple.

Type: Dessert.
Origin: France, recorded 1870.
Parentage: Unknown.
Flowering: Early.
Other names: Calleville de Maussion, Calville Maussion, Kalvil Mossion and Maussion's Calville.

Calville Rouge D'Hiver

The rounded to slightly conical, somewhat thick-skinned, irregular fruits, around 6cm (2¼in) across, are bright yellow-green with a strong bright red flush and yellow dots. The creamy white flesh is rather soft and moderately juicy with a somewhat sweet flavour.

Note: This variety is vigorous and hardy, performing well in cold situations. It does best in fertile soil. The fruits can sometimes be small.

Right: As its French name suggests, Calville Rouge d'Hiver is a good winter apple.

Type: Culinary.
Origin: Possibly Brittany, France, recorded c.1600.
Parentage: Unknown.
Flowering: Mid-season.
Other names: Achte Rote Winter Calville, Blutroter Calville, Calville d'Anjou, Calville Imperiale, Coeur de Boeuf, Cushman's Black, Gallwill Rusch, Le Général, Passe Pomme d'Hiver, Rambour Turc, Red Winter Calville, Roode Paasch, Roter Winter Calville and Winter Red Calville.

Captain Kidd

Type: Dessert.
Origin: Twyford, Hawkes Bay, NZ, 1962 (introduced 1969).
Parentage: Cox's Orange Pippin (female) x Delicious (male).
Flowering: Mid-season.

The fruits are slightly conical and around 6cm (2¼in) across. They are heavily flushed red and can show some russeting. The white flesh is crisp, sweet and juicy with a rich, aromatic flavour.

Note: This variety is a more highly coloured sport of Kidd's Orange Red.

Right: Captain Kidd can be relied on to fruit well.

Carrara Brusca

Type: Dessert.
Origin: Italy, 1958.
Parentage: Unknown.
Flowering: Mid-season.

The flattened fruits can be up to 7cm (2¾in) across or more. They are bright green with a red flush and some russeting. The yellowish flesh is firm and crisp with a subacid flavour.

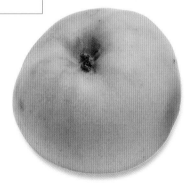

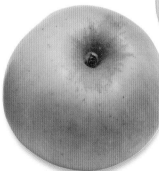

Note: This variety is rare in cultivation. Cankers have been reported.

Catshead

Type: Culinary.
Origin: England, UK, before 1600s.
Parentage: Unknown.
Flowering: Mid-season.
Other names: Apfelmuser, Coustard, Crede's Grosser, Wilhelm's Apfel, Duke of York, Green Codlin, Green Costard, Grenadier, Herefordshire Goose, Herrenapfel, Katzenkopf, Loggerhead, Monstrous Pigs Snout, Pomme de Royal Costard, Schafsnase, Stoke Leadington, Tankard, Terwin's Goliat, Tête de Seigneur and Tête du Chat.

The fruits of this unusual variety have a very distinctive, angular shape and are up to 7cm (2¾in) across or more. Fruits have a green skin. The texture of the whitish flesh is coarse and rather dry and the taste is sharp and subacid.

Note: The fruits cook to a firm, sharp-flavoured purée. Young trees may not crop well.

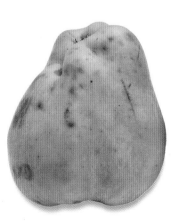

Cavallotta

The rounded but slightly irregular fruits are around 6cm (2¼in) across. The skins are bright yellowish green and the flesh is creamy white and firm with an acid flavour.

Type: Dessert.
Origin: Italy, 1958.
Parentage: Unknown.
Flowering: Mid-season.

Note: This variety is spur-fruiting.

Cheddar Cross

The conical fruits are around 7cm (2¾in) across and pale dull yellowish green with a red flush. The firm, fine-textured, white flesh is somewhat acid with little flavour.

Note: This variety is resistant to scab. Growth is dense and trees readily form spurs.

Type: Dessert.
Origin: Long Ashton Research Station, Bristol, UK, 1916 (introduced 1949).
Parentage: Allington Pippin (female) x Star of Devon (male).
Flowering: Early.

Chelmsford Wonder

The flattened, somewhat irregular fruits are around 7cm (2¾in) across. They are dull greenish yellow with red striping. The near white flesh is firm, juicy and fine-textured with a subacid flavour.

Type: Culinary.
Origin: Chelmsford, Essex, UK, c.1870 (introduced 1890).
Parentage: Unknown.
Flowering: Mid-season.
Other names:
Chudo Shelmsforda, Merveille de Chelmsford and Wunder von Chelmsford.

Note: Fruits store well for several months. The flavour remains acidic after cooking.

Chivers Delight

Type: Dessert.
Origin: Histon, Cambridgeshire, UK, 1936.
Parentage: Unknown (possibly involving Cox's Orange Pippin).
Flowering: Mid-season.

The rounded fruits are around 6cm (2¼in) across. They have bright green skins with a strong red flush. The creamy white flesh is crisp and juicy with a sweet, pleasant flavour.

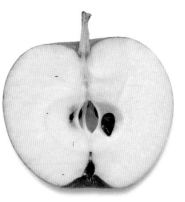

Note: Susceptible to canker. Fruits store well. This variety was popular during the early part of the 20th century.

Christmas Pearmain

Type: Dessert.
Origin: Kent, UK, first recorded 1893.
Parentage: Unknown.
Flowering: Early.
Other name: Bunyard's Christmas Pearmain.

The rounded fruits, around 6cm (2¼in) across, are green with a dark red flush. The flesh is yellowish white, crisp and juicy and has a pleasant, sweet flavour.

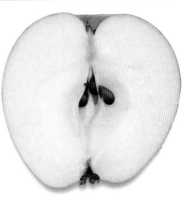

Note: Trees are generally healthy and crop well.

Claygate Pearmain

Type: Dessert.
Origin: Claygate, Surrey, UK, exhibited 1821.
Parentage: Unknown.
Flowering: Mid-season.
Other names: Archerfield Pearmain, Bradley's Pearmain, Brown's Pippin, Doncaster Pearmain, Empress Eugenie, Formosa Nonpareil, Formosa Pippin, Fowler's Pippin, Mason's Ribston Pearmain, Parmen Kleigatskii, Pearmain de Claygate, Pomme de Claygate, Ribston Pearmain, Summer Pearmain and Winter Pearmain.

The rounded fruits, often more than 6cm (2¼in) across, are dull yellow-green with a pinkish red flush and striping and some thin russeting and dotting. The yellowish white flesh is firm, crisp, rather coarse-textured and juicy with a rich aromatic flavour.

Note: Fruits can be stored for around four months. Trees are not vigorous, staying neat and compact, but crop freely, showing some resistance to scab. This variety is a good choice for a small garden.

Clemens

The slightly flattened, irregular fruits are around 6cm (2¼in) across. They are bright yellowish green with a red flush. The whitish flesh is soft, with a sweet, subacid flavour.

Type: Dessert.
Origin: Belgium, 1948.
Parentage: Unknown.
Flowering: Mid-season.

Note: Trees are vigorous.

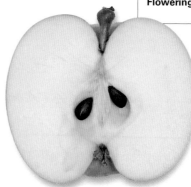

Cockett's Red

The slightly flattened, somewhat irregular fruits are around 6cm (2¼in) across. They are light yellowish green with a usually even, bright red flush. The whitish flesh is firm and sweet in flavour, sometimes sharp when first picked.

Type: Dessert.
Origin: Wisbech, Cambridgeshire, UK, 1929.
Parentage: Unknown.
Flowering: Mid-season.
Other names: Marguerite Henrietta and One Bite.

Note: Fruits store well, the flavour becoming more mellow. This variety was popular for making toffee apples.

Cola

The distinctly conical fruits are around 5cm (2in) across or more. They are an even bright yellowish green in colour. The whitish flesh is coarse in texture with a subacid flavour.

Note: This variety is well suited to growing in a warm Mediterranean climate and does well in coastal situations.

Type: Dessert.
Origin: Italy, early 1900s.
Parentage: Unknown.
Flowering: Mid-season.

Coquette d'Auvergne

Type: Dessert.
Origin: France, 1947.
Parentage: Unknown.
Flowering: Late.

Note: Trees are weak-growing. Nowadays, this variety is rare in cultivation.

The rather conical fruits are around 6cm (2¼in) across. The skins are light yellow-green with a pronounced dark red flush. The whitish flesh is sometimes tinged orange immediately beneath the skin. It is soft and rather mealy in texture.

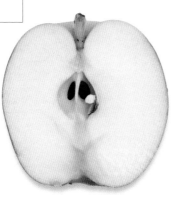

Cornish Aromatic

Type: Dessert.
Origin: Cornwall, UK, recorded 1813 but probably much older.
Parentage: Unknown.
Flowering: Late.
Other names: Aromatic, Aromatic Pippin, Aromatic Russet, Aromatique de Cornouailles, Cornwalliser Gewurzapfel and Siberian Russet.

The handsome fruits, around 6cm (2¼in) across, are rounded but may be knobbly. The red flush is broken by some spotting and russeting. The creamy white flesh is firm and rather dry. The flavour is rich, spicy and aromatic.

Note: This old English variety is thought to have been grown in Cornwall for many centuries. Trees bear freely.

Cornish Gilliflower

Type: Dessert.
Origin: Found in a cottage garden near Truro, Cornwall, UK, introduced in 1813.
Parentage: Unknown.
Flowering: Mid-season.
Other names: Calville d'Angleterre, Cornish Juli Flower, Cornwalliser Nelkenapfel, Gilliflower, Julie Flomer, July Flower, Kalvil angliiskii, Nelken Apfel, Pomme Regelans, Red Gilliflower and Regalan.

The irregular, bumpy fruits, up to around 8cm (3in) across, are dull yellow-green with a pinkish red flush with a webbing of rough russeting. The creamy white flesh is firm and rather dry with a sweet and rich aromatic flavour.

Note: This variety is tip-bearing, seldom setting abundant crops. It was an important variety in the 19th century. The flowers are clove scented. Fruits store well for three months or longer. For the best flavour, pick them as late as possible.

Above: Cornish Gilliflower is one of the most desirable of dessert apples, because of its rich flavour.

Cortland

The fruits are flattened and rather irregular and can be up to 7cm (2¾in) across or more. They are bright greenish yellow with an uneven deep red flush. The white flesh is moderately juicy and slightly coarse in texture but with a sweet, refreshing flavour.

Note: The skins of this variety can be tough. Despite its early flowering, it crops well in cold areas. Cut fruits are slow to brown, so are suitable for use in fruit salads.

Type: Dessert.
Origin: New York State Agricultural Experiment Station, Geneva, USA, 1898.
Parentage: Ben Davis (female) x McIntosh (male).
Flowering: Early.
Other names: Cartland, Courtland and Courtlandt.

Cottenham Seedling

The fruits are irregularly rounded and around 7cm (2¾in) across. They are bright yellowish green with a pinkish red flush. The whitish flesh is firm, coarse-textured and juicy with a sharp, distinctly acid flavour.

Note: This is a fine cooking apple with very attractive blossom. Late flowering makes it useful for frost-prone areas.

Type: Culinary.
Origin: Cottenham, Cambridgeshire, UK, 1924.
Parentage: Dumelow's Seedling (female) x Unknown.
Flowering: Late.

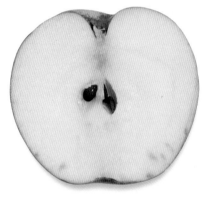

Court Pendu Plat

The flattened fruits, around 5cm (2in) across, are bright yellow with a bright orange and red flush and some spotting and striping. The creamy white flesh is very firm, fine-textured and juicy with a rich, sweet, slightly aromatic flavour.

Note: This excellent old variety possibly dates back to Roman times but it remains of more than just historic interest. It was called the 'wise apple' because it flowers late and hence escapes frost damage in cold areas. Fruits are also suitable for cooking.

Type: Dessert.
Origin: Europe, first described 1613 but believed to be much older.
Parentage: Unknown.
Flowering: Very late.
Other names: Belin, Belle de Senart, Capendu, Coriander Rose, Courte Queue, Garron's Apple, Kasapgel, Pomme de Berlin, Princesse Noble Zoete, Prudente, Reinette de Belges, Reinette de Portugal, Reinette Plate d'Hiver, Reinette Rose, Rode Korpendu, Roter Kurzstiel, Russian Apple, Wise Apple, Wollaton Pippin and Zlatousek Kratkostopkaty.

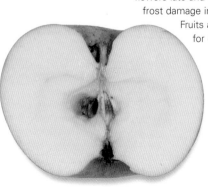

Cox's Orange Pippin

Type: Dessert.
Origin: Buckinghamshire, UK, 1825.
Parentage: ?Ribston Pippin (female) x Unknown.
Flowering: Mid-season.
Other names: Apelsinnyi renet, Cox Orangen Reinette, Cox's Pomeranzen Pepping, Coxova Reneta, Kemp's Orange, Koksa Pomaranczowa, Orange de Cox, Reinette Orange de Cox, Renet Coksa, Renet Cox Portocaliu, Reneta Coxa pomaranzowa, Russet Pippin and Verbesserte Muscat Reinette.

The rounded fruits are up to 5cm (2in) across, sometimes smaller. They are yellowish green with a red stripe and an orange flush. The creamy white flesh is crisp and juicy with an intensely aromatic flavour.

Note: This is sometimes regarded as the best of all English apples. It does best in warm, dry climates – elsewhere, it can be prone to scab and canker. The flavour improves in storage.

Crawley Beauty

Type: Dessert and culinary.
Origin: Crawley, Sussex, UK, c.1870, introduced 1906.
Parentage: Unknown.
Flowering: Very late.
Other names:
Ratcliff Sargeant and Ratcliffe Sargeant.

The rounded fruits, around 6cm (2¼in) across, are bright green with a red flush and some spotting. The whitish flesh is slightly coarse in texture and rather dry. The flavour is sharp and slightly sweet.

Note: Late flowering makes this disease-resistant variety useful for areas where spring frosts are likely. Growth is vigorous and upright. It is apparently identical with the French variety Novelle France.

Crimson Queening

Type: Dessert.
Origin: England, first recorded 1831 but probably much older.
Parentage: Unknown.
Flowering: Mid-season.
Other names: Crimson Quoining, Herefordshire Queening, Quining, Red Queening, Scarlet Queening, Summer Queening and Summer Quoining.

This old English variety is notable for the pointed shape of its fruits, which are around 5cm (2in) across. They are bright green with an even dark red flush. The creamy white flesh is soft and dryish, becoming mealy. The flavour is only moderately sweet.

Note: Trees are weak-growing. The fruits can be stored for three to four months.

Cusset Blanc

The flattened, slightly irregular fruits are around 6cm (2¼in) across. They are bright yellowish green with some flushing. The creamy white flesh is firm and coarse with a sharp flavour.

Note: Late flowering makes this a suitable variety for growing in cold areas.

Type: Dessert.
Origin: France, 1947.
Parentage: Unknown.
Flowering: Very late.

D'Arcy Spice

The oblong-shaped fruits, around 5cm (2in) across or more, are green with a crimson flush and pronounced russeting. The whitish flesh is firm, fine-textured and juicy with a characteristic spicy, aromatic flavour.

  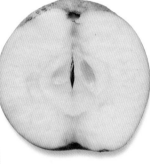

Note: The fruits of this excellent variety can be stored for four or five months, sometimes longer. Trees are moderately vigorous.

Type: Dessert.
Origin: Found in the garden of The Hall, Tolleshunt d'Arcy, Essex, UK, 1785 (but possibly older; introduced 1848 as Baddow Pippin).
Parentage: Unknown.
Flowering: Mid-season.
Other names: Baddow Pippin, Essex Spice, Pepin de Baddow, Spice, Spice Apple, Spring Ribston, Spring Ribston Pippin, Spring Ribstone and Winter Ribston.

Dalice

Above: Dalice is one of many dessert apples bred from Cox's Orange Pippin.

Note: Trees are moderately vigorous.

The rounded, very slightly conical fruits are around 6cm (2¼in) across. The skins are bright green flushed and marked with bright red. The creamy white flesh is coarse, soft and dry with a subacid to sweet, insipid flavour.

Type: Dessert.
Origin: Hastings, Sussex, UK, between 1933 and 1937.
Parentage: Cox's Orange Pippin (female) x Unknown.
Flowering: Mid-season.

Dark Red Staymared

Type: Dessert.
Origin: Barber County, VA, USA, introduced 1927.
Parentage: Winesap (female) x Unknown.
Flowering: Mid-season.
Other name: Dark-red Staymared.

The rounded to somewhat conical fruits, around 6cm (2¼in) across, are bright-green with a strong dark red flush and some striping. The pale yellow flesh is juicy with a light aromatic flavour.

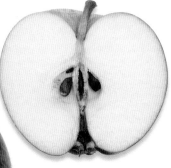

Note: This triploid is a more highly coloured sport of Stayman's Winesap. They are bright green with a heavy, deep red flush.

Dawn

Type: Dessert.
Origin: ?Ware Park Gardens, Hertfordshire, UK, 1940.
Parentage: Unknown.
Flowering: Mid-season.

The rounded (but sometimes slightly pointed) fruits are around 6cm (2¼in) across and bright yellow-green with a bright red flush. The crisp white flesh has a sweet, sharp flavour that is somewhat reminiscent of raspberries.

Note: This variety is self-sterile. Trees are moderately vigorous.

Left: A suitable pollination partner nearby will ensure good fruiting.

de Flandre

Type: Dessert.
Origin: France, 1876.
Parentage: Unknown.
Flowering: Late.
Other name: Figue.

The somewhat flattened fruits, around 6cm (2¼in) across, are bright green with a strong red flush. The creamy white flesh is firm and coarse with a slightly sweet, subacid and aromatic flavour.

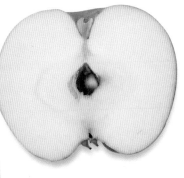

Note: This variety is believed to show some resistance to blackspot. Trees are moderately vigorous.

De Vendue l'Eveque

The rounded fruits, around 6cm (2¼in) across, are an even bright green, lightly speckled with pale yellowish white dots. The creamy white flesh is crisp with a tart flavour.

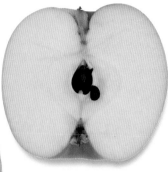

Type: Culinary.
Origin: France, 1948.
Parentage: Unknown.
Flowering: Late.

Note: This variety is commonly used in France as a cider apple. Late flowering makes it suitable for growing in cold areas.

Right: This variety is grown in the Aube department of France.

Delcorf

Type: Dessert.
Origin: Malicorne, France, 1956 and introduced into commerce 1976.
Parentage: Stark Jonagrimes (female) x Golden Delicious (male).
Flowering: Mid-season.
Other names: Ambassy Dalili Delbarestivale, Delcorf Estivale and Estivale Monidel.

Note: Trees are of average vigour. Fruits bruise easily.

The rounded to slightly oblong fruits, around 7cm (2¾in) across, are bright yellow-green with a strong pinkish or orange-red flush and some flecking. The creamy white flesh is fairly crisp and juicy and very sweet, but with a hint of sharpness.

Above: Delcorf is grown commercially in both France and England.

Delicious

The irregular fruits, around 6cm (2¼in) across or more, are yellow-green with a strong dark red flush. The whitish flesh is very firm, very sweet and juicy with a highly aromatic flavour.

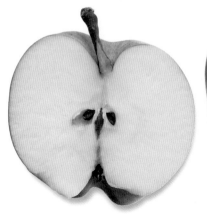

Type: Dessert.
Origin: Peru, Iowa, USA, *c*.1880 (introduced 1895).
Parentage: Unknown.
Flowering: Mid-season.
Other names: Cervena prevazhodna, Delicious rosso, Hawkeye, Piros Delicious, Prevoshodnoe krasnoe and Stark Delicious.

Note: Fruits develop their best flavour in warm areas. The skin can be very tough.

Delgollune

The conical fruits, around 6cm (2¼in) across, are bright greenish yellow with a pinkish red flush. The whitish flesh is crisp and juicy with a sweet, lightly aromatic flavour.

Note: Late flowering makes this variety suitable for growing in areas with late spring frosts.

Type: Dessert.
Origin: Delbard Nurseries, France, 1962.
Parentage: Golden Delicious (female) x Lundbytorp (male).
Flowering: Very late.
Other name: Delbard Jubilee.

Left: Delgollune is a popular commercial variety in France and has been used in breeding programmes.

Delnimb

Type: Dessert.
Origin: Malicorne, France, 1960s.
Parentage: Maigold (female) x Grive Rouge (male).
Flowering: Very late.

The rounded fruits, around 6cm (2¼in) across, are an even bright yellow-green. The creamy white flesh is rather coarse but juicy with a fairly rich, sweet, subacid flavour.

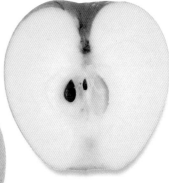

Note: The late flowering of this variety makes it suitable for growing in areas that are prone to late spring frosts.

Devonshire Quarrenden

The flattened, slightly irregular fruits, around 7cm (2¾in) across, are bright yellow-green with a strong dark purplish red flush. The creamy white flesh, sometimes stained red, is sweet, crisp and juicy with a distinctive aromatic flavour.

Note: This variety is a triploid. Trees are hardy and crop freely.

Type: Dessert.
Origin: Believed to be Devon, UK, but possibly originally France, first recorded 1678.
Parentage: Unknown.
Flowering: Early.
Other names: Annat Scarlet, Englischer Scharlach Peppin, Morgenrotapfel, Pepin alyi, Pippin Scarlet, Pomme Impériale, Quarrendon du Comité de Devon, Quarrington, Red Quarrenden, Sack, Scarlet Pippin, Scharlach Pepping, Sharlakhovyi pepin and Tsyganka.

Diamond Jubilee

Type: Dessert and culinary.
Origin: Kent, UK, 1889.
Parentage: Unknown.
Flowering: Mid-season.

The rounded fruits, around 7cm (2¾in) across, are bright green or greenish yellow. The whitish flesh is firm and crisp with a subacid and slightly aromatic flavour.

Far left: Skins of this variety show an even colouring.

Note: This old variety was named to commemorate Queen Victoria's diamond jubilee.

Diana

The rounded fruits, around 7cm (2¾in) across, are bright greenish yellow with a strong dark red flush. The whitish flesh is sweet, soft and juicy.

Note: The flavour is similar to McIntosh. Trees are moderately vigorous.

Type: Dessert.
Origin: Former Yugoslavia, 1967.
Parentage: Unknown.
Flowering: Mid-season.

Dillington Beauty

The slightly flattened, rather irregular fruits, around 7cm (2¾in) across, are dull yellowish green with some flushing and spotting. The whitish flesh is soft and rather coarse with a subacid flavour.

Type: Dessert.
Origin: New Zealand, 1872.
Parentage: Unknown.
Flowering: Mid-season.

Note: Formerly popular as a garden variety in New Zealand, Dillington Beauty has become rare in cultivation. Trees are moderately vigorous.

Directeur van de Plassche

Type: Dessert.
Origin: Institute for Horticultural Plant Breeding, Wageningen, Netherlands, 1935.
Parentage: Cox's Orange Pippin (female) x Jonathan (male).
Flowering: Mid-season.

The rounded fruits, around 6cm (2¼in) across, are bright greenish yellow with a bright red flush. The creamy white flesh is juicy with a slightly subacid flavour.

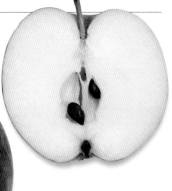

Note: Trees are moderately vigorous.

Dorée de Tournai

Type: Dessert.
Origin: Tournai, Belgium, 1817.
Parentage: Unknown.
Flowering: Early.
Other names: Doree de Tournay, Gold Apfel von Tournay and la Dorade.

The irregular, somewhat square fruits, around 7cm (2¾in) across, are dull yellowish green. The flesh is firm and crisp with a sweet, subacid, rich, aromatic flavour.

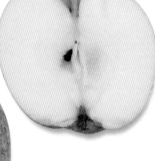

Note: This variety is nowadays rare in cultivation outside historic gardens.

Dorsett Golden

The irregular fruits, around 7cm (2¾in) across, are yellowish green with a strong bright red flush. The creamy white flesh is juicy with a sweet, light, aromatic flavour.

Note: This variety is an excellent choice for warm and coastal areas. The young trees bear freely.

Type: Dessert.
Origin: Nassau, New Providence Islands, 1953.
Parentage: Golden Delicious (female) x Unknown.
Flowering: Late.

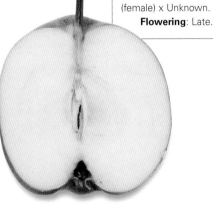

Double-Red Baldwin

Type: Dessert.
Origin: Salisbury, New Hampshire, USA, 1924.
Parentage: Unknown.
Flowering: Early.

The flattened, irregular fruits, around 6cm (2¼in) across, are bright yellow-green with a strong dark red flush. The yellowish flesh is coarse-textured and juicy with a sweet, subacid flavour.

Note: This variety is a more brightly coloured sport of Baldwin.

Left: The skins of this variety ripen to a very deep red on the side nearest the sun.

Dugamel

The rounded, slightly knobbly fruits, around 6cm (2¼in) across, are bright green with a strong and even dark red flush. The whitish flesh is firm and juicy with a pleasant, faintly aromatic flavour.

Type: Dessert.
Origin: France, date unknown.
Parentage: Unknown.
Flowering: Mid-season.

Note: This variety is a more highly coloured clone of Melrose.

Duke of Devonshire

The flattened fruits, around 5cm (2in) across, are bright yellow-green and heavily russeted. The creamy white flesh is firm, fine-textured and rather dry with a rich, nutty, intense sweet-sharp flavour.

Note: Fruits store well, developing their best flavour after one to two months. Trees are moderately vigorous.

Type: Dessert.
Origin: Holker Hall, Lancashire, UK, 1835 (introduced 1875).
Parentage: Unknown.
Flowering: Mid-season.
Other names: Devonshire Duke, Duc de Devonshire, Herzog von Devonshire, Holker and Holker Pippin.

Dunn's Seedling

Type: Dessert.
Origin: Kew, Melbourne, Australia, first recorded 1890.
Parentage: Unknown.
Flowering: Early.
Other names: Chenimuri, Dunn's Favourite, Dunns, Monroe's Favourite, Munroe's Favourite, Ohenimuri and Ohinemuri.

The rounded, slightly bumpy fruits, around 6cm (2¼in) across, are bright yellow-green with some flushing. The creamy white flesh is crisp and hard with a sweet, subacid flavour.

Note: This variety is important historically as one of the first to be grown widely in Australia. Trees are moderately vigorous.

Dutch Mignonne

Type: Dessert and culinary.
Origin: ?Netherlands, before 1771.
Parentage: Unknown.
Flowering: Early.
Other names: Belle Reinette de Caux, Casseler Reinette, Christ's Golden Reinette, Contor, Copmanshorpe Crab, Copmanshorpe Russet, Craft Angry, de Laak, Dutch Minion, Grosse-Reinette Rouge Tiquetee, Hollandische Goldreinette, Paternoster, Rawle's Reinette, Reinette Imperatrice, Stettiner Pepping, Thorpe Grabe and Vermillon d'Andalousie.

The flattened fruits, around 6cm (2¼in) across, are bright green with a light flush. The creamy yellow flesh is firm and juicy with a slightly acid, not very sweet, faintly aromatic flavour.

Note: Trees bear freely and are suitable for training as espaliers. Fruits store well.

Right: This old variety readily forms spur systems that carry regularly shaped fruits.

Easter Orange

Type: Dessert.
Origin: Winchester, Hampshire, UK, 1897.
Parentage: Unknown.
Flowering: Mid-season.

The rounded fruits, around 5cm (2in) across, are yellow-green with a strong red flush. The creamy white flesh is crisp and firm with a sweet and aromatic flavour.

Note: The fruits are also suitable for cooking.

Left: When ripe, the fruits of this variety have a very intense flavour.

Egremont Russet

The slightly flattened fruits, around 6cm (2¼in) across, are yellow-green with heavy russeting. The creamy white flesh is firm, fine textured and rather dry, with a very distinctive rich, nutty flavour.

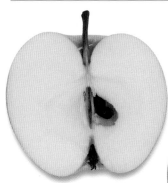

Note: This is probably the best-known and most popular of the russet apples. Trees, which are hardy and compact, are partially self-fertile.

Type: Dessert.   **Origin**: ?England,   first recorded 1872.   **Parentage**: Unknown.   **Flowering**: Early.   **Other name**: Egremont.

Above: Egremont Russet is a classic English russet apple from the Victorian era.

Elan

The rounded fruits, around 7cm (2¾in) across, are greenish yellow with red flushing and striping. The creamy white flesh is crisp, sweet and juicy.

Type: Dessert.   **Origin**: IVT, Wageningen,   Netherlands, before 1983.   **Parentage**: Golden   Delicious (female) x   James Grieve (male).   **Flowering**: Very early.

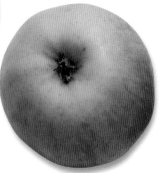

Note: This variety is tip-bearing. Trees are moderately vigorous.

Elise Rathke

The rounded fruits, around 5cm (2in) across, are yellowish green with a red flush and striping. The creamy white flesh is fine and soft with a subacid and moderately sweet and spicy flavour.

Type: Dessert.   **Origin**: Pravst, nr Gdansk,   Poland, or Elbinge, Germany,   first recorded 1884.   **Parentage**: Unknown.   **Flowering**: Mid-season.   **Other names**: Elisa Rathké,   Elisa Rathke, Elisa Ratk, Eliza   Ratke and Rote Reinette.

Note: This variety has a drooping habit and is good in a confined space.

Ellison's Orange

Type: Dessert.
Origin: Bracebridge and at Hartsholme Hall, Lincolnshire, UK, first recorded 1904 and introduced 1911.
Parentage: Cox's Orange Pippin (female) x Calville Blanc (male) (probably Calville Blanc d'Hiver).
Flowering: Mid-season.

The rounded to slightly conical fruits, around 6cm (2¼in) across, are yellow-green with a strong dark red flush and striping. The creamy white flesh is soft and juicy, like a pear, with a rich, strong aniseed flavour.

Note: The fruits are not suitable for long-term storing. The flavour is considered one of the most complex of all dessert apples. Trees are generally disease resistant and easy to grow.

Above: This variety is one of the best offspring of Cox's Orange Pippin.

Elmore Pippin

The bright greenish yellow, rounded fruits, around 5cm (2in) across, show some spotting. The creamy white flesh is firm with an intense, sweet-sharp flavour.

Note: Fruits can be stored for up to five months. Trees are moderately vigorous.

Type: Dessert.
Origin: ?UK, before 1949.
Parentage: Unknown.
Flowering: Mid-season.

Right: The fruits of Elmore Pippin stay on the tree until late autumn.

Eri Zagarra

Type: Culinary.
Origin: France (Basque Country), 1973.
Parentage: Unknown.
Flowering: Mid-season.

The slightly flattened fruits, around 6cm (2¼in) across, are greenish yellow with a red flush and some russeting. The creamy white flesh is tart in flavour.

Note: Fruits cook well.

Left: Eri Zagarra is an excellent cooking apple but somewhat rare in cultivation.

Esopus Spitzenburg

The somewhat conical fruits, around 6cm (2¼in) across, are bright greenish-yellow with a strong red flush. The whitish flesh is crisp and tender with a rich aromatic flavour.

Note: This old American apple was widely grown in the USA in the 19th century and was the traditional choice for apple pies. It does best in warm areas.

Type: Dessert.
Origin: Esopus, Ulster County, NY, USA, before 1790.
Parentage: Unknown.
Flowering: Mid-season.
Other names: Aesopus Spitzenberg, Aesopus Spitzenburg, Aesopus Spitzenburgh, Esopus, Esopus Spitzenberg, Esopus Spitzenburgh, Ezop Spitzenburg, Spitzenberg, Spitzenburg, True Spitzenberg and True Spitzenburg.

Etlins Reinette

The fruits are irregular in shape and can be up to around 7cm (2¾in) across. They are bright yellow-green with some spotting. The creamy white flesh is fine and crisp with a sweet, slightly subacid, aromatic flavour.

Note: This variety commemorates a noted German pomologist. Trees are very vigorous.

Type: Dessert.
Origin: Landenberg estate, Germany, 1866.
Parentage: Unknown.
Flowering: Early.
Other names: Etlin's Reinette, Ettlin's Reinette, Reinette d'Etlin and Reinette Ettlin's.

Fara Nume

The slightly conical fruits, around 6cm (2¼in) across, are dull yellow-green with some spotting. The creamy white flesh is soft and fine with a sweet, subacid flavour.

Type: Dessert.
Origin: Romania, 1948.
Parentage: Unknown.
Flowering: Mid-season.

Note: Fara nume is a Romanian phrase that translates as 'without a name'.

Right: The fine, speckled russeting on the fruits is characteristic of this variety.

Faversham Creek

Type: Culinary.
Origin: A seedling found growing in salt water in Faversham Creek, Kent, UK, 1970s.
Parentage: Unknown.
Flowering: Mid-season.

The slightly flattened fruits, around 6cm (2¼in) across, are bright yellow-green with a pinkish to orange-red flush and some striping. The yellowish flesh is coarse and dry with an acid flavour.

Note: This variety is very rare in cultivation. Fruits cook to a creamy consistency with very good flavour.

Fenouillet de Ribours

Type: Dessert
Origin: La Rouairie garden, Maine-et-Loire, France, first fruited 1840.
Parentage: Unknown.
Flowering: Mid-season.

The irregular, sometimes knobbly or ribbed fruits, up to around 7cm (2¾in) across, are bright green with a red flush and some greyish or bronze russeting and some white spotting. The white flesh is fine in texture with a sweet, subacid, aniseed-perfumed flavour.

Note: The fruits are late to ripen on the tree. They are prized for their unusual flavour.

Feuillemorte

Type: Dessert.
Origin: France, 1948.
Parentage: Unknown.
Flowering: Very late.
Other name: Feuille Morte.

The somewhat flattened fruits are bright yellow-green with a strong red flush and striping. The white flesh is firm and fine with a subacid and distinctive flavour.

Note: This is one of the latest varieties to flower.

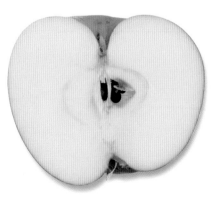

Finasso

The flattened fruits, around 6cm (2¼in) across, are yellowish green with a strong red flush. The whitish flesh is firm and fine with a slightly subacid flavour.

Type: Dessert.
Origin: France, 1949.
Parentage: Unknown.
Flowering: Late.

Note: Late flowering makes this a suitable variety for frost-prone areas.

Right: This moderately vigorous variety crops well.

Fireside

Type: Dessert.
Origin: Minnesota Agricultural Experiment Station, Excelsior, USA, 1917 (introduced commercially 1943).
Parentage: McIntosh x Longfield.
Flowering: Early.

The rounded fruits, around 6cm (2¼in) across, are bright green with a red flush and striping. The white flesh is firm and crisp with a sweet, subacid, aromatic flavour.

Note: Trees are vigorous, hardy and resistant to cedar apple rust. The fruits store well.

Firmgold

The conical, uneven fruits, around 6cm (2¼in) across, are greenish yellow with darker spotting. The flesh is firm, crisp and juicy with a sweet flavour.

Type: Dessert.
Origin: Zillah, WA, USA, date not recorded.
Parentage: A chance seedling found growing among some Starkspur Golden Delicious and Starkrimson Red Delicious trees.
Flowering: Early.

Note: Trees are prone to biennial bearing if not thinned correctly.

Florina

Type: Dessert.
Origin: Station de Recherches d'Arboriculture Fruitière, Angers, France, date not recorded.
Parentage: Complex, involving Rome Beauty, Golden Delicious, Starking, Simpsons Giant Limb and Jonathan.
Flowering: Early.

Note: This tip-bearing variety is resistant to scab.

The rounded fruits, around 6cm (2¼in) across, are bright yellow-green with a strong red flush and some spotting. The whitish flesh is rather tart and acid in flavour.

Fon's Spring

Type: Dessert.
Origin: Milbury Heath, Falfield, Gloucestershire, UK, 1948.
Parentage: John Standish (female) x Cox's Orange Pippin (male).
Flowering: Late.
Other name: Eden.

The slightly flattened fruits, around 6cm (2¼in) across, are bright yellow-green with a strong red flush. The white flesh is firm and fairly juicy with a sweet, subacid flavour, rather like Cox's Orange Pippin.

Note: Late flowering makes this a suitable variety for growing in cold districts where late frosts are common.

Forge

Type: Dessert.
Origin: East Grinstead, Sussex, before 1851.
Parentage: Unknown.
Flowering: Mid-season.
Other names: Der Schmiedeapfel, Forge Apple, Schmiede Apfel, Schmiedeapfel and Sussex Forge.

Note: The fruits are also suitable for cooking. Trees bear freely.

The rounded, rather uneven fruits, around 6cm (2¼in) across, are bright green with a red flush. The white flesh is crisp and very juicy with a pleasant, aromatic but somewhat sharp flavour.

Fortosh

The conical, unevenly shaped fruits, around 7cm (2¾ in) across, are bright green with a red flush and streaks. The pink-tinged white flesh is soft and juicy with a moderately sweet, slightly acid flavour.

Type: Dessert.
Origin: Central Experimental Farm, Ottawa, Canada, 1928.
Parentage: Unknown.
Flowering: Early.

Note: Trees are very vigorous.

Right: Fruits of this variety have a distinctive shape and colouring.

Foster's Seedling

The slightly flattened fruits, around 6cm (2¼ in) across, are bright green with red flushing and flecks. The white flesh is tender with an acid and vinous flavour.

Type: Culinary.
Origin: Maidstone, Kent, UK, *c.*1893.
Parentage: Unknown.
Flowering: Late.

Note: Fruits cook to a purée with a very sharp flavour. This variety is self-sterile so a compatible pollinator is required.

Fraise de Buhler

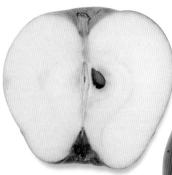

The very irregular fruits, around 7cm (2¾ in) across, are yellow-green with a red flush and striping. The whitish flesh is firm and fine with a subacid flavour.

Type: Dessert.
Origin: ?Buhl, nr Baden, Germany, before 1947.
Parentage: Unknown.
Flowering: Early.

Note: The name of this variety suggests the fruits may have a strawberry-like flavour. Trees are very vigorous.

Franc-Bon-Pommier

Type: Dessert.
Origin: France, 1950.
Parentage: Unknown.
Flowering: Late.
Other name: Franc-Bon-Pommier (Moselle).

Note: The blossom of this variety, sometimes used for cider making, is susceptible to fireblight.

Left: The Franc-Bon-Pommier originates from the north of France.

The somewhat flattened, slightly irregular fruits, around 6cm (2¼in) across, are green with a strong red flush and some striping. The white flesh is firm with a slightly sweet flavour.

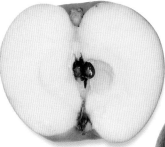

France Deliquet

Note: Trees are moderately vigorous.

The somewhat knobbly and irregular, flattened fruits, around 7cm (2¾in) across, are bright yellow-green with a red flush and some russeting. The creamy white flesh is firm, fine and crisp with a slightly sweet, slightly subacid flavour.

Type: Dessert.
Origin: Angers, France, 1950.
Parentage: Unknown.
Flowering: Late.

Above: Fruits are borne on spurs in clusters.

Francis

Type: Dessert.
Origin: Essex, UK, early 20th century.
Parentage: Cox's Orange Pippin (female) x Unknown.
Flowering: Mid-season.

The rounded to slightly conical fruits, around 6cm (2¼in) across, are bright yellow-green with a pinkish red flush and some striping and dotting. The creamy white flesh is firm, fine and crisp with a very sweet and aromatic flavour.

Note: Trees are moderately vigorous.

Freiherr von Berlepsch

The slightly flattened, somewhat irregular fruits, around 6cm (2¼in) across, are yellow-green with a pinkish red flush and some russeting. The creamy white flesh is crisp and very juicy with a subacid flavour.

Note: Trees are very vigorous, doing best in a sheltered position. They can be prone to canker and fungal diseases. Fruits can be stored for up to six months.

Type: Dessert.
Origin: Grevenbroich, Rheinland, Germany, c.1880.
Parentage: Ananas Reinette (female) x Ribston Pippin (male).
Flowering: Mid-season.
Other names: Freiherr de beri, Baron de Berlepsch, Berlepsch, Berlepschs Goldrenette, Freiherr von Berlepsch Gold-Reinette, Goldrenette Freiherr von Berlepsch, Reinette dorée de Berlepsch, Reinette Freiherr von Berlepsch, Renet Berlepsch and Renet zolotoi Berlepsha.

Frémy

The rounded fruits, around 6cm (2¼in) across, are clear green, generously splashed and marked with russeting over the entire surface. The yellowish flesh is firm and fine with a sweet, subacid and aromatic flavour.

Note: The flavour is similar to that of a Reinette apple. Trees are very vigorous.

Type: Dessert.
Origin: Chère, France, c.1830–40.
Parentage: Unknown.
Flowering: Unknown.
Other names: de Fremy and Gelineau.

French Crab

The rounded fruits, around 6cm (2¼in) across, are bright green with some spotting and russeting and sometimes a dull red flush. The white flesh, distinctly tinged green, is very firm, coarse-textured and a little juicy and acid.

Note: Trees are very hardy and bear freely. The fruits cook well with a strong aroma. They can be stored for up to six months or even longer.

Left: French crab is a cooking apple of fine quality.

Type: Culinary.
Origin: Thought to be France, brought to England late 1700s.
Parentage: Unknown.
Flowering: Mid-season.
Other names: Amiens Long Keeper, Bobin, Claremont Pippin, Easter Pippin, Green Beefing, Grüner Oster, Iron King, Ironside, Ironstone, Ironstone Pippin, John Apple, Robin, Somerset Stone Pippin, Three Years Old, Tunbridge Pippin, Two Years Apple, Winter Greening, Winter Queening, Yorkshire Robin and Young's Long Keeper.

Fuji

Type: Dessert.
Origin: Horticultural Research Station, Nakahara, Japan, 1939 (named 1962).
Parentage: Ralls Janet (female) x Delicious (male).
Flowering: Mid-season.
Other name: Fuji INRA Type 4 – Nagafu (No.2) INFEL 6671

The rounded fruits, around 6cm (2¼in) across, are yellow-green with a pink-red flush and flecking. The dull white flesh is crisp and juicy with a slightly subacid flavour.

Note: This popular commercial variety does best in areas with warm summers. Scab and fireblight may be a problem in some areas. Fruits store well.

Fukunishiki

The rounded, slightly irregular fruits, around 6cm (2¼in) across, are yellow-green with a pinkish-red marbled flush. The creamy-white flesh is firm and crisp with a sweet flavour that is somewhat reminiscent of pear drop sweets.

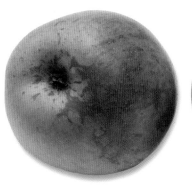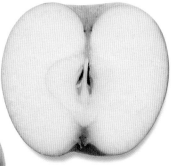

Type: Dessert.
Origin: Aomori Apple Experiment Station, Japan, 1933 (named 1949).
Parentage: Ralls Janet (female) x Delicious (male).
Flowering: Mid-season.

Note: Fruits need a long, warm summer to ripen fully.

Right: *Fukunishiki is an attractive apple with a very distinctive taste when ripe.*

Galloway Pippin

Type: Culinary.
Origin: Wigtown, Galloway, UK, 1871 (but thought to be much older).
Parentage: Unknown.
Flowering: Mid-season.
Other names: Croft en Reich, Croft St Andrews, Gallibro, Gallibro Pippin, Galloway, Galway's Pippin, Graft-en-Reich, Pepin Galloveiskii and Pepin Galloway.

The flattened, slightly uneven fruits, to around 7cm (2¾in) across, are bright yellow-green with some spotting. The creamy white flesh is firm, crisp and juicy with a sharp, subacid flavour.

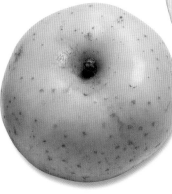

Note: The fruits of this old Scottish variety cook well but are best used early rather than storing.

Gambafina

Type: Dessert.
Origin: Carraglio, province of Cuneo, Italy, *c*.1900.
Parentage: Unknown.
Flowering: Mid-season.

The flattened, slightly irregular fruits, around 6cm (2¼ in) across, are bright yellow with a strong dark red flush and some striping. The greenish white flesh is soft with a sweet subacid flavour.

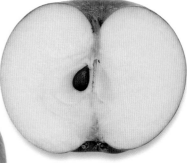

Note: This variety shows excellent disease resistance.

Gascoyne's Scarlet

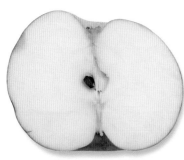

Note: This variety produces an attractive pink juice. Trees are very vigorous.

The very irregular fruits, around 6cm (2¼ in) across, are light yellowish green with a pinkish red flush. The whitish flesh is firm, fine-textured and slightly juicy and sweet, but with very little flavour.

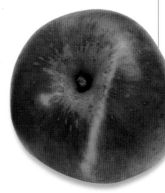

Type: Dessert and culinary.
Origin: Maidstone, Kent, UK, 1871.
Parentage: Unknown.
Flowering: Mid-season.
Other names: Cramoisie de Gascoigne, Friedrich August von Sachesen, Gascoigne's Scarlet, Gascoigne's Seedling, Malinovoe Gaskonskoe, Rhum von England and Schöner von Rusdorf.

George Carpenter

Note: The flavour is similar to Blenheim Orange. Trees are very vigorous.

The attractive, rounded fruits, around 8cm (3in) across, are yellow-green with a strong red flush. The white flesh is firm, fine-textured and juicy with a sweet, aromatic flavour.

Type: Dessert.
Origin: West Hall Gardens, Byfleet, Surrey, UK, 1902.
Parentage: Blenheim Orange (female) x King of the Pippins (male).
Flowering: Mid-season.

Gewürzluiken

Type: Dessert.
Origin: Germany, 1951.
Parentage: Unknown.
Flowering: Mid-season.

The rounded fruits are yellow-green with a strong red flush and striping. The whitish flesh is firm with a sweet subacid flavour.

Note: Flowers show some frost resistance. Fruits store well.

Giambun

Type: Dessert.
Origin: Italy, 1958.
Parentage: Unknown.
Flowering: Late.

The long, conical fruits, around 5cm (2in) across, are bright yellow-green with a dark red flush. The creamy white flesh is firm and coarse with a subacid flavour.

Note: Trees are moderately vigorous.

Left: The shape of the ripe fruits is very distinctive.

Gian André

Type: Dessert.
Origin: Italy, 1958.
Parentage: Unknown.
Flowering: Late.

The conical, irregular fruits, around 7cm (2¾in) across, are bright yellow-green with a red flush. The creamy white flesh is firm, fine and tender with an insipid flavour.

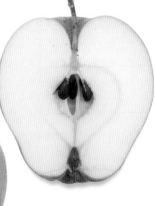

Above: Fruits of Gian André are slightly ridged and bumpy.

Note: Late flowering makes this a suitable variety for growing in cold districts. Trees are weak-growing.

Glengyle Red

The rounded fruits, around 7cm (2¾ in) across, are bright yellow with a red flush. The creamy white flesh is coarse-textured and juicy but with little flavour.

Type: Dessert and culinary.
Origin: Balannah, South Australia, 1914.
Parentage: A more highly coloured sport of Rome Beauty.
Flowering: Late.

Note: The skins of this variety tend to be tough. Trees are moderately vigorous.

Gloria Mundi

The irregular, sometimes oblong, heavily ribbed fruits, often more than 8cm (3in) across, are bright green. The soft, creamy white flesh is coarse-textured and dry with a subacid taste.

Note: The precise origins of this variety are in doubt owing to conflicting historical records.

Type: Culinary.
Origin: Germany or USA, 1804.
Parentage: Unknown.
Flowering: Mid-season.
Other names: American Mammoth, Baltimore, Belle Dubois, Belle Josephine, Copp's Mammoth, Glazenwood, Grosse de St Clement, Herrenapfel, Josephine, Kinderhook Pippin, Mammoth, Melon, Mississippi, Monstrous Pippin, Mountain Flora, Ox Apple, Pfundapfel, Pound, Ruhm der Welt, Slava Mira, Spanish Pippin, Titus Pippin and Vandyne Apple.

Golden Delicious

The slightly conical, sometimes irregular fruits, to 7cm (2¾ in) across, are yellow. The creamy white flesh is crisp and juicy with a sweet, aromatic flavour.

Type: Dessert.
Origin: Clay County, West VA, USA, 1905.
Parentage: ?Grimes Golden (female) x Unknown.
Flowering: Mid-season.
Other names: Arany Delicious, Delicios auriu, Stark Golden Delicious, Yellow Delicious, Zlatna prevazhodna and Zolotoe prevoshodnoe.

Note: This self-fertile variety does best in warm areas, where it is easy to grow. In some areas, scab, fireblight and rust may be a problem. Trees can be prone to biennial bearing.

Golden Knob

Type: Dessert.
Origin: Enmore Castle, Somerset, UK, late 1700s.
Parentage: Unknown.
Flowering: Mid-season.
Other names: Golden Nobb, Kentish Golden Knob, Old Lady and Old Maid.

The irregular fruits, around 5cm (2in) across, are bright yellow with heavy russeting. The flesh is firm with an intense, nutty, sweet-sharp flavour.

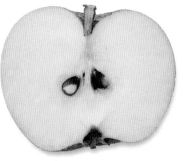

Note: Trees are vigorous and hardy and bear freely.

Golden Russet

Type: Culinary and dessert.
Origin: New York, USA, 1845.
Parentage: Seedling of English Russet.
Flowering: Early.

Note: Fruits can be stored for around three months. This variety is excellent for cider making. Trees are scab resistant.

The rounded fruits, of medium size, are greyish green to bronze with a coppery orange flush and russeting. The creamy white flesh is fine-grained, crisp and juicy with a sweet flavour.

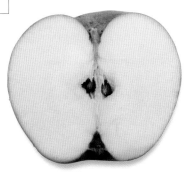

Right: Golden Russet is an excellent eating apple of fine quality.

Goldjon

Type: Dessert.
Origin: Turin University, Italy, date not recorded.
Parentage: Golden Delicious (female) x Jonathan (male).
Flowering: Mid-season.

The slightly conical, somewhat irregular fruits, around 7cm (2¾ in) across, are bright yellow-green with a pinkish red flush. The creamy white flesh is crisp and juicy with a sweet flavour.

Note: This variety is suitable for juicing.

Far left: The colouring of the ripe fruits is attractive.

Granny Giffard

The rounded to conical fruits, around 6cm (2¼in) across, are light green with a pinkish red flush and some striping and spotting. The yellowish white flesh is fine and tender with a subacid flavour.

Type: Culinary and dessert.
Origin: Minster, near Margate, Kent, UK, exhibited 1858.
Parentage: Unknown.
Flowering: Late.
Other name: Granny Gifford.

Note: Fruits can be stored for three to four months. Trees are moderately vigorous.

Granny Smith

The rounded fruits, around 6cm (2¼in) across, are an even bright green with lighter flecking. The creamy white flesh is firm, rather coarse-textured and juicy with a refreshing, subacid flavour.

Note: This variety, which does best in warm areas, was raised by Mrs Thomas Smith. Born in Peasmarsh, Sussex, UK, in 1800, she emigrated to Australia in 1838. In some areas, powdery mildew and fireblight may cause problems. The fruits store well.

Type: Dessert.
Origin: Ryde, NSW, Australia, before 1868.
Parentage: ?French Crab (female) x Unknown.
Flowering: Early.

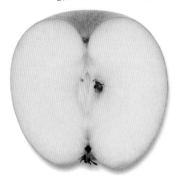

Grantonian

The rounded fruits, more than 8cm (3in) across, are bright green. The creamy white flesh is coarse, mealy and soft with a slightly subacid flavour.

Note: This variety is self-sterile so a compatible pollination partner is required for successful fruiting. The fruits store well.

Type: Culinary.
Origin: Nottingham, UK, 1883.
Parentage: Unknown.
Flowering: Mid-season.

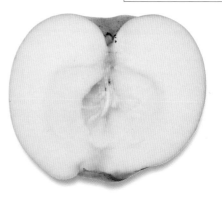

Gravenstein

Type: Culinary and dessert.
Origin: Schleswig-Holstein, Italy or Southern Tyrol; arrived in Denmark *c.*1669.
Parentage: Unknown.
Flowering: Early.
Other names: A. Grafenstein, Blumencalvill, Calville Gravenstein, de Comte, Diels Sommerkönig, Early Congress, Ernteapfel, Gelber Gravensteiner, Graasten, Gravstynke, Ohio Nonpareil, Paradiesapfel, Petergaard, Prinzessinapfel, Rippapfel, Romarin de Botzen, Sabine, Stroemling, The Gravenstein Apple and Tom Harryman.

The thin-skinned, somewhat uneven fruits, up to 8cm (3in) across, are yellow-green with orange-red mottling and streaking. The yellowish white flesh is crisp, rather coarse-textured and juicy with a pleasant mixture of sweetness and acidity and a distinctive flavour.

Note: This variety is a triploid. It was declared the national apple of Denmark in 2005. Trees are vigorous, developing a large crown, and are prone to biennial bearing. Susceptible to leaf spots, fungal disease and bitter pit but resistant to canker. Fruits can be stored for around two to three months.

Left: Gravenstein is a historic variety that has remained in cultivation.

Green Purnell

Type: Dessert.
Origin: Worcestershire, UK. Recorded 1945 but believed to be much older.
Parentage: Unknown.
Flowering: Mid-season.

The irregular, somewhat flattened fruits, around 7cm (2¾in) across, are bright green with a red flush. The creamy white flesh is fine-textured with a slightly sweet, subacid flavour.

Note: Though rare in cultivation nowadays, this variety has been used in the restoration of old orchards in the British Midlands. Trees are moderately vigorous.

Far left: Fruits can show some spotting and russeting.

Greensleeves

Type: Dessert.
Origin: East Malling Research Station, Maidstone, Kent, UK, 1966.
Parentage: James Grieve (female) x Golden Delicious (male).
Flowering: Very early.

The rounded, occasionally oblong to conical fruits, around 7cm (2¾in) across, are bright yellow-green with some russeting. The creamy white flesh, sometimes tinged pink-orange, is crisp and juicy with a mild, refreshing taste.

Note: This is a prolific variety. Trees are partially tip-bearing and bear fruit when young. Early flowering makes it unsuitable for use in very cold areas.

Right: Greensleeves is a good garden apple with a pleasant flavour.

Grimes Golden

Type: Dessert.
Origin: Brook County, West VA, USA, 1804.
Parentage: Unknown.
Flowering: Early.
Other names: Dorée de Grimes, Grimes, Grimes Goldapfel, Grimes Golden Pippin, Grimes Yellow Pippin and Zolotoe Graima.

Note: Young trees bear reliably and show some resistance to fireblight and apple cedar rust. The fruits are suitable for cider making.

The rounded fruits, around 7cm (2¾in) across, are bright greenish yellow. The creamy white flesh is crisp, juicy and fine-textured with a moderately sweet and flavour.

Right: Grimes Golden is a probable parent of the popular Golden Delicious variety.

Groninger Kroon

Note: This variety is resistant to apple scab. Trees are moderately vigorous.

The conical, sometimes almost oblong fruits, around 6cm (2¼in) across, are yellowish green with a pinkish red flush. The white flesh is very fine and firm with a slightly sweet flavour.

Type: Dessert.
Origin: Netherlands, before 1944.
Parentage: Unknown.
Flowering: Mid-season.
Other name: Groningen Kroon.

Gronsvelder Klumpke

Note: This variety is a sport of Eijsdener Klumpke. Trees are very vigorous.

The somewhat irregular, slightly oblong fruits, around 6cm (2¼in) across, are bright green with a strong dark red flush. The creamy white flesh is firm and fine-textured with a subacid flavour.

Type: Dessert.
Origin: Netherlands and Belgium, 1948.
Parentage: Unknown.
Flowering: Late.
Other names: Rood Klumpke and Sabot de Gronsveld.

Gros-Api

The flattened, irregular fruits, up to 7cm (2¾in) or more across, are bright yellowish green with a pinkish red flush and some russeting. The white flesh is firm and fine-textured with a sweet, subacid and perfumed flavour.

Type: Dessert.
Origin: Brittany, France, recorded 1628.
Parentage: Unknown.
Flowering: Mid-season.
Other names: Api Blanc, Api Bolshoe, Api Double, Api Grande, Api Grosse, Api rose, Dieu, Double Api, Double Rose, Drap d'Or (Villeneuve d'Agen), Gros Api, Grosser Api, Large Lady Apple, Passe Rose, Poma Rosa, Rose de l'Angenais, Rose de Provence, Rose Double Api, Rosenapfel, Rosenapi, Rubenapfel, Rubin and Vermillon Rubis.

Note: Fruits are wind-resistant. Mature trees crop freely.

Gros-Locard

Type: Culinary and dessert.
Origin: France, before 1849.
Parentage: Unknown.
Flowering: Late.
Other names: de Locard, Gro-Lokar, Gros-Locar, Locard Bicolore, Locard Groseille and Pomme de Locard.

The irregular fruits, around 7cm (2¾in) across, are bright yellow-green with some russeting. The creamy white flesh is crisp with a sweet and slightly acid flavour.

Note: Trees are vigorous. The fruits are suitable for juicing.

Grosse Mignonnette d'Herbassy

Type: Dessert.
Origin: France, first described 1934.
Parentage: Unknown.
Flowering: Mid-season.
Other names: Cabassou, Demoiselle and Mignonnette d'Herbassy.

The flattened fruits, around 7cm (2¾in) across, are bright yellow-green with a red flush. The flesh is fairly firm with a subacid and slightly sweet flavour.

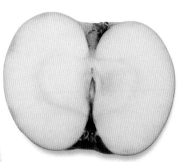

Note: Fruits can be stored for several months.

Grvena Lepogvetka

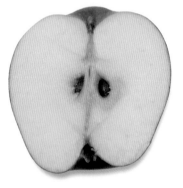

The conical, almost pear-shaped fruits, around 6cm (2¼in) across, are bright yellow with a dark red flush and some striping. The creamy white flesh has a sweet, subacid flavour.

Type: Dessert.
Origin: Former Yugoslavia, 1975.
Parentage: Unknown.
Flowering: Mid-season.

Note: Trees are moderately vigorous.

Gustavs Dauerapfel

The somewhat oblong fruits, around 6cm (2¼in) across, are bright yellow-green with a strong red flush. The creamy white flesh is firm and fine-textured with a sweet, slightly subacid and perfumed flavour.

Note: Fruits store for up to five months. Trees are moderately vigorous.

Type: Dessert.
Origin: Wadenswil, Switzerland, first described 1899.
Parentage: Unknown.
Flowering: Early.
Other names: Gustav Dauerapfel, Gustav Durabil and Gustavovo trvanlive.

Gyógyi Piros

The rounded fruits, around 7cm (2¾in) across, are bright greenish yellow with a strong dark red flush and some flecking. The creamy white flesh is fairly firm and fine-textured with a subacid and slightly sweet flavour.

Type: Dessert.
Origin: Romania or Hungary, first recorded 1860.
Parentage: Unknown.
Flowering: Early.
Other names: Gyogyer roter, Roter Gyogger and Royii de Geoagiu.

Note: Trees are moderately vigorous.

Hamvas Alma

The somewhat irregular fruits, to 8cm (3in) across, are bright greenish yellow with a red flush and some flecking. The creamy white flesh is fairly fine and soft with a sweetish subacid flavour.

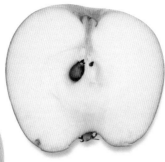

Type: Dessert.
Origin: Hungary, 1948.
Parentage: Unknown.
Flowering: Mid-season.

Note: Trees are moderately vigorous.

Right: Trees bear soft-fleshed fruit with plenty of fruity acidity.

Haralson

Type: Dessert.
Origin: Excelsior, MN, USA, selected 1913 and introduced 1923.
Parentage: Malinda (female) x Unknown.
Flowering: Mid-season.

The rounded fruits, around 7cm (2¾in) across, are bright yellow-green with a strong dark red flush. The creamy white flesh is crisp and juicy.

Note: The fruits can also be cooked and hold their shape well. Stored fruits retain their flavour well. Trees are vigorous with a tendency to biennial bearing.

Harry Pring

Type: Dessert.
Origin: Surrey, UK, 1911.
Parentage: Unknown.
Flowering: Mid-season.

The rounded fruits, around 6cm (2¼in) across, are yellow-green with a pinkish- to orange-red flush. The creamy white flesh has a savoury flavour.

Note: Trees are moderately vigorous. This variety is self-sterile so a compatible pollination partner is needed for good fruiting.

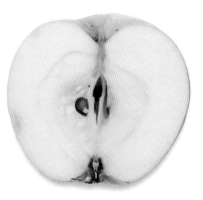

Harvey

The irregular, slightly flattened fruits, around 7cm (2¾ in) across, are bright yellow-green with some russeting. The creamy white flesh is firm, coarse-textured and very dry with a subacid and perfumed flavour.

Note: This variety is of considerable historic interest. Trees are moderately vigorous.

Type: Culinary.
Origin: Norfolk, UK, first mentioned 1629 by English botanist Parkinson.
Parentage: Unknown.
Flowering: Mid-season.
Other names: Doctor Harvey, Doctor Harvey's Apple, Golden Warrior, Harvey Apple and The Doctor.

Hawthornden

The flattened fruits, around 7cm (2¾ in) across, are bright greenish yellow with a red flush. The creamy white flesh is firm and coarse with a subacid flavour.

Note: Trees are generally healthy and vigorous and crop freely. Canker and woolly aphids may cause problems.

Type: Culinary.
Origin: Scotland, UK, 1780.
Parentage: Unknown.
Flowering: Mid-season.
Other names: Apfel von Hawthornden, Epine blanche, Glogowka, Hagendornsapfel, Haley, Hawley, Hawthornden Old, Hawthornden Red, Hawthornden White, Hawthorndenske, Hlohovske, Lincolnshire Pippin, Lord Kingston, Shoreditch White, Weeler's Kernel, Weisser Hawthornden, Wheeler's Kernel, White Apple and White Hawthornden.

Hejocsabai Sarga

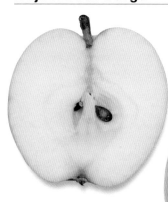

The rounded fruits, around 7cm (2¾ in) across, are bright yellow-green. The very white flesh has a sweet, almost scented flavour.

Note: Hejocsabai is a district in Miskolc, an industrial city in north-eastern Hungary.

Type: Dessert.
Origin: Hungary, 1948.
Parentage: Unknown.
Flowering: Mid-season.

Herefordshire Beefing

The somewhat flattened, slightly irregular fruits, around 7cm (2¾in) across, are bright yellow-green with a strong orange to dark red flush and some russeting and spotting. The yellowish white flesh is firm and fine-textured with a moderately acid flavour.

Note: Fruits can be stored for around two to three months. They are very heavy for their size.

Left: Ripening fruits are dark and shiny.

Type: Culinary.
Origin: Herefordshire, UK, known in the late 1700s.
Parentage: Unknown.
Flowering: Late.
Other names: Hereford Beaufin, Hereford Beefing, Herefordshire and Herefordshire Beaufin.

High View Pippin

Type: Dessert.
Origin: Ernest Hill, Weybridge, Surrey, UK, 1911.
Parentage: Sturmer Pippin (female) x Cox's Orange Pippin (male).
Flowering: Mid-season.

The slightly conical fruits, around 7cm (2¾in) across, are dull yellow-green with a broken red flush. The creamy white flesh is firm, fine-textured and juicy with a sweet, pleasant, aromatic flavour.

Note: Fruits store well. Trees are moderately vigorous.

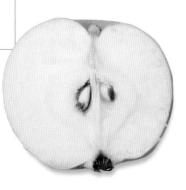

Histon Favourite

Type: Dessert and culinary.
Origin: Histon, Cambridgeshire, UK, first recorded 1883.
Parentage: Unknown.
Flowering: Early.
Other names: Chiver's Seedling, Chivers' Seedling and Histon Favorite.

The somewhat flattened, sometimes irregular fruits, around 7cm (2¾in) across, are yellow-green with a pinkish red flush. The creamy white flesh is rather soft, fine textured and juicy flesh with a faint flavour that is only a little sweet.

Note: Fruits can be stored for two to three months. Trees are moderately vigorous.

Hoary Morning

Type: Culinary.
Origin: ?Somerset, UK, first recorded 1819.
Parentage: Unknown.
Flowering: Mid-season.
Other names: Bachelor's Glory, Bedu Pteter Morgen Apfel, Blendon Seedling, Brouillard, Dainty, Downey, Downy, General Johnson, Harmat alma, Honeymoon, Mela pruinosa, Morgenduft, New Margil, Pruhaty ploskoun, Sam Rawlings, Utrennyaya rosa and Webster's Harvest Festival.

The flattened fruits, around 7cm (2¾ in) across, are yellowish green with a red flush that often appears as striping. The whole surface is covered with a thick bloom, like frost. The creamy white flesh is firm, rather coarse-textured and dry with no flavour and little acidity.

Note: Fully ripe fruits are also edible raw. Trees are moderately vigorous.

Hog's Snout

The knobbly, irregular fruits, around 7cm (2¾ in) across, are bright yellow-green with some russeting. The creamy white flesh is soft with a slightly acid flavour.

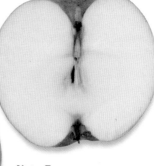

Type: Dessert.
Origin: UK, 1947.
Parentage: Unknown.
Flowering: Early.

Note: Trees are moderately vigorous.

Right: This variety is grown almost as much for the charm of its name as for the fruit itself.

Hohenzollern

The slightly flattened, somewhat irregular fruits, around 7cm (2¾ in) across, are bright yellow-green with some russeting. The flesh is crisp and coarse with a slightly sweet flavour.

Type: Dessert.
Origin: Probably Germany, 1947.
Parentage: Unknown.
Flowering: Mid-season.

Note: Some sources indicate a French origin for this variety. Trees are very vigorous.

Far right: This apple commemorates a notable German aristocratic family.

Holstein

Type: Dessert.
Origin: Eutin, Holstein, Germany, *c.*1918.
Parentage: Unknown, but possibly involving Cox's Orange Pippin.
Flowering: Early.
Other names: Holstein Cox, Holsteiner Cox, Holsteiner Gelber Cox and Vahldiks Cox Seedling No.III.

The somewhat oval but irregular fruits, to 8cm (3in) across, are yellow-green with a broken red flush. The creamy white flesh is firm, slightly coarse-textured and juicy with a little acidity and a sweet, richly aromatic flavour.

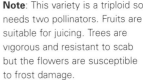

Note: This variety is a triploid so needs two pollinators. Fruits are suitable for juicing. Trees are vigorous and resistant to scab but the flowers are susceptible to frost damage.

Horei

Type: Dessert.
Origin: Aomori Apple Experiment Station, Japan, 1931, introduced 1949.
Parentage: Ralls Janet (female) x Golden Delicious (male).
Flowering: Mid-season.

The slightly conical fruits, around 7cm (2¾in) across, are bright yellow-green with an even red flush. The creamy white flesh is very firm with a fairly sweet flavour.

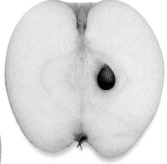

Note: The skins of the fruits are high in vitamins. Trees are weak growing.

Houblon

Type: Dessert.
Origin: Welford Park, Newbury, Berkshire, UK, first recorded 1901.
Parentage: Peasgood's Nonsuch (female) x Cox's Orange Pippin (male).
Flowering: Mid-season.

The rounded fruits, around 7cm (2¾in) across, are bright green with a red flush and striping. The creamy white flesh is firm, slightly coarse-textured and moderately juicy with a little acidity and a good aromatic, slightly aniseed taste.

Note: This variety is self-sterile so a suitable pollination partner is needed for good fruiting. Trees are moderately vigorous.

Howgate Wonder

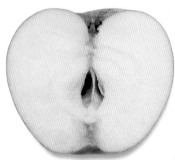

The rounded but sometimes uneven fruits, often much more than 7cm (2¾in) across, are bright greenish yellow with a red flush and striping. The creamy white flesh is firm, fine-textured and juicy, quite sweet when ripe and with a faint aromatic flavour.

Note: The fruits cook well. Fully ripe, they are also edible raw. This variety is partially self-fertile. Trees are vigorous and crop heavily.

Type: Culinary.
Origin: Bembridge, Isle of Wight, UK, 1915–16, introduced 1932.
Parentage: Blenheim Orange (female) x Newton Wonder (male).
Flowering: Mid-season.

Hubbardston Nonsuch

The rounded but sometimes uneven fruits, around 7cm (2¾in) across, are bright greenish yellow with a strong bright red flush. The creamy white flesh is firm and fine-textured with a sweet, subacid flavour.

Note: Trees bear regular and heavy crops of evenly sized fruits. Trees are moderately vigorous.

Type: Dessert.
Origin: Hubbardston, MA, USA, first recorded 1832.
Parentage: Unknown.
Flowering: Mid-season.
Other names: American Blush, American Nonpareil, Farmer's Profit, Hubardston Pippin, Hubbardston Old Town Pippin, Hubbardston Pippin, John May, Monstreuse d'Amerique, Nonesuch, Nonpareille de Hubbardston, Nonsuch, Old Town Pippin, Orleans, Sans Pareille d'Hubbardston, Sondergleichen von Hubbardston and Van Vleet.

Idared

The rounded fruits, around 7cm (2¾in) across, are bright green with a strong bright crimson-red flush and some indistinct streaking. The white, green- or pink-tinged flesh is firm, crisp and fine-textured with a sweet and pleasant vinous flavour.

Right: This sweet red apple is renowned for its keeping qualities.

Type: Dessert and culinary.
Origin: Idaho Agricultural Experiment Station, Moscow, USA, introduced 1942.
Parentage: Jonathan (female) x Wagener (male).
Flowering: Early.

Note: Trees tolerate heavy soil. They can be susceptible to fungal diseases. Young trees crop well. For the best colour, fruits need good exposure to sun. They store well over a long period.

Ildrod Pigeon

Type: Dessert.
Origin: Island of Fyn, Denmark, *c*.1840.
Parentage: Unknown.
Flowering: Early.
Other names: Eldrau Pigeon, Eldrod Pigeon, Eldrott Duvapple, Feuerroter Taubenapfel, Golubok ognenno-krasnyi, Ilrood Pigeon, Morke rod Pigeon, Pigeon rouge feu, Taubenapfel Feuerroter and Yldrod Pigeon.

The somewhat oblong fruits, around 7cm (2¾in) across, are bright greenish yellow with a red flush. The white flesh is firm, crisp and fine-textured with a sweet, subacid and slightly aromatic flavour.

Note: This variety is susceptible to powdery mildew. Some viruses can also cause problems.

Ingol

Type: Dessert.
Origin: Jork Fruit Research Station, Hamburg, Germany, 1954.
Parentage: Ingrid Marie (female) x Golden Delicious (male).
Flowering: Mid-season.

The flattened fruits, around 7cm (2¾in) across, are greenish yellow with a pinkish red flush and some striping. The creamy white flesh is soft but juicy with a rich flavour.

Note: This variety is resistant to bitter pit. Fruits store very well but lose flavour after four months. Trees are moderately vigorous.

Ingrid Marie

Type: Dessert.
Origin: Island of Fyn, Denmark, 1910.
Parentage: ?Cox's Orange Pippin (female) x Unknown.
Flowering: Mid-season.

The flattened fruits, around 7cm (2¾in) across, are yellow with a pinkish red flush and some spotting. The creamy white flesh is firm, crisp, fine-textured and juicy with a fair flavour.

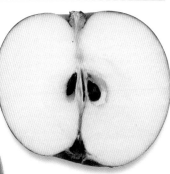

Note: Fruits can crack during some seasons. They are best eaten straight from the tree. Trees are moderately vigorous.

Jacquin

The conical fruits, around 7cm (2¾in) across, are bright yellowish green. The creamy white flesh is firm and crisp with a moderately sweet flavour.

Type: Dessert.
Origin: Boisbunel, France, recorded 1872.
Parentage: Unknown.
Flowering: Mid-season.

Note: Fruits are suitable for juicing and cider making. Trees are moderately vigorous.

Right: Jacquin is local to the Meurthe-et-Moselle department in the Lorraine region of France.

James Grieve

Left: James Grieve is a famous apple, formerly grown widely throughout Europe.

The rounded fruits, up to around 7cm (2¾in) across, are bright yellow-green with a bright orange-red flush and some streaking and spotting. The creamy white flesh is rather soft but very juicy with a good refreshing flavour.

Type: Culinary and dessert.
Origin: Edinburgh, Scotland, UK, first recorded 1893.
Parentage: Pott's Seedling or Cox's Orange Pippin (female) x Unknown.
Flowering: Mid-season.
Other names: Dzems Griw, Grieve and Jems Griv.

Note: Trees crop heavily, thriving in cool areas. Fruits do not store well. Bitter pit can be a problem. Commercially, this variety is often used for juicing and cider making. Red James Grieve is a sport.

Jansen von Welten

The very irregular fruits, around 8cm (3in) across, are yellowish green with a strong red flush and some spotting. The creamy white flesh is fairly firm with a sweet, aromatic, nutty flavour.

Note: Trees, of moderate vigour, crop freely. They are best trained as pyramids.

Type: Dessert.
Origin: Welten, nr Aachen, Germany, 1823.
Parentage: Unknown.
Flowering: Mid-season.
Other names: Couronne des Pommes, Fausen of Wellen, Jansen de Welten, Jansen van Welten, Jansen von Wetton, Reinette von Welten, Rosen Apfel von Welten and Rosenapfel von Welten.

Jean Tondeur

Type: Dessert.
Origin: France, 1947.
Parentage: Unknown.
Flowering: Late.

The flattened fruits, around 7cm (2¾in) across, are bright greenish yellow with a red flush. The white flesh is soft and fine with a subacid flavour.

  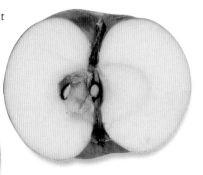

Note: This variety is local to the Marne department of north-eastern France. Trees are moderately vigorous.

Jersey Black

Type: Dessert.
Origin: New Jersey, USA, recorded 1817.
Parentage: Unknown.
Flowering: Mid-season.
Other names: Black American, Black Apple, Black Apple of America, Black Jersey, Dodge's Black and Small Black.

The uneven, very knobbly fruits, to 9cm (3¼in) across, are yellowish green with a dark red flush. The creamy-white flesh is crisp and rather coarse with a sweet, subacid, aromatic flavour.

Note: This variety is self-sterile, so a compatible pollination partner is required for successful fruiting.

 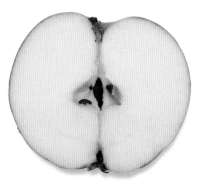

Jonagored

Type: Dessert.
Origin: Halen, Belgium, introduced 1985.
Parentage: Golden Delicious (female) x Jonathan (male).
Flowering: Very early.

Note: Early flowering makes this triploid variety suitable only for areas where late frosts are rare.

The knobbly, slightly conical fruits, around 7cm (2¾in) across, are yellow-green with a strong dark red flush that can be patchy and some striping. The creamy white flesh is fine-textured and juicy with a sweet and rich flavour.

Above: This variety is a sport mutation of Jonagold.

Jonathan

The irregular fruits, to 8cm (3in) across, are bright greenish-yellow with a strong bright red flush. The creamy-white flesh is soft, fine-textured, fairly juicy and sweet.

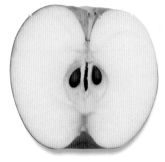

Note: Trees, which are naturally small, can be susceptible to fungal diseases. It is a popular variety in North America. It is partially self-fertile but best with a pollinator. The fruits store well.

Type: Dessert.
Origin: Woodstock, Ulster Co., NY, USA.
Parentage: ?Esopus Spitzenburg (female) x Unknown.
Flowering: Mid-season.
Other names: Djonathan, Dzhonatan, Dzoneth, Esopus Spitzenberg (New), King Philip, Philip Rick, Pomme Jonathan and Ulster Seedling.

Far left: This American variety is named after Jonathan Hasbrouck, who discovered the apple.

Josephine

The more or less rounded but uneven fruits, around 7cm (2¾in) across, are bright green with net-like russeting over the skin. The cream flesh is fine with a somewhat sweet flavour.

Note: This variety should not be confused with Belle Joséphine (correctly, Gloria Mundi). Trees are very vigorous.

Type: Dessert.
Origin: France, 1947.
Parentage: Unknown.
Flowering: Mid-season.

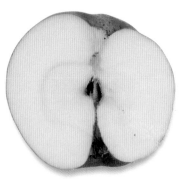

Joybells

The flattened, irregular fruits, around 7cm (2¾in) across, are pale greenish yellow with a strong pinkish red flush and some russeting. The creamy white flesh is crisp and juicy with a sweet and pleasant flavour.

Type: Dessert.
Origin: Godalming, Surrey, UK; records show that trees were grafted *c.*1914.
Parentage: Unknown.
Flowering: Mid-season.
Other name: Joy Bells.

Note: Trees, which crop heavily, are moderately vigorous.

Far left: Its pretty markings make Joybells a particularly attractive apple.

Jumbo Ohrin

Type: Dessert.
Origin: Nakajima Tenkohen Fruit Nurseries, Japan, 1985.
Parentage: ?Golden Delicious (female) x ?Indo (male).
Flowering: Early.

The rather uneven, somewhat square fruits, around 7cm (2¾in) across, are bright green with a red flush. The creamy white flesh is crisp and juicy.

Note: Jumbo Ohrin is one of the most important commercial apple varieties in Japan.

Jupp's Russet A

Type: Dessert.
Origin: New Zealand, 1951.
Parentage: Unknown.
Flowering: Mid-season.

Note: Though it commemorates an English grower, this has been a valued variety in New Zealand.

Left: *Russeting is a characteristic of this apple, as its name suggests.*

The rounded fruits, around 7cm (2¾in) across, are yellowish green with a light red flush and some russeting. The greenish white flesh is firm and fine with a sweet subacid flavour.

Kandile

Type: Dessert.
Origin: Bulgaria, 1957.
Parentage: Unknown.
Flowering: Mid-season.

The slightly flattened fruits, around 7cm (2¾in) across, are bright greenish yellow with a red flush and striping. The creamy white flesh is firm and fine with a subacid flavour.

Note: This variety should not be confused with a much older variety known as Kandil Sinap, which is also sometimes grown as Kandile.

Kenneth

The rounded, occasionally irregular fruits, around 7cm (2¾ in) across, are dull green with a dark red flush. The creamy white flesh is somewhat coarse and soft with a subacid and sweet flavour.

Type: Dessert.
Origin: Rhyl, Wales, UK, 1920.
Parentage: Unknown.
Flowering: Mid-season.

Note: This variety is named in honour of its breeder, Kenneth McCreadie. Trees are moderately vigorous.

Right: Fruits of this variety can be variously shaped and of different sizes.

Keswick Codlin

The conical fruits, around 7cm (2¾ in) across or more, are clear bright green with an orange flush and some spotting. The yellowish white flesh is soft, rather coarse-textured and with an acid flavour.

Note: This is an excellent garden variety that crops prolifically. The flesh is very juicy when freshly picked but becomes dry and mealy after a few weeks' storage. Fruits cook to a sweet purée.

Left: Keswick Codlin is an easy apple variety to grow.

Type: Culinary.
Origin: Found on a rubbish heap at Gleaston Castle near Ulverston, Lancashire, UK, recorded 1793.
Parentage: Unknown.
Flowering: Early.
Other names: Codlin de Keswick, Everbearing, Keswick, Keswick Codling, Keswicker Kuchenapfel, Kodlin kesvikskii, Pinder's Apple and White Codlin.

Kidd's Orange Red

The rounded fruits (sometimes lumpy), around 7cm (2¾ in) across, are yellow with a bright orange-red flush somewhat broken by russeting. The creamy white flesh is firm, crisp and juicy with a sweet, rich, aromatic flavour.

Type: Dessert.
Origin: Greytown, Wairarapa, New Zealand, 1924.
Parentage: Cox's Orange Pippin (female) x Delicious (male).
Flowering: Mid-season.
Other names: Delco, Kidd's Orange and Kidd's Oranje Roode.

Note: Trees crop reliably but seldom heavily – hence this variety has not become popular commercially. They benefit from thinning.

King David

Type: Dessert.
Origin: Washington County, AR, USA, found 1893 in a hedgerow.
Parentage: ?Jonathan (female) x Winesap or Arkansas Black (male).
Flowering: Mid-season.

The rounded but uneven fruits, around 7cm (2¾in) across, are yellow-green with a dark red flush and some striping. The creamy white flesh is rather coarse with a subacid, slightly sweet flavour.

  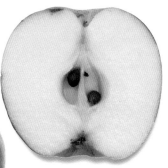

Note: Trees, ultimately large, bear very early and are resistant to fireblight. The fruits store well.

King of the Pippins

Type: Dessert.
Origin: UK or France, first recorded 1800.
Parentage: Unknown.
Flowering: Mid-season.
Other names: Aranyparmen, Pearmain, English Winter Golden Pear, George I, Gold Parmane, Goldreinette, Hampshire Yellow, Herzogs Reinette, Jones' Southampton Yellow, King of Pippins, Orange Pearmain, Pike's Pearmain, Reinette d'Oree, Seek no Farther, Shropshire Pippin and Winter Pearmain.

The rounded fruits, around 7cm (2¾in) across, are bright greenish yellow with a strong red flush. The white flesh is firm and juicy with a sharp and slightly aromatic subacid flavour.

Note: Formerly Golden Winter Pearmain. Identical to Reine des Reinettes grown in France. Trees do not do well in cold, heavy soils. It is partially self-fertile.

King's Acre Pippin

Type: Dessert.
Origin: King's Acre Nurseries, Hereford, recorded 1897, introduced 1899.
Parentage: ?Sturmer Pippin (female) x ?Ribston Pippin (male).
Flowering: Mid-season.
Other names: Cranston's, Cranston's Pippin and Ribston Pearmain.

The rounded fruits, up to around 6cm (2¼in) across or more, are yellow-green with a red flush and some russeting. The creamy white flesh is firm, coarse-textured and juicy with a rich, strong, aromatic flavour.

Note: The fruits store well for one to two months. This variety is a triploid. Bitter pit can be a problem.

Kis Erno Tabornok

Type: Dessert.
Origin: Hungary, 1948.
Parentage: Unknown.
Flowering: Mid-season.

Note: This unusual apple is not widely grown outside its native Hungary.

Left: This variety honours a Hungarian member of the military.

The somewhat flattened, uneven fruits, around 7cm (2¾ in) across, are bright green with a red flush that can show as patches. The creamy-white flesh is tough with a slightly sweet flavour.

Kitchovka

The slightly irregular fruits, around 6cm (2¼ in) across, are yellow with a pinkish red flush. The creamy white flesh is firm and rather coarse with a subacid and slightly sweet flavour.

Type: Dessert.
Origin: Bulgaria, 1957.
Parentage: Unknown.
Flowering: Mid-season.

Note: Trees are very vigorous.

Above: Fruits within a cluster are of uneven shape.

Klunster

The flattened, slightly irregular fruits, around 7cm (2¾ in) across, are bright green, sometimes with a reddish flush and some russeting. The white flesh is firm and fine with a subacid flavour.

Type: Dessert.
Origin: Jork Fruit Research Station, nr Hamburg, Germany, 1951.
Parentage: Unknown.
Flowering: Mid-season.

Note: Trees are very vigorous.

Right: This variety generally crops well.

Knobby Russet

The irregular fruits, around 7cm (2¾in) across, have a distinctively warty appearance and are dull yellow-green with some scaly russeting. The white flesh is firm and rather dry with a fairly strong flavour.

Note: This variety is self-sterile so a suitable pollination partner is needed for good fruiting. Trees are moderately vigorous.

Type: Dessert.
Origin: Midhurst, Sussex, UK, 1820.
Parentage: Unknown.
Flowering: Early.
Other names: Knobbed Russet, Old Maid's, Old Maids, Winter, Winter Apple and Winter Russet.

Kolacara

Type: Dessert.
Origin: Former Yugoslavia, 1936.
Parentage: Unknown.
Flowering: Early.
Other names: Kolatchara and Koltchara.

The flattened, somewhat uneven fruits, around 7cm (2¾in) across or more, are greenish yellow with a bright red flush and striping. The creamy white flesh is firm and coarse with a subacid flavour.

Note: This variety is a triploid so needs two pollination partners. Trees are very vigorous.

Kougetsu

Type: Dessert.
Origin: Aomori Apple Experimental Station, Japan, date unknown.
Parentage: Golden Delicious (female) x Jonathan (male).
Flowering: Very early.

The rounded, slightly uneven fruits, around 7cm (2¾in) across, are bright yellowish green with a bright red flush and some spotting. The cream flesh is coarse in texture.

Note: Early flowering makes this variety suitable only for areas where late frosts are rare.

La Gaillarde

The rounded fruits, around 6cm (2¼in) across, are green with a red flush. The creamy white flesh is coarse and crisp with a subacid sweet flavour.

Note: This variety is self-sterile so a suitable pollination partner is needed for good fruiting. Trees are very vigorous.

Type: Culinary and dessert.
Origin: Angers, France, 1930.
Parentage: Unknown.
Flowering: Mid-season.

La Nationale

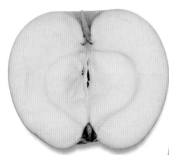

The rounded fruits, around 7cm (2¾in) across, are green with a red flush. The whitish flesh is firm with a sweet flavour.

Type: Dessert.
Origin: Sainte-Romain-au-Mont d'Or, Rhône, France, 1871.
Parentage: Unknown.
Flowering: Late.
Other names: Bernardin, Bourget, Cusset à Fruits Rouges, Cusset Rouge, Déesse nationale and Natsionalnoe.

Note: Late flowering makes this a suitable variety for cold areas. Fruits can also be used for cooking.

Lady Henniker

The rather knobbly, somewhat flattened and irregular fruits, around 7cm (2¾in) across, are light green with a red flush that can show as flecking. The whitish flesh is firm, coarse-textured and rather dry with a fairly acid but fair flavour.

Type: Culinary and dessert.
Origin: Thornham Hall, Eye, Suffolk, UK, between 1840 and 1850, introduced 1873.
Parentage: Unknown.
Flowering: Mid-season.
Other names: Henniker, Lady Hennicker and Ledi Genniker.

Note: This popular garden variety is self-sterile so a suitable pollination partner is needed for good fruiting. Trees are very vigorous.

Lady Sudeley

Type: Dessert.
Origin: Petworth, Sussex, UK, *c*.1849, introduced 1885.
Parentage: Unknown.
Flowering: Mid-season.
Other names: Jacob's Strawberry and Lady Sudely.

The rounded, slightly irregular, ribbed fruits, around 7cm (2¾in) across, are bright yellow-green with a pinkish red flush and some streaking and russeting. The creamy yellow flesh is firm and juicy with a somewhat acid but good flavour.

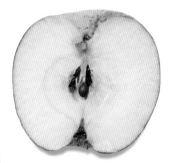

Note: Trees are small, compact and moderately vigorous. A tip-bearer.

Lady Williams

Type: Dessert.
Origin: Donnybrook, Western Australia, *c*.1935.
Parentage: ?Granny Smith (female) x Jonathan or ?Rokewood (male).
Flowering: Early.

Note: Fruits need a long summer to ripen fully. Trees are moderately vigorous.

The rounded fruits, around 6cm (2¼in) across, are dull light green with a dark red flush. The creamy white flesh is firm and crisp.

Landsberger Reinette

Type: Dessert.
Origin: Landsberg/Warthe, Brandenburg, Germany, *c*.1840.
Parentage: Unknown.
Flowering: Early.
Other names: Buchardt Renette, Landsberg, Landsberger, Landsberger Renette, Landsberska, Landsberska Reneta, Reinette de Landsberg, Renet landsbergskii, Reneta Gorzawska, Reneta Landsberska and Surprise.

The rounded fruits, around 7cm (2¾in) across, are bright green. The whitish flesh is soft, fine-textured and very juicy with a sweet and refreshing flavour.

Note: Fruits store well. They are also suitable for cooking.

Lane's Prince Albert

Type: Culinary.
Origin: Berkhamstead, Hertfordshire, UK, *c*.1840, introduced 1850.
Parentage: Russet Nonpareil (female) x Dumelow's Seedling (male).
Flowering: Mid-season.
Other names: Albert Lanskii, Lane, Lane's, Lane's Albert, Perkins' A. 1, Prince Albert, Prince Albert de Lane, Prinz Albert, Profit, Victoria and Albert.

The slightly uneven fruits, more than 7cm (2¾ in) across, are bright green with a red flush and some flecking. The creamy white flesh is very juicy with an acid flavour.

Note: The fruits cook well. Trees crop freely. Trees are moderately vigorous.

Lawyer Nutmeg

Note: This variety originated with David Lawyer. Trees are moderately vigorous.

The slightly flattened, somewhat uneven fruits, around 7cm (2¾ in) across, are bright yellow green with a slight red flush. The creamy white flesh has a rich and spicy flavour reminiscent of nutmeg.

Type: Dessert.
Origin: Plains, MT, USA, date unknown.
Parentage: ?Wismer Dessert (female) x ?Apple Crab (male).
Flowering: Mid-season.

Laxton's Royalty

Note: Fruits are late to ripen. They can be stored for three to four months. Trees are moderately vigorous.

The somewhat flattened fruits, to 8cm (3in) across, are mid-green with a dark red flush. The yellowish white flesh is hard and crisp with a slightly sweet to subacid taste.

Type: Dessert.
Origin: Bedford, UK, 1908, introduced 1932.
Parentage: Cox's Orange Pippin (female) x Court Pendu Plat (male).
Flowering: Late.

Laxton's Superb

The rounded, slightly uneven fruits, around 7cm (2¾in) across, are dull green with a dull red flush. The creamy white flesh is firm and very juicy with a sweet, pleasant and refreshing flavour.

Note: Trees, which are vigorous and spreading, are prone to biennial bearing.

Type: Dessert.
Origin: Bedford, UK, 1897, introduced 1922.
Parentage: Wyken Pippin (female) x Cox's Orange Pippin (male).
Flowering: Mid-season.
Other names: Laxton Superb, Laxtons Superb and Superb.

 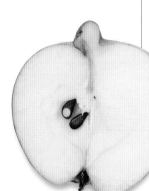

Type: Culinary.
Origin: Harwich, Essex, UK, 1883.
Parentage: Unknown.
Flowering: Early.

Leather Jacket

The somewhat flattened fruits, around 7cm (2¾in) across, are bright yellow-green with some spotting. The creamy white flesh is somewhat acid in flavour.

Note: The fruits cook well.

Left: The skins of this variety have a rather greasy appearance and feel.

Leathercoat Russet

Type: Dessert.
Origin: England, UK, first recorded 1597.
Parentage: Unknown.
Flowering: Early.
Other name: Royal Russet.

The irregular, somewhat flattened fruits, around 7cm (2¾in) across, are dull green with some russeting. The greenish yellow flesh is tender with a sweet, subacid flavour.

  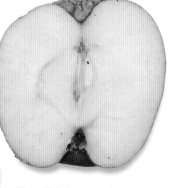

Note: This is a very vigorous variety that is best grown on a dwarfing rootstock.

Legana

The rounded, slightly conical fruits, around 6cm (2¼in) across, are yellowish green with a red flush. The creamy white flesh is firm and fine with a sweet, subacid flavour.

Type: Dessert.
Origin: Legana, Tasmania, Australia, c.1940.
Parentage: Democrat (female) x Delicious (male).
Flowering: Mid-season.

Note: This variety is weak-growing so may not do well on a dwarfing rootstock.

Right: Legana is named after a rural town that contained several apple orchards.

Leonie de Sonnaville

The flattened fruits, around 6cm (2¼in) across, are dull greenish yellow with a strong red flush. The creamy white flesh is sweet and juicy with an aromatic flavour.

Type: Dessert.
Origin: Institute for Horticultural Plant Breeding (IVT), Wageningen, Netherlands, 1974.
Parentage: Cox's Orange Pippin (female) x Jonathan (male).
Flowering: Late.

Note: This variety is a partial tip-bearer. Trees are moderately vigorous.

Levering Limbertwig

The slightly flattened fruits, around 6cm (2¼in) across, are bright green with a strong red flush. The yellowish flesh is fairly firm with a subacid flavour.

Type: Dessert.
Origin: Ararat, VA, USA, date unknown.
Parentage: Unknown.
Flowering: Mid-season.
Other name: Limbertwig.

Note: A larger-fruited mutation of Limbertwig. It is very vigorous, so is suitable for growing on a dwarfing rootstock. Fruits ripen late.

Lille

Type: Dessert.
Origin: France, 1948.
Parentage: Unknown.
Flowering: Late.

The rounded fruits, around 5cm (2in) across, are bright green with a deep pinkish red flush. The greenish white flesh is fine with a subacid flavour.

Note: Late flowering makes this a suitable variety for growing in areas where late spring frosts are likely.

Lodgemore Nonpareil

Type: Dessert.
Origin: Lodgemore, Stroud, Gloucestershire, UK, c.1808.
Parentage: Unknown.
Flowering: Late.
Other names: Clissold's Seedling, Lodgemore Seedling, Non Pareille de Lodgemore and Nonpareille de Lodgemore.

The somewhat irregular fruits, around 6cm (2¼in) across, are bright yellow-green, dotted with grey and with some russeting. The creamy white flesh is firm, crisp and juicy with a sweet and perfumed flavour.

Note: Trees crop freely. Fruits can be stored for several months, retaining good flavour.

Lombarts Calville

Type: Dessert.
Origin: Zundert, Netherlands, 1906.
Parentage: ?Calville Blanc D'Hiver (female) x Unknown.
Flowering: Mid-season.
Other names: Lombarts Kalvill, Lombartscalville and Witte Winter Lombartscalville.

The slightly conical fruits, around 6cm (2¼in) across, are a shiny yellowish green. The creamy white flesh is firm, fairly coarse and soft with a sweet subacid flavour.

Note: Trees are moderately vigorous. Fruits can be stored for around three months.

Long Bider

Type: Culinary.
Origin: East Malling Research Station, Maidstone, Kent, UK, 1948.
Parentage: Unknown.
Flowering: Unknown.
Other name: Longbider.

The flattened fruits, around 6cm (2¼in) across, are yellowish green with some spotting. The flesh is creamy white.

Note: The fruits cook well.

Longney Russet

The rounded but slightly irregular fruits, to 7cm (2¾in) across, are green with heavy russeting and a red flush that can appear as spotting. The creamy white flesh is fine, hard and dry with a subacid flavour.

Note: The fruits are suitable for cider making. The fruits store well, retaining good flavour.

Type: Dessert.
Origin: Gloucestershire, UK, 1949 (probably older).
Parentage: Unknown.
Flowering: Mid-season.

  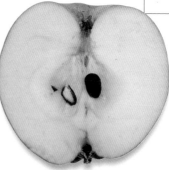

Lord Burghley

The slightly conical fruits, around 7cm (2¾in) across, are bright golden yellow-green with a strong red flush. The yellowish white flesh is very firm, fine-textured and rather dry with a sweet and rich aromatic flavour.

Type: Dessert.
Origin: Burghley, Stamford, Lincolnshire, UK, 1843, introduced 1865.
Parentage: Unknown.
Flowering: Late.
Other names: Bergli, Lord Burghleigh and Lord Burleigh.

Note: The fruits keep well in storage, retaining good flavour for up to five months.

Lord Grosvenor

Type: Culinary.
Origin: Unknown but believed to be new in 1872.
Parentage: Unknown.
Flowering: Mid-season.

The very irregular, sometimes quince- or pear-like fruits, around 8cm (3in) across or more, are bright yellow-green to straw yellow with a few spots and some traces of thin russeting. The white flesh is soft, tender and juicy with an acid to subacid flavour.

Note: The fruits cook well. They can be stored for two to three months.

Lord Hindlip

Type: Dessert.
Origin: Worcestershire, UK, 1896.
Parentage: Unknown.
Flowering: Mid-season.

The roughly conical, somewhat irregular fruits, around 7cm (2¾in) across, are yellow-green with some russeting and a strong red flush. The creamy white flesh is fairly firm, very fine-textured and juicy with a good aromatic flavour.

Note: Trees are moderately vigorous. This variety is self-sterile, so a suitable pollination partner is needed for good fruiting.

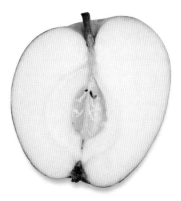

Lord Lambourne

Type: Dessert.
Origin: Bedford, UK, 1907, introduced 1923.
Parentage: James Grieve (female) x Worcester Pearmain (male).
Flowering: Early.

The slightly flattened but uniform fruits, around 6cm (2¼in) across, are bright yellow-green with a strong orange-red flush and some streaking. The creamy white flesh is slightly coarse-textured and juicy with a strong, sweet and somewhat aromatic flavour.

Note: The same parents produced Katy and Elton Beauty. Trees, of moderate vigour, are easy to grow and crop well. They are partially self-fertile but fruit best in the presence of a pollinator.

Above: Lord Lambourne is a classic dessert apple, with a uniform shape and a pretty flush.

Mabbot's Pearmain

Type: Dessert.
Origin: Kent, UK,
first described 1883.
Parentage: Unknown.
Flowering: Mid-season.
Other names: Canterbury,
Mabbut's Pearmain,
Parmaene von Mabbott,
Parmane von Mabot,
Parmane von Mabott,
Pearmain de Mabbot and
Pearmain de Mabbott.

Note: Fruits can be stored for
up to around three months.
Trees are moderately vigorous.

The rounded fruits, up to around 7cm (2¾in) across, are
bright yellow-green with a pinkish red flush and some
spotting and grey russeting. The yellowish white flesh
is fairly crisp, somewhat coarse-textured and juicy with
a slightly acid, pleasant aromatic flavour.

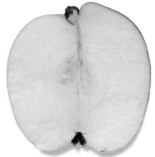

*Above: Fruits can turn bright red
on the side that is exposed to
the sun.*

Macwood

The somewhat irregular, rounded to conical fruits, around
6cm (2¼in) across, are bright green with a strong dark red
flush. The white flesh is firm and somewhat coarse with a
sweet, perfumed flavour.

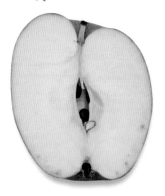

Type: Dessert.
Origin: Central Experimental
Farm, Ottawa, Canada, 1936.
Parentage: McIntosh
(female) x Forest (male).
Flowering: Early.

Note: Needs a sheltered position
to protect the flowers in frost-
prone areas.

*Right: Dark red apples such as
this one are always popular.*

Madoue Rouge

The irregular fruits, around 6cm (2¼in) across, are yellow-
green with a red flush. The yellowish flesh is tough with a
sweet subacid flavour.

Type: Dessert.
Origin: Nieul (Haute-Vienne),
France, described 1947.
Parentage: Unknown.
Flowering: Very late.
Other name: Madou.

Note: Late flowering
makes this a suitable
variety for cold districts.
It is local to the Limousin
province of France.

Malling Kent

Type: Dessert.
Origin: East Malling Research Station, Maidstone, Kent, UK, 1949.
Parentage: Cox's Orange Pippin (female) x Jonathan (male).
Flowering: Mid-season.

The conical fruits, around 6cm (2¼in) across, are bright greenish yellow with a pinkish red flush and some streaking. The creamy white flesh is slightly coarse-textured and fairly juicy with a pleasant aromatic flavour.

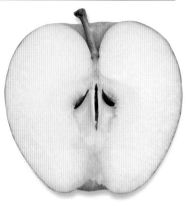

Note: Trees are of moderate vigour. The flavour is similar to that of Cox's Orange Pippin.

Mannington's Pearmain

Type: Dessert.
Origin: Uckfield, Sussex, UK, c.1770, introduced 1847.
Parentage: Unknown.
Flowering: Mid-season.
Other names: Mannington Pearmain, Mannington's Parmaene, Mannington's Parmane, Pearmain de Mannington and Pomme de Mannington.

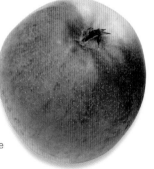

The rounded to flattened fruits, around 7cm (2¾in) across, are light greenish yellow with thin russeting and a pinkish red flush. The flesh is greenish white to yellow, firm, fine-textured and moderately juicy with a slightly aromatic flavour.

Note: This variety was produced from seed found in cider pomace. To develop their fullest flavour, fruits are best allowed to hang on the tree for as long as possible before picking. Young trees bear well.

Margil

Type: Dessert.
Origin: Europe, known in England before 1750 (possibly of French origin).
Parentage: Unknown.
Flowering: Early.
Other names: Fail-me-Never, Gewurz Reinette, Herefordshire Margil, Kleine Granat-Reinette, Margil Hook, Munches Pippin, Muscadet, Never Fail, Reinette Muscat, Reinette Sucrée, Renet Muscat, Renetta Moscata, Small Ribston, Sucrée d'Hiver and White Margil.

The rounded to conical fruits, around 6cm (2¼in) across, are bright yellow-green with a strong orange-red flush and some streaking, with a tendency to russeting. The creamy white to yellow flesh is firm and rather dry with a sweet aromatic taste.

Note: This is one of the oldest dessert varieties grown in England. The flavour is similar to Braeburn. Early flowering makes this variety susceptible to frost damage. Of moderate vigour, it is suitable for training as an espalier. Crops may be small.

Mariborka

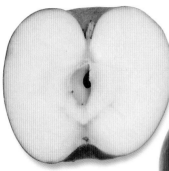

The somewhat flattened, slightly irregular fruits, around 6cm (2¼in) across, are bright green with a strong red flush and some light streaking. The whitish flesh is crisp and juicy with a rich, aromatic flavour.

Note: Late flowering makes this a suitable variety for areas where late frosts are common.

Type: Dessert.
Origin: Institut Za Vocarstvo, Cacak, former Yugoslavia, date unknown.
Parentage: Golden Pearmain (female) x Jonathan (male).
Flowering: Late.

Marie Doudou

The rather flattened, irregular fruits, around 6cm (2¼in) across, are dull pale green with a strong dull red flush and some russeting. The white flesh is tinged green and is fairly tough with a subacid flavour.

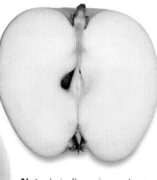

Note: Late flowering makes this a suitable variety for cold districts.

Right: Marie Doudou is local to north-western France.

Type: Dessert.
Origin: France, described 1948.
Parentage: Unknown.
Flowering: Very late.

Marie-Joseph d'Othée

The flattened fruits, to 5cm (2in) across, are bright greenish yellow with a pinkish red flush with some streaking and russeting. The greenish white flesh is firm with a sweet subacid flavour.

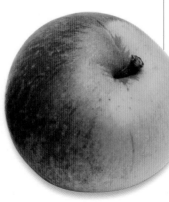

Note: This is a large tree, suitable for orchards, and generally healthy and productive. The fruits store well.

Type: Dessert.
Origin: Liège, Belgium, 1947.
Parentage: Unknown.
Flowering: Late.
Other names: de Fer, Ijzerappel, Marie-José, Pomme de Deux Ans, Pomme de Fer, Reine Marie d'Otlée and Reine Marie Joseph d'Othée.

Marie-Louise Ducote

The rounded fruits, around 6cm (2¼in) across, are light yellow-green with some spotting and russeting. The greenish white flesh is tender with a sweet flavour.

Type: Dessert.
Origin: France, 1947.
Parentage: Unknown.
Flowering: Late.

Note: This variety is spur-bearing.

Right: This dainty-looking apple has a very pleasant taste.

Marie-Madeleine

Type: Dessert.
Origin: France, 1947.
Parentage: Unknown.
Flowering: Late.
Other name:
Marie Madeleine.

The rounded to conical fruits, around 6cm (2¼in) across, are pale green with russeting. The greenish white flesh is coarse, crisp and juicy with a subacid flavour.

Note: Besides being excellent as an eating apple, this variety is also good for cider making.

Marosszeki Piros Paris

Type: Dessert.
Origin: Maros-Torda, Hungary, first recorded in 1598.
Parentage: Unknown.
Flowering: Early.
Other names: Grosse-Pomme-Paris, Maros Szeki, Paris, Paris Alma, Paris Apfel, Paris de Moros, Paris jaune, Paris vert, Pomme Paris, Pomme Paris, Rouge de Marosszek and Rother Parisapfel.

The rounded fruits, around 6cm (2¼in) across, are bright yellow-green with a red flush. The white flesh has a subacid, aromatic flavour.

Note: This is an apple of great antiquity. Its place of origin is presently in central Romania (eastern Transylvania).

May Queen

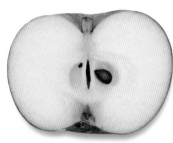

The flattened, irregular fruits, around 7cm (2¾in) across, are bright green with a deep red flush and some striping. The yellow flesh is firm and compact with an unusual, sometimes astringent flavour.

Note: This variety is self-sterile, so a suitable pollination partner is required for successful fruiting. The fruits store well.

Right: May Queen has a notable crunchy texture.

Type: Dessert.
Origin: Worcester, UK, 1888.
Parentage: Unknown.
Flowering: Mid-season.

McIntosh

Note: Trees, of moderate vigour, can be vulnerable to canker in humid areas. They are resistant to powdery mildew and cedar apple rust. Fruits store well but can lose flavour. This variety has given rise to several sports.

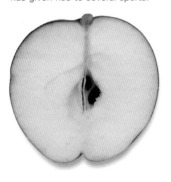

The rounded, often irregular fruits, around 7cm (2¾in) across, are bright green with a strong dark bluish red flush and some striping and flecking. The white flesh is rather soft, fine-textured and very juicy with a sweet, pleasant vinous flavour.

Type: Dessert.
Origin: Dundela, Dundas County, Ontario, Canada, 1796, introduced *c*.1870.
Parentage: ?Fameuse or Saint Lawrence (female) x Unknown.
Flowering: Early.
Other names: M'Intosh, Mac Intosh, Mac Intosh Red, Mac-Intosh, Mac-Intosh Red, MacIntosh, MacIntosh Red, Mackintosh, Mackintosh Red, Makintos, Mc-Intosh Red, McIntosh Red and Mekintos.

McLellan

The flattened fruits, around 7cm (2¾in) across or more, are bright green. The whitish flesh is fairly firm, fine and very tender with a sweet subacid flavour.

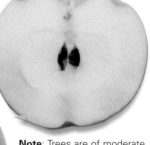

Note: Trees are of moderate vigour. The fruits ripen in late autumn.

Type: Dessert.
Origin: Woodstock, CT, USA, *c*.1780.
Parentage: Unknown.
Flowering: Early.
Other names: Lilac, M'Clellan's, M'Lellan, M'Lellan's, Mac-Lellan, MacLellan, Martin, Mc Lellan, McClelan, McClellan and Mek-Lellan.

Megumi

Type: Dessert.
Origin: South Korea, 1967.
Parentage: Ralls Janet x Jonathan.
Flowering: Late.

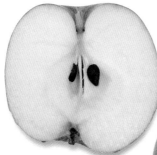

The somewhat conical fruits, around 7cm (2¾in) across, are bright yellowish green with a pinkish red flush. The creamy white flesh is firm and coarse with a very sweet flavour.

Note: Trees crop freely but are weak-growing so should not be on very dwarfing rootstocks.

Melon

Type: Dessert.
Origin: East Bloomfield, Ontario County, NY, USA, *c.*1800, introduced 1845.
Parentage: Unknown.
Flowering: Mid-season.
Other names: Amerikanischer Melonen Apfel, Amerikansk Melonaeble, Melon Apple, Melon de Norton, Melon Norton, Norton, Norton Watermelon, Norton's Melon, Pomme Melon d'Amérique, Pomme Norton and Watermelon.

The rounded but irregular, rather bluntly angular fruits, around 7cm (2¾in) across, are bright lemon yellow tinged with green with a red flush and some flecking and veiny russeting. The yellowish white flesh is firm, fine, crisp and tender with a subacid and aromatic flavour.

Note: Trees are susceptible to frost damage and are weak-growing, so unsuitable for very dwarfing rootstocks. They crop heavily but are prone to biennial bearing; fruits should be thinned. Stored fruits are best before the end of winter.

Mère de Ménage

Type: Culinary.
Origin: Known in the late 1700s.
Parentage: Unknown.
Flowering: Mid-season.
Other names: Bellefleur de France, Brietling, Burton's Beauty, Capp Mammoth, Femme de Ménage, Flanders Pippin, Gelbe Tellerapfel, German Spa, Gloria Mundi, Harlow Pippin, Libra, Livre, Lord Combermere, Menagerie, Mère-de-Ménage, Pfund, Queen Emma, Rambour d'Amérique, Red German, Riesenapfel, Teller and Winter Colmar.

The somewhat irregular, sometimes flattened fruits, up to around 7cm (2¾in) across or more, are bright yellow-green with a strong dark red flush and some streaking and russeting. The greenish flesh is firm, crisp, rather coarse-textured and rather dry with an acid flavour.

Above: Mère de Ménage is a beautiful apple of first-rate quality.

Note: Fruits can be stored for three to four months.

Merton Beauty

Type: Dessert.
Origin: John Innes Institute, Merton, London, UK, 1933.
Parentage: Ellison's Orange (female) x Cox's Orange Pippin (male).
Flowering: Mid-season.

The rounded fruits, up to around 7cm (2¾in) across, are bright yellow-green with a pinkish red flush and some russeting. The creamy white flesh is firm, fine-textured and juicy with a distinct aniseed flavour.

Note: Trees are moderately vigorous. Fruits are best eaten within two weeks of picking.

Above: The attractive Merton Beauty is easy to grow and always gives a good crop.

Merton Russet

The rounded, slightly conical fruits, around 6cm (2¼in) across, are bright yellowish green with heavy russeting. The creamy white flesh is firm, crisp and tender with a sweet subacid flavour.

Type: Dessert.
Origin: John Innes Horticultural Institute, Merton, London, UK, 1921 (named 1943).
Parentage: Sturmer Pippin (female) x Cox's Orange Pippin (male).
Flowering: Early.

Note: Trees are very vigorous. The variety does best on a dwarfing rootstock.

Mimi

The rounded, slightly irregular fruits, around 6cm (2¼in) across, are bright yellow-green with a strong dark red flush and some flecking. The yellow flesh is fine and soft with a sweet subacid flavour.

Type: Dessert.
Origin: Horticultural Laboratory, Wageningen, Netherlands, 1935.
Parentage: Jonathan (female) x Cox's Orange Pippin (male).
Flowering: Mid-season.

Note: Trees are moderately vigorous.

Minister von Hammerstein

The flattened, irregular fruits, around 7cm (2¾in) across, are bright yellow-green. The creamy white flesh is firm with a sweet, subacid flavour.

Type: Dessert.
Origin: Geisenheim, Germany, 1882.
Parentage: Landsberger Reinette (female) x Unknown.
Flowering: Early.
Other names: Gammershtein, Hamerstainska, Hammerstein and Hammerstenovo.

Note: Trees are moderately vigorous. They can be vulnerable to mildew and canker in poor growing conditions.

Mitchelson's Seedling

Type: Culinary.
Origin: Kingston upon Thames, Surrey, UK, 1851.
Parentage: Unknown.
Flowering: Mid-season.
Other names: Mitchellson's Seedling, Mitchelson and Mitchelson's Seedling of Hogg.

The rounded but slightly irregular fruits, around 7cm (2¾in) across, are deep yellow-green with a light pinkish red mottled flush and some delicate russeting. The yellowish white flesh is firm and crisp with an acid flavour.

Note: Fully ripe fruits can also be eaten raw. They can be stored for two to three months.

Monarch

Type: Culinary.
Origin: Chelmsford, Essex, UK, 1888, introduced 1918.
Parentage: Peasgood's Nonsuch (female) x Dumelow's Seedling (male).
Flowering: Mid-season.

The rounded fruits, around 7cm (2¾in) across, are bright yellow-green with a red flush and some striping. The white flesh is rather soft, somewhat coarse-textured and juicy with a subacid flavour.

Note: The fruits bruise very easily. They cook to a juicy purée, not as sharp as Bramley. Trees, which are vigorous, are partially self-fertile.

Montfort

Type: Dessert.
Origin: Woodford Green, Essex, UK, *c*.1928.
Parentage: Unknown.
Flowering: Mid-season.

Note: This variety is self-sterile, so a suitable pollination partner is required for successful fruiting. Fruits can be stored for up to four months.

The flattened fruits, around 6cm (2¼ in) across, are bright greenish yellow with a red flush. The greenish white flesh is firm and crisp with a subacid flavour.

Above: Montfort is an apple with an attractive appearance and a mellow flavour.

Montmedy

The somewhat flattened fruits, around 6cm (2¼ in) across, are yellow-green with a strong red flush and some russeting.

Note: Late flowering makes this a suitable variety for growing in areas where spring frosts are likely.

Type: Dessert.
Origin: Italy, recorded 1864.
Parentage: Unknown.
Flowering: Late.

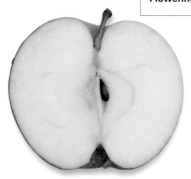

Mors de Veau

The slightly rounded but irregular fruits, around 6cm (2¼ in) across, are yellow-green with a strong dark red flush. The greenish white flesh is firm and fine with a subacid flavour.

Note: This variety is rare in cultivation.

Type: Dessert.
Origin: Switzerland, 1948.
Parentage: Unknown.
Flowering: Late.

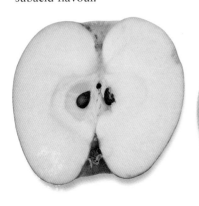

Moss's Seedling

The rounded fruits, around 7cm (2¾ in) across, are yellow-green with a red flush that appears as stripes and flecks. The creamy white flesh is crisp and juicy.

Type: Dessert.
Origin: Newport, Shropshire, UK, *c.*1955.
Parentage: Unknown.
Flowering: Mid-season.

Note: The flavour is similar to that of Cox's Orange Pippin.

Right: Ripening fruits develop a characteristic striping and flecking on the skins.

Mother

Type: Dessert.
Origin: Boston, Worcester County, MA, USA, recorded 1844.
Parentage: Unknown.
Flowering: Mid-season.
Other names: American Mother, Gardener's Apple, Mother Apple, Mother of America, Mother of the Americans, Mutter Apfel, Mutterapfel, Queen, Queen Anne and Queen Mary.

The conical, irregular fruits, around 6cm (2¼ in) across, are bright yellow-green with a strong dark red flush, sometimes with a mottled or streaked appearance. The yellowish white flesh is fairly firm and very juicy with a distinctive aromatic flavour.

Note: The skins of this variety are very waxy. The fruits need full sun to develop their best flavour. Trees are partially self-fertile.

Moti

Type: Dessert.
Origin: Muntii Apuseni, Romania, 1958.
Parentage: Unknown.
Flowering: Late.
Other names: Moate and Motate.

The rounded, sometimes slightly bumpy fruits, around 7cm (2¾ in) across, are bright yellow-green. The creamy white flesh is very firm with a sweet subacid flavour.

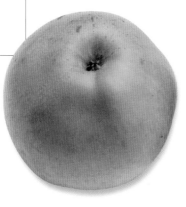

Note: Late flowering makes this a suitable variety for growing in areas where spring frosts are likely.

Mount Rainier

The conical fruits, around 6cm (2¼in) across, are dull yellow-green with a deep red flush. The yellowish flesh is fine and crisp with a very sweet, aromatic flavour.

Type: Dessert.
Origin: ?Netherlands, by 1929.
Parentage: Unknown.
Flowering: Early.

Note: Trees are moderately vigorous.

Right: Fruits have the reddest colouring on the face that is most exposed to the sun.

Museau de Lièvre

Note: Fruits can be stored for five to six months.

The name Museau de Lièvre is generic, referring to a family of apples with a similar shape but differing in colour and flavour. Fruits are tall and conical and about 5cm (2in) across. The creamy white flesh can be very acidic to sweet and fragrant, depending on the variety.

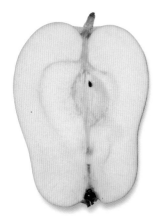

Type: Dessert.
Origin: France.
Parentage: Unknown.
Flowering: Variable.
Selected forms:
Museau de Lièvre blanc, Museau de Lièvre jaune, Museau de Lièvre rouge, Museau de Lièvre rouge du Béarn and Museau de Lièvre de septembre.

Mutsu

The irregular fruits, up to around 7cm (2¾in) across or more, are bright yellow-green with some russeting. The creamy white flesh is firm, fine-textured and juicy with a slightly sweet, somewhat acid but refreshing and pleasant flavour.

Note: This variety is a triploid. It is very susceptible to apple scab, fireblight and powdery mildew. Fruits can be stored for three to six months. They are also suitable for cider making.

Left: This variety is named after the Mutsu Province of Japan, where it is assumed it was first grown.

Type: Dessert and culinary.
Origin: Japan, 1930.
Parentage: Golden Delicious (female) x Indo (male).
Flowering: Mid-season.
Other name: Crispin.

Neild's Drooper

The somewhat irregular fruits, around 6cm (2¼in) across, are bright yellow-green with a strong red flush and some russeting. The greenish white flesh is crisp, tender and watery with an acid flavour.

Note: The tree has an unusual weeping habit, hence the name.

Left: Ripe fruits of this variety have a very complex flavour.

Type: Culinary and dessert.
Origin: Woburn, Bedfordshire, UK, 1915–16.
Parentage: Unknown.
Flowering: Late.

Nemtesc cu Miezul Rosu

Type: Dessert.
Origin: Romania, 1948 (but probably much older).
Parentage: Unknown.
Flowering: Early.
Other name: Cu Miezul Rosu.

The conical fruits, around 6cm (2¼in) across, are bright yellow-green with a strong red flush and some striping. The flesh is soft and coarse with a subacid flavour.

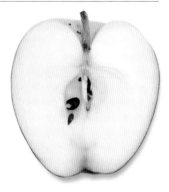

Note: This spur-bearing variety is native to Romania and has been the subject of fertility studies.

Neue Goldparmane

Type: Dessert.
Origin: Germany, 1951.
Parentage: ?Golden Winter Pearmain (female) x Parker's Grey Pippin (male).
Flowering: Early.
Other names: Strauwaldts Goldparmane and Strauwaldts Neue Goldparmane.

Note: Early flowering makes this variety unsuitable for areas where hard spring frosts are likely.

The rounded to slightly conical fruits, around 6cm (2¼in) across, are light green with an orange-red flush and some uneven russeting. The pale yellow flesh is firm and fine with a sweet, rich flavour.

Newton Wonder

The slightly flattened, rounded to irregular fruits, more than 6cm (2¼in) across, are bright green with a strong red, sometimes striped, flush. The creamy white flesh is rather coarse-textured and moderately juicy with a subacid flavour.

Note: The fruits cook well, with a light, fluffy texture, producing a sweeter purée than a Bramley. They store well. Trees, which are vigorous, show good disease resistance. They are partially self-fertile.

Type: Culinary.
Origin: King's Newton, Melbourne, Derbyshire, UK, introduced *c.*1887.
Parentage: ?Dumelow's Seedling (female) x ?Blenheim Orange (male).
Flowering: Mid-season.

Newtown Pippin

The slightly flattened, somewhat irregular fruits, around 6cm (2¼in) across, are bright green with some russeting and darker spotting. The creamy white flesh is firm, fine-textured and juicy with a trace of richness.

Note: This variety was made famous by Thomas Jefferson, who grew them in his orchard at Monticello.

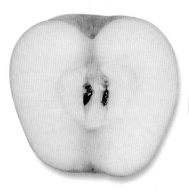

Type: Dessert.
Origin: Newtown, Long Island, New York, USA, by 1759.
Parentage: Unknown.
Flowering: Mid-season.
Other names: Albemarle, American Newtown Pippin, Back Creek, Brookes Pippin, Coxe's Green Newton Pippin, Green Winter Pippin, Hampshire Greening, Hunt's Mountain Pippin, Neujorker Reinette, New York Greening, New York Pippin, Ohio Green Pippin, Pepin Vert de Newtown, Virginia Pippin, White Newtown Pippin and Yellow Newtown Pippin.

Newtown Spitzenburg

The rounded but slightly conical fruits, around 6cm (2¼in) across, are bright green with a deep red flush and some spotting. The creamy yellow flesh is firm and coarse with a sweet subacid flavour.

Note: This variety is sometimes confused with Esopus Spitzenburg. Trees are vigorous but prone to biennial bearing. The fruits store well.

Type: Dessert.
Origin: Newtown, Long Island, NY, USA, recorded 1817.
Parentage: Unknown.
Flowering: Early.
Other names: Barrett's Spitzenberg, Burlington, Burlington Spitzenberg, English Spitzenberg, Joe Berry, Kounty, Kountz, Matchless, Ox-Eye, Queen of the Dessert, Spiced Ox-Eye, Spitzemberg, Spitzenburgh and Vandevere of New York.

Nolan Pippin

Type: Dessert.
Origin: Colchester, Essex, England, UK, 1920.
Parentage: Unknown.
Flowering: Mid-season.

The slightly flattened, somewhat irregular fruits, around 6cm (2¼in) across, are green with uneven cinnamon brown russeting. The white flesh is crisp and hard with a sweet subacid flavour.

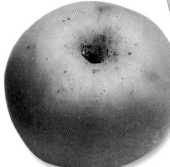

Note: Trees are vigorous. Fruits store well.

Nonpareil

Type: Dessert.
Origin: ?France, introduced into England mid-1500s.
Parentage: Unknown.
Flowering: Early.
Other names: Alter Nonpareil, Bespodobnoe starinnoe, Duc d'Arsell, English Nonpareil, Golden Russet Nonpareil, Groene Reinette, Gruener Reinette, Hunt's Nonpareil, Loveden's Pippin, Nonpareil Old, Original Nonpareil, Pomme Poire, Reinette Franche, Reinette Nonpareil, Reinette Sans Pareille, Reinette Verte and Unvergleichliche Reinett.

The irregular, flattened fruits, up to around 6cm (2¼in) across or more, are yellowish green with uneven russeting and spotting. The greenish white flesh is fine-textured and juicy with a slightly acid and pleasant aromatic flavour.

Note: Trees are healthy and bear well. The fruits store well.

Nonsuch Park

Type: Dessert.
Origin: England, UK, described 1831.
Parentage: Unknown.
Flowering: Mid-season.
Other names: Nonesuch Park and Nonsuch Park Apple.

The slightly flattened fruits, around 6cm (2¼in) across, are bright yellow-green with some spotting. The greenish white flesh is firm and crisp.

Note: This variety commemorates a deer hunting park established by Henry VIII of England. The fruits have waxy skins.

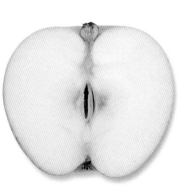

Norfolk Royal

The conical fruits, around 7cm (2¾in) across, are bright yellow-green with a strong red flush that can appear as striping. The creamy white flesh is moderately firm, crisp and very juicy with a sweet and pleasant, melon-like flavour.

Type: Dessert.
Origin: North Walsham, Norfolk, UK, *c.*1908.
Parentage: A chance seedling.
Flowering: Mid-season.

Note: The fruits are best eaten soon after picking as they do not store well. Norfolk Royal Russet is a russeted sport of this variety.

Norman's Pippin

The rounded fruits, around 6cm (2¼in) across, are bright green with light russeting. The greenish white flesh is soft with a sweet, rich flavour.

Type: Dessert.
Origin: ?Flanders, recorded 1900.
Parentage: Unknown.
Flowering: Mid-season.

Note: Trees can lack vigour. Fruits can be used for juicing or cider making.

Right: *Fruits show even colouring and a waxy skin when ripe.*

Normandie

The slightly irregular fruits, around 6cm (2¼in) across, are bright green with a strong dark red flush and some striping. The greenish white flesh is soft and dry with an insipid flavour.

Note: Late flowering makes this a suitable variety for growing in areas with late frosts.

Type: Dessert.
Origin: ?France, 1948.
Parentage: Unknown.
Flowering: Very late.

Northern Greening

Type: Culinary.
Origin: ?England, UK, first recorded 1826.
Parentage: Unknown.
Flowering: Mid-season.
Other names: Cowarn Queening, Cowarne Queening, Cowarne Seedling, Gruener Englischer Pepping, John, Kirk Langley Pippin, Langley Pippin, Old Northern Greening, Verte du Nord, Walmer Court and Woodcock.

The rounded, slightly irregular fruits, around 6cm (2¼in) across, are yellow-green with a red flush and some spotting and russeting. The creamy white flesh is moderately firm, a little coarse-textured and juicy with an acid flavour.

Note: This variety is probably the ancestor of many Victorian culinary apples. The fruits store well. Trees are productive and disease resistant. They tolerate cold winters.

Northern Spy

Type: Dessert.
Origin: East Bloomfield, NY, USA, *c.*1800, introduced 1840.
Parentage: Unknown.
Flowering: Late.
Other names: King Apple, King's Apple, Severnui Razvedchik, Severnui Shpion, Spaeher des Nordens, Spaher des Nordens and Spy.

Note: This variety is resistant to woolly aphid and has been used as a parent in the breeding of resistant rootstocks and varieties. Trees, which are vigorous, are prone to biennial bearing. Fruits are late to ripen and store well.

The irregular fruits, around 7cm (2¾in) across, are yellow-green with a strong dark red flush and some spotting. The yellow flesh is fairly firm, juicy and sweet with a pleasant flavour.

Above: Fruits develop a red flush where they are exposed to the sun.

Nottingham Pippin

Type: Dessert.
Origin: ?Nottingham, UK, by 1815.
Parentage: Unknown.
Flowering: Mid-season.
Other names: Pepping von Nottingham and Pippin of Nottingham.

The irregular, somewhat flattened fruits, around 6cm (2¼in) across, are bright yellow-green with some russeting. The white flesh is fine and tender with a sweet, vinous flavour.

Note: Trees are vigorous and bear freely. This variety is self-sterile, so a suitable pollination partner is required.

Nova Easygro

Type: Dessert.
Origin: Canadian Department Agricultural Research Station, Kentville, Nova Scotia, 1956, introduced 1971.
Parentage: Spartan (female) x Scab Resistant seedling (male).
Flowering: Mid-season.

The slightly irregular fruits, around 6cm (2¼in) across, are bright greenish yellow with a strong red flush and some striping. The whitish flesh is firm, crisp and moderately juicy with a subacid and pleasant flavour.

  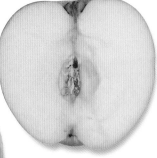

Note: Trees, which are vigorous, are resistant to scab and cedar apple rust, and show some resistance to fireblight and mildew.

Old Fred

The flattened fruits, up to 7cm (2¾in) across, are dull yellow-green with a pinkish red flush and some striping. The creamy white flesh is firm and fine with a subacid flavour.

Note: Old Fred, rare in cultivation, was named after the nurseryman who bred it.

Type: Dessert.
Origin: Eynsham, Oxford, UK, exhibited 1944.
Parentage: Allington Pippin (female) x Court Pendu Plat (male).
Flowering: Mid-season.

  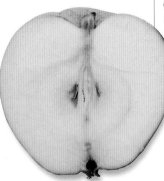

Ontario

The somewhat flattened, irregular fruits, around 7cm (2¾in) across or more, are bright yellow-green with a very strong dark red flush and some striping. The creamy white flesh is crisp and very juicy with a rather acid flavour.

Type: Dessert and culinary.
Origin: Paris, Ontario, Canada, c.1820.
Parentage: Wagener (female) x Northern Spy (male).
Flowering: Mid-season.
Other name: Ontarioapfel.

Note: The flowers are weather resistant. The fruits, which store well, tend to bruise easily. They cook well, breaking up completely. Trees are moderately vigorous. There is also a tetraploid clone (with four sets of chromosomes).

Opalescent

Type: Dessert.
Origin: Xenia, OH, USA, introduced 1899.
Parentage: Unknown.
Flowering: Mid-season.

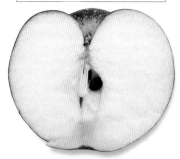

The conical fruits, around 6cm (2¼in) across, are bright yellow-green with a strong red flush. The creamy white flesh is firm and crisp with a sweet, strawberry-like taste.

Note: This variety is a parent of Shenandoah. The fruits are also suitable for cooking.

Right: Its excellent flavour has made Opalescent a very popular variety.

Orin

Type: Dessert.
Origin: Fukushima Prefecture, Japan, before 1942.
Parentage: Golden Delicious (female) x Indo (male).
Flowering: Very early.

The conical fruits, around 6cm (2¼in) across, are bright yellow-green with russeting and spotting. The creamy white flesh is firm and juicy with a sweet and aromatic, honeyed flavour.

Note: This variety is a triploid, so two pollinators will be needed for fruiting. Trees are tip-bearing.

Orleans Reinette

Above: This variety develops a complex flavour as it ripens.

The somewhat flattened fruits, around 6cm (2¼in) across, are yellow-green with an orange-red flush and some striping and light russeting. The creamy white flesh is firm, fine-textured and only a little juicy with a pleasant, Blenheim-like flavour.

Note: Trees are moderately vigorous, hardy and crop well. They fruit best in a warm location.

Type: Dessert.
Origin: Unknown, but assumed to be French, first described 1776.
Parentage: Unknown.
Flowering: Late.
Other names: Aurore, Cardinal Pippin, Doerell's Grosse Gold Reinette, Madam Calpin, New York Reinette, Pearmain d'Or, Reinette d'Aix, Reinette de Breil, Reinette Golden, Reinette Triomphante, Ronde Belle-Fleur, Starklow's Bester, Triumph Reinette, Winter Ribston, Yellow German Reinette and Zimnii Shafran.

Osnabrücker Reinette

The rounded fruits, around 6cm (2¼in) across, are bright green with some uneven russeting. The creamy white flesh is fine and tender with a sweet and very vinous flavour.

Note: Fruits can be stored for up to five months. Trees are vigorous initially, developing a large, rounded crown.

Type: Dessert.
Origin: Osnabrück, Hannover, Germany, by 1802.
Parentage: Chance seedling.
Flowering: Mid-season.
Other names: De Grawe Foos-Renet, Franz Joseph von Eggers Reinette, Französische Goldereinette, Gold-Reinette, Graawe Fos-Renet, Graue Osnabrücker Reinette, Graue Reinette von Canada, Osnabrücker grau überzogene Reinette, Reinette Aigre, Reinette d'Osnabrück, Reinette Grise d'Osnabrück, Renet Osnabrukskii and Rotgraue Kelch-Reinette.

Oxford Conquest

The slightly irregular, rather flattened fruits, around 6cm (2¼in) across or more, are dull yellow-green with an orange-red flush and some russeting. The creamy white flesh is rather tough with an acid flavour.

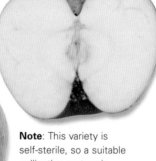

Note: This variety is self-sterile, so a suitable pollination partner is needed for reliable fruiting.

Type: Dessert.
Origin: Eynsham, Oxford, UK, 1927.
Parentage: Blenheim Orange (female) x Court Pendu Plat (male).
Flowering: Mid-season.

Oxford Hoard

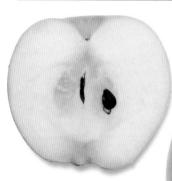

The irregular fruits, around 6cm (2¼in) across, are bright yellowish green with some spotting. The creamy white flesh is coarse, firm and tough with a sweet and aromatic flavour.

Note: Trees are very vigorous. The skins of the fruits can be quite waxy.

Type: Dessert.
Origin: Eynsham, Oxford, UK, exhibited 1943.
Parentage: Sturmer Pippin (female) x Golden Russet (male).
Flowering: Early.

Parker's Pippin

Type: Dessert.
Origin: ?England, before 1800.
Parentage: Unknown.
Flowering: Early.
Other names: Broker's Pippin, Graue Reinette, Jadrnac Parkeruv, Kozhanyi renet, Lederapfel, Parker, Parker Peppin, Parker's Grey Pippin, Parkerova, Parkers Grauer Pepping, Parsker's Pippin, Pepin Gris de Parker, Peppina Parker, Pippin de Parker, Pomme Parker, Poppina Parker, Reinette Grise de Pfaffenhofen, Sanct-Nicolas Reinette, Spencer's Pippin and Zizzen-Apfel.

The rounded to oblong fruits, around 6cm (2¼in) across, are light green with russeting. The creamy white flesh is fairly crisp and firm with a subacid and slightly aromatic flavour.

Note: This variety performs well on a dwarfing rootstock. It is one of the parents of Neue Goldparmane.

Peck's Pleasant

Type: Dessert.
Origin: Rhode Island, USA, recorded 1832.
Parentage: Unknown.
Flowering: Mid-season.
Other names: Dutch Greening, Peck, Peck Pleasant, Waltz Apple and Watts Apple.

The rounded, slightly irregular fruits, around 6cm (2¼in) across, are bright green to yellow with some lighter flecking and spotting; an orange-red flush can sometimes partly deepen to pink. The yellowish flesh is crisp with a sweet, subacid, aromatic flavour.

Note: Trees are prone to biennial bearing. They are moderately vigorous.

Pero Dourado

Type: Dessert.
Origin: Portugal, 1952.
Parentage: Unknown.
Flowering: Mid-season.

Above: The pointed shape of the fruits is characteristic.

The conical to oblong fruits, around 6cm (2¼in) across, are bright yellow-green with a pinkish red flush and some russeting. The creamy white flesh is firm and fine with a subacid flavour.

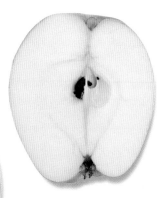

Note: This variety is rare in cultivation but has been used as a subject for research into cultivar identification.

Petit Pippin

The rounded to slightly irregular fruits, around 6cm (2¼ in) across, are bright yellow-green with some darker spotting and russeting. The creamy white flesh is soft with a sweet, aromatic flavour.

Note: The fruits are best in late summer.

Type: Dessert.
Origin: East Malling Research Station, Kent, UK, 1948.
Parentage: Unknown.
Flowering: Mid-season.

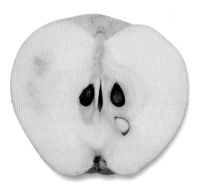

Pig's Nose Pippin

The roughly conical fruits, around 6cm (2¼ in) across, are yellow-green with a bright red flush and some russeting in dots and patches. The creamy white flesh is fine and crisp with a sweet flavour.

Type: Dessert.
Origin: ?Hereford, UK, described 1884.
Parentage: Unknown.
Flowering: Mid-season.

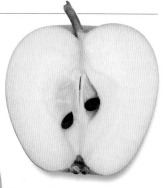

Note: Fruits can be stored until mid-winter only.

Right: Pig's Nose Pippin is often grown simply for the appeal of its curious name.

Pigeon de Jérusalem

Type: Dessert.
Origin: France, recorded late 1600s.
Parentage: Unknown.
Flowering: Mid-season.
Other names: Coeur de Pigeon, Gros Pigeon Rouge, Gros Pigeonnet rouge, Gros-Coeur de Pigeon, Jérusalem, Pigeon, Pigeon d'Hiver, Pigeon Rouge, Pigeonnet de Jérusalem and Pomme de Jérusalem.

The roughly conical, very irregular fruits, around 6cm (2¼ in) across, are light green with a strong pinkish red flush and some striping; the whole surface is covered with a bluish bloom. The white flesh is firm and fine with a subacid and slightly perfumed flavour.

Note: Trees are vigorous and crop freely. The fruits are also suitable for cooking.

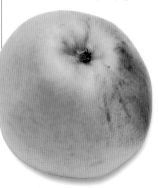

Pink Lady

Type: Dessert.
Origin: Australia, 1979.
Parentage: A selection of Cripps Pink (Lady Williams x Golden Delicious).
Flowering: Mid-season.

The slightly conical to oblong fruits, around 6cm (2¼ in) across, are yellow with a distinctive pinkish orange flush. The creamy white flesh is crisp, firm and very sweet.

Note: This variety needs a long summer to ripen and produce the characteristic flush. It is susceptible to rosy apple aphid and scab. Trees crop heavily and the fruits store well. It is an important commercial variety.

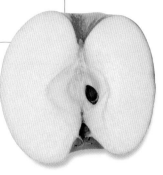  

Pinner Seedling

Type: Dessert.
Origin: Pinner, Middlesex, UK, 1810.
Parentage: Unknown.
Flowering: Mid-season.
Other names: Carel's Seedling, Carle's Seedling, Carrel's Seedling, Carrell's Seedling, Pinner and Pinners Seedling.

The rounded, slightly conical, sometimes irregular fruits, around 7cm (2¾ in) across, are bright green with a pinkish red flush and some russeting (sometimes almost covering the fruit). The whitish flesh, tinged with green, is crisp, juicy and sweet in flavour.

Note: The fruits store well. They can be used for juicing and cider making.

Pitmaston Pineapple

Type: Dessert.
Origin: Witley, UK, c.1785.
Parentage: Golden Pippin (female) x Unknown.
Flowering: Early.
Other names: Ananas de Pitmaston, Pine-Apple, Pineapple, Pineapple Pippin, Pitmaston Pine, Pitmaston Pine Apple and Reinette d'Ananas.

The somewhat conical fruits, around 6cm (2¼ in) across, are dull yellow-green with some fine russeting. The creamy white to yellowish flesh is firm and juicy with a sweet, rich, distinctive flavour.

Note: The flavour is similar to that of a pineapple, hence the name. Trees are small and upright, so suitable for small gardens.

Far right: This old English variety has an unusual flavour.

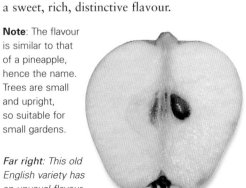

Pixie

The somewhat flattened fruits, around 6cm (2¼ in) across, are bright greenish yellow with a strong red flush and some striping and russeting. The creamy white flesh is crisp and fairly juicy with a good aromatic, somewhat sharp flavour.

Type: Dessert.
Origin: National Fruit Trials, Wisley, Surrey, UK, 1947.
Parentage: Cox's Orange Pippin or Sunset (female) x Unknown.
Flowering: Mid-season.

Note: This variety, which grows well on a dwarfing rootstock, is disease resistant. Trees can over-crop, so fruit should be thinned. The fruits store well.

Pomme Crotte

The flattened, irregular fruits, up to around 7cm (2¾ in) across or more, are bright yellow-green with a strong dark red flush. The creamy white flesh is sweet and juicy.

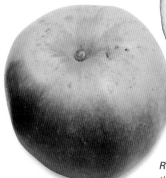

Type: Dessert.
Origin: France, 1947.
Parentage: Unknown.
Flowering: Mid-season.

Note: Trees are moderately vigorous.

Right: Fruits turn dark red where the skin is exposed to the sun.

Pomme d'Amour

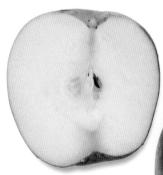

The rounded, slightly irregular fruits, around 6cm (2¼ in) across, are bright yellow-green with an orange-red flush and some striping. The yellowish white flesh is firm with a slightly sweet, slightly subacid flavour.

Type: Dessert.
Origin: France, 1947.
Parentage: Unknown.
Flowering: Mid-season.

Note: Trees are moderately vigorous.

Far right: The name of this variety, Pomme d'Amour, means 'toffee apple' in French.

Pomme d'Enfer

Type: Dessert.
Origin: Allier, France, 1948.
Parentage: Unknown.
Flowering: Mid-season.

The rounded to slightly conical fruits, around 7cm (2¾in) across or more, are dull green with a strong red flush and mottled russeting. The greenish white flesh has an acid flavour.

Note: Trees can lack vigour. Picked fruits have been used in France to scent the interiors of wardrobes.

Pomme de Choux à Nez Creux

Type: Culinary.
Origin: Cher, France, 1948.
Parentage: Unknown.
Flowering: Late.

The flattened, rather irregular fruits, around 7cm (2¾in) across or more, are bright yellow-green with some russeting. The yellowish flesh is soft, juicy and acid.

Note: Late flowering makes this variety suitable for growing where spring frosts are likely.

Left: Fruits of this variety show variegated colouring.

Pomme de Fer

Type: Dessert.
Origin: France, described 1948.
Parentage: Unknown.
Flowering: Mid-season.

The flattened fruits, around 7cm (2¾in) across, are bright yellow-green with a red flush and some striping. The flesh is creamy white.

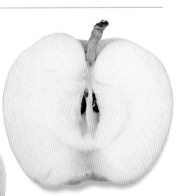

Note: This variety is a parent of Canada Baldwin. The fruits store well and can also be used in cooking.

Pomme de Feu

The rounded fruits, around 6cm (2¼in) across, are bright yellowy green with waxy skins. The creamy white flesh is firm and fine, with a slightly subacid flavour.

Note: This variety is rare in cultivation.

Type: Culinary.
Origin: France, 1948.
Parentage: Unknown.
Flowering: Late.

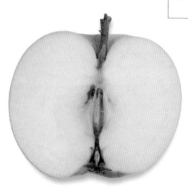

Pomme de Glace

The slightly flattened, slightly irregular fruits, around 7cm (2¾in) across, are bright green with some russeting. The greenish white flesh is firm with an acid flavour.

Type: Culinary.
Origin: France, 1948.
Parentage: Unknown.
Flowering: Late.

Note: This variety gets its name (which translates as 'ice apple') from the frosty appearance of the fruits. These can be stored for three to four months.

Pomme Noire

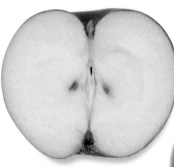

The rounded, slightly irregular fruits, around 6cm (2¼in) across, are bright green with a very dark red flush. The pale green flesh is grainy with a sweet flavour.

Type: Dessert.
Origin: France, 1973.
Parentage: Unknown.
Flowering: Late.
Other names: Grosse Pomme Noire, Black American, Black Apple and Violette Glacée.

Note: Fruits can be stored for up to five months. Trees are moderately vigorous.

Pommerscher Krummstiel

Type: Dessert.
Origin: Berlin Technical University, Germany, 1967.
Parentage: Unknown.
Flowering: Mid-season.

The irregular fruits, around 7cm (2¾in) across or more, are bright green with a strong red flush. The whitish flesh has a fairly rich, slightly aromatic flavour.

Note: Fruits store well. The flavour is best four weeks after picking.

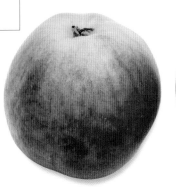  

Prairie Spy

Type: Dessert.
Origin: University of Minnesota Fruit Breeding Farm, Excelsior, USA, 1951.
Parentage: Unknown.
Flowering: Mid-season.

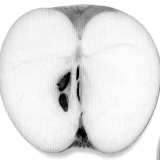

The rounded fruits, around 6cm (2¼in) across, are bright yellow-green with a strong dark red flush and some russeting. The greenish white flesh is firm and fine with a sweet, subacid flavour.

Note: Trees are vigorous and long-lived; they bear young. The flavour of the fruits improves in storage.

Type: Dessert.
Origin: Netherlands, 1945.
Parentage: Present van Engeland (female) x Brabant Bellefleur (male).
Flowering: Early.

Present van Holland

The conical to oval fruits, around 6cm (2¼in) across, are bright yellow-green with a bright red flush. The white flesh is firm and coarse with a subacid flavour.

Note: Trees can lack vigour, so this variety is unsuitable for growing on a dwarfing rootstock.

Right: *The oval shape of the fruits is characteristic.*

Prinses Beatrix

The uneven fruits, up to around 7cm (2¾in) across or more, are yellow-green with a bright red flush and some striping and flecking. The creamy white flesh is firm, fine and rather tough with a subacid flavour.

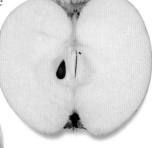

Type: Dessert.
Origin: Horticultural Laboratory, Wageningen, Netherlands, 1935.
Parentage: Cox's Orange Pippin (female) x Jonathan (male).
Flowering: Mid-season.

Note: This attractive variety is rather unusual in cultivation.

Prinses Irene

The slightly irregular fruits, around 6cm (2¼in) across, are bright yellow-green with a red flush and some striping and flecking. The greenish white flesh is crisp with a subacid flavour.

Type: Dessert.
Origin: Horticultural Laboratory, Wageningen, Netherlands, 1935.
Parentage: Jonathan (female) x Cox's Orange Pippin (male).
Flowering: Early.

Note: Trees are weak-growing, so are unsuitable for use with a dwarfing rootstock.

Prinses Margriet

The rounded to slightly flattened fruits, around 6cm (2¼in) across, are yellow-green with a red flush and some flecking and russeting. The cream flesh is tinged green and has an acid flavour.

Type: Dessert.
Origin: Horticultural Laboratory, Wageningen, Netherlands, 1935, introduced 1955.
Parentage: Jonathan (female) x Cox's Orange Pippin (male).
Flowering: Mid-season.

Note: Trees are moderately vigorous.

Prinses Marijke

Type: Dessert.
Origin: Horticultural Laboratory, Wageningen, Netherlands, 1935, introduced 1952.
Parentage: Jonathan (female) x Cox's Orange Pippin (male).
Flowering: Mid-season.

Note: Trees are weak-growing, so are unsuitable for use with a dwarfing rootstock.

The rounded, slightly flattened fruits, around 7cm (2¾ in) across, are bright green with a dark red flush and some russeting. The creamy white flesh is fine, firm and crisp with a fairly sweet, subacid, aromatic flavour.

Queen Cox

Type: Dessert.
Origin: Appleby Fruit Farm, Kingston Bagpuize, Berkshire, UK, 1953.
Parentage: ?Ribston Pippin (female) x Unknown.
Flowering: Mid-season.

The rounded fruits, around 6cm (2¼ in) across, are green with a red flush and some striping. The creamy white flesh is firm, slightly acid and juicy with a rich, aromatic flavour.

Note: This variety is a more highly coloured clone of Cox's Orange Pippin.

Racine Blanche

Type: Culinary.
Origin: France, 1947.
Parentage: Unknown.
Flowering: Late.

Note: Late flowering makes this variety suitable for growing in areas where late frosts are likely.

The slightly flattened, somewhat irregular fruits are bright yellow-green with a red flush and some russeting. The yellowish flesh is rather coarse with an acid flavour.

Rampale

The flattened, somewhat irregular fruits, up to around 6cm (2¼in) across, are yellow-green with a red flush and some flecking and russeting. The whitish flesh is crisp with a sweet, vinous, perfumed flavour.

Note: Late flowering makes this variety suitable for growing in areas where late frosts are likely.

Type: Dessert.
Origin: France, 1947.
Parentage: Unknown.
Flowering: Late.

Reale d'Entraygues

The conical to oblong fruits, up to around 8cm (3in) across or more, are bright yellow-green with some spotting. The yellowish white flesh is very firm with a very sweet, perfumed flavour.

Note: This variety is normally grown as a standard. Avoid hot sites.

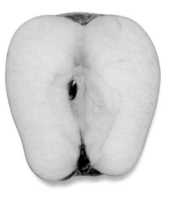

Type: Dessert.
Origin: France, recorded 1947 but probably much older.
Parentage: Unknown.
Flowering: Mid-season.
Other name: Reinette de Pons.

Réaux

The flattened, somewhat irregular fruits, around 6cm (2¼in) across, are bright green with a strong red flush. The creamy white flesh is firm and fine with a sweet, subacid, slightly aromatic flavour.

Type: Dessert.
Origin: France, recorded 1895.
Parentage: Unknown.
Flowering: Late.
Other name: Reau.

Note: This variety is grown in the Meuse, Marne and Argonne departments of France. Fruits can be stored for up to five months.

Red Dougherty

Type: Dessert.
Origin: Twyford, Hawkes Bay, New Zealand, introduced 1930.
Parentage: Unknown.
Flowering: Mid-season.

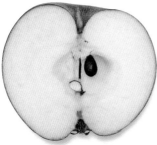

Note: This variety has been used in recent breeding programmes to produce apples suitable for dry climates.

The rounded fruits, around 6cm (2¼ in) across, are yellow-green with a pinkish red flush and some striping and flecking. The greenish white flesh is firm, fine and hard with a sweet subacid taste.

Red Granny Smith

Type: Dessert.
Origin: Western Australia, date unknown.
Parentage: ?Granny Smith (female) x ?Jonathan (male).
Flowering: Mid-season.
Other names: Batt's Seedling and Red Gem.

The rounded to slightly conical fruits, around 6cm (2¼ in) across, are bright green with a strong red flush and some striping and flecking. The creamy white flesh is firm and crisp with a subacid flavour.

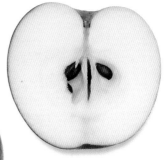

Note: Trees are moderately vigorous. Lady Williams is sometimes grown under this name.

Red Statesman

Type: Dessert.
Origin: New Zealand, discovered 1914.
Parentage: Unknown.
Flowering: Mid-season.
Other name: Warrior.

The rounded fruits, around 6cm (2¼ in) across, are bright green with a strong red flush and some striping and spotting. The pale creamy white flesh is firm with a sweet, subacid to acid flavour.

Note: This variety is a more highly coloured clone of the Australian variety Statesman.

Reid's Seedling

The rounded, sometimes slightly irregular or conical fruits, up to around 7cm (2¾ in) across, are light green with a carmine red flush and some streaking and russet specks. The creamy white flesh is somewhat coarse with a sweet subacid flavour.

Type: Dessert.
Origin: Richill, Co. Armagh, Ireland, *c.*1880–90.
Parentage: Unknown.
Flowering: Mid-season.

Note: The flesh is sometimes spotted with pink.

Reinette à Longue Queue

The rounded to conical fruits, around 6cm (2¼ in) across or more, are bright yellowish green. The greenish white flesh is firm and rather coarse with a sweetish, slightly aromatic flavour.

Type: Dessert.
Origin: France, recorded 1831.
Parentage: Unknown.
Flowering: Mid-season.
Other names: Reinette à la Longue Queue and Reinette à Longue Quene.

Note: This variety is mentioned in *Loudon's Encyclopedia of Gardening* (1822). Fruits have the best flavour eaten soon after picking in summer. They do not store well.

Reinette Clochard

The rounded fruits, around 6cm (2¼ in) across, are bright green with some russeting and spotting. The yellowish flesh is fine with a sweet, subacid, perfumed flavour.

Type: Culinary and dessert.
Origin: France, known mid-1800s.
Parentage: Unknown.
Flowering: Mid-season.
Other names: Clochard, Clochard de Gatine, de Parthenay, Reinette Clocharde, Reinette de Parthenay, Reinette Parthenaise, Reinette von Clochard, Renet Kloshar, Rochelle and Roux brillant.

Note: This variety has been grown under many different names, so its lineage is difficult to trace. Trees, of average vigour, crop regularly.

Reinette d'Anjou

Type: Dessert.
Origin: Belgium or Germany, first mentioned 1817.
Parentage: Unknown.
Flowering: Mid-season.
Other name: Reinette Blanche.

The rounded to slightly conical fruits, around 7cm (2¾in) across, are bright yellow-green with a strong pink to red flush. The creamy white flesh is firm and fine with a subacid, slightly sweet, slightly aromatic flavour.

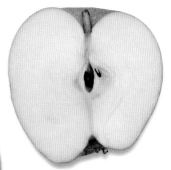

Note: This variety, still grown commercially in France, is similar to Reinette Verte. Trees are hardy, vigorous and bear well. The fruits can be stored for up to five months.

Reinette de Brucbrucks

Type: Dessert.
Origin: France, 1947.
Parentage: Unknown.
Flowering: Mid-season.

The flattened, very irregular fruits, around 7cm (2¾in) across, are green with a strong red flush and some russeting. The creamy white flesh is firm and coarse in texture with a subacid, sweet flavour.

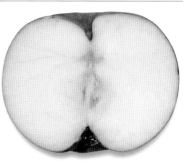

Note: Trees are very vigorous, so are best grown on dwarfing rootstocks.

Reinette de France

Type: Dessert.
Origin: France, 1948.
Parentage: Unknown.
Flowering: Very late.
Other names: Court-pendu de Tournay and Reinette d'Orléans.

The rounded, slightly flattened fruits, up to around 7cm (2¾in) across, are bright yellow-green with a red flush and some russeting. The yellowish white flesh is firm with a subacid, sweet and slightly aromatic flavour.

Note: Trees are very hardy and moderately vigorous.

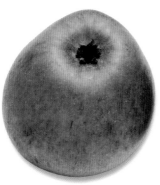

Reinette de Lucas

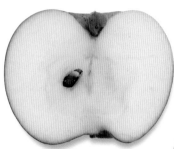

The somewhat flattened, rather irregular fruits, around 7cm (2¾in) across, are bright yellow-green with a strong dark red flush and some russeting. The creamy white flesh is firm, crisp and fine with a subacid and slightly sweet flavour.

Note: Trees are moderately vigorous.

Type: Dessert.
Origin: ?Belgium, recorded 1872.
Parentage: Unknown.
Flowering: Mid-season.
Other names: Lucas' Reinette, Lucas's Reinette and Reinette Lucas.

Reinette de Mâcon

The somewhat flattened, slightly irregular fruits, around 6cm (2¼in) across or more, are dull green with a red flush and dark russeting. The creamy white flesh is firm and fine with a slightly sweet, subacid flavour.

Note: Early flowering makes this an unsuitable variety for areas where late frosts are likely.

Type: Dessert.
Origin: France, probably Mâcon (Seine-et-Loire), first recorded 1628.
Parentage: Unknown.
Flowering: Early.
Other names: Allman grarenett, Allman laderrenett, Carpentin, Damason Reinette, Double Reinette de Mascon, Laderrenett, Leder Reinette, Leder-Apfel, Lederreinette, Rainette Double de Mazerus, Reinette Damson, Reinette Double de Maserus, Renet Damason, Reneta Damazonska and Styryjskie slynne jablko skorzane.

Reinette de Metz

The slightly flattened, somewhat irregular fruits, around 6cm (2¼in) across, are dull yellow-green with a light red flush and some spotting and russeting. The white flesh is fairly fine and tender with a sweet, subacid and slightly aromatic flavour.

Type: Dessert.
Origin: ?France, described 1934.
Parentage: Unknown.
Flowering: Early.

Note: Early flowering makes this an unsuitable variety for areas where late frosts are likely.

Reinette du Canada

The very irregular, somewhat flattened fruits, around 7cm (2¾ in) across, are dull yellow-green with some russeting and spotting. The creamy white flesh is firm, rather dry and coarse-textured with a sweet and moderate flavour.

Type: Culinary and dessert.
Origin: ?Normandy, France, first mentioned 1771.
Parentage: Unknown.
Flowering: Mid-season.
Other names: Amerikanischer Romanite, Bamporta, Canada Blanc, Canada Pippin, Forbes's Large Portugal, German Green, Hollandische Reinette, Janura, Kaiser-Reinette, Mala Janura, Portugal Russet, Rambour de Paris, Reinette Grandville, Reinette Incomparable, Reinette Virginale, Sternreinette, Wahr Reinette, Weisse Antillische Winter Reinette and White Pippin.

Note: This variety is a triploid. The trees are vigorous and very productive. The fruits store well.

Reinette Dubuisson

Type: Dessert.
Origin: France, 1950.
Parentage: Unknown.
Flowering: Mid-season.

The somewhat flattened, irregular fruits, up to around 7cm (2¾ in) across, are bright yellow-green with a light red flush and some russeting. The greenish white flesh, tinged orange, is firm and coarse with a subacid flavour.

Note: Fruits can be stored for up to six months. Trees are usually very productive and trouble-free.

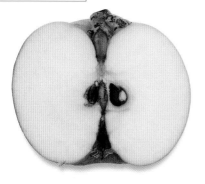

Reinette Marbrée

Type: Dessert.
Origin: Netherlands, described 1760.
Parentage: Unknown.
Flowering: Mid-season.
Other names: Character, Character of Drap d'Or, Charakter Reinette, Cimetière, Concombre des Chartreux, Drap d'Or, Gestrickte Herbst Reinette, Gestrickte Reinette, Heilige Julians Apfel, Julien, Karakter Reinette, Neetjes Apple, Netz Reinette, Pomme de Caractère, Reinette Brodée, Reinette Caractère, Reinette Filée, Reinette Valkenier, Saint Julian and Seigneur d'Orsay.

The rounded, slightly flattened fruits, up to around 7cm (2¾ in) across, are dull yellow-green with a marbling of russeting. The whitish flesh is compact, juicy and firm with a very sweet and perfumed flavour.

Note: Trees are moderately vigorous. Fruits can be stored for four months or more.

Reinette Simirenko

The rounded, somewhat irregular fruits, around 6cm (2¼in) across or more, are bright green with some russeting. The greenish white flesh is tender and crisp with a subacid flavour.

Note: Trees are moderately vigorous, bearing heavily even when young. The ripened fruits persist on the tree.

Type: Dessert.
Origin: Ukraine, described 1895.
Parentage: Unknown.
Flowering: Mid-season.
Other names: Reinette de Simirenko, Reinette Verte de Simirenko, Reinette Verte Incomparable, Renet Filibera, Renet P. F. Simirenko, Renet Simirenko, Simirenko, Simirenkova Reneta, Wood's Greening, Zelenyi renet Simirenko and Zeleomi renet Simirenko.

Reinette Thouin

The rounded to conical fruits, around 6cm (2¼in) across, are bright yellow-green with russeting and spotting. The greenish white flesh is firm, crisp and coarse with a subacid flavour.

Note: Trees are vigorous and productive. Training is possible, but this variety does best when grown as a standard.

Type: Dessert.
Origin: Beaumont, nr Montmorency, France, 1822.
Parentage: Unknown.
Flowering: Mid-season.
Other names: Bonne Thouin, Renet Tuen, Thouin's Reinette and Thouins Reinette.

Reinette Verte

The rounded, slightly flattened fruits, around 7cm (2¾in) across, are yellowish green with a reddish flush and some greyish russeting and spotting. The yellowish white flesh is tender and juicy with a sweet, vinous, highly aromatic flavour.

Type: Dessert.
Origin: Unknown.
Parentage: Unknown.
Flowering: Late.

Note: The fruits can be stored for up to four months or longer. They are suitable for juicing.

Far right: Fruits develop a very sweet flavour as they ripen.

Ribston Pippin

Type: Dessert.
Origin: Ribston Hall, Yorkshire, UK, from seed brought from Rouen, and planted *c.*1707.
Parentage: Unknown.
Flowering: Early.
Other names: Beautiful Pippin, Formosa, Glory of York, Granatreinette, Jadrnac Ribstonsky, Kaiser Reinette, Lord Raglan, Nonpareille, Pepin de Ribston, Pomme Granite, Poppina Ribston, Reinette de Traves, Reinette Grenade Anglaise, Ribstone, Ribstonov Pepin, Ridge, Rockhill's Russet and Travers.

The slightly irregular fruits, up to around 7cm (2¾in) across, are yellow-green to dull yellow with an orange-red flush and striping and some russeting. The creamy yellow flesh is firm, fine-textured and moderately juicy with a rich aromatic flavour.

Note: This is a probable parent of the Cox's Orange Pippin variety. The flavour is best about one month after picking but fruits can be stored for a further two to three months in optimum conditions. Trees are vigorous and crop well but can be prone to canker in damp soils. Some protection is advisable in cold areas.

Right: Ribston Pippin is an historic variety that is still worth growing.

Richard Delicious

Type: Dessert.
Origin: Unknown.
Parentage: Unknown; presumed to be a sport of Delicious.
Flowering: Mid-season.

The rounded to conical fruits, around 6cm (2¼in) across, are green with an even, bright red flush. The creamy white flesh is sweet and juicy.

Note: This variety is important commercially in Himachal Pradesh, north India. It is also used in breeding programmes. The fruits can be stored for up to four months.

Roanoke

Type: Dessert.
Origin: Virginia Polytechnic Institute, Blacksburg, USA, introduced 1949.
Parentage: Red Rome (female) x Schoharie (Northern Spy cross) (male).
Flowering: Late.

The rounded fruits, around 6cm (2¼in) across, are bright yellow-green with a strong dark red flush. The creamy white flesh is crisp and juicy with a mild flavour.

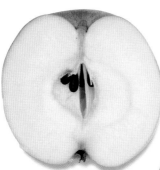

Note: Trees are moderately vigorous. The name commemorates an important city in Virginia.

Rode Wagenaar

The conical, slightly uneven fruits, around 6cm (2¼in) across, are green with a strong dark red flush. The creamy white flesh is crisp and juicy with a refreshing flavour.

Note: Trees are moderately vigorous.

Type: Dessert.
Origin: IVT, Wageningen, Netherlands, 1963.
Parentage: Unknown.
Flowering: Early.

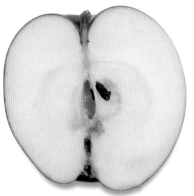  

Rosa du Perche

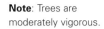

The very uneven, slightly flattened fruits, up to around 7cm (2¾in) across, are green with a strong red flush. The white flesh is fairly fine with a sweet and perfumed flavour.

Type: Dessert.
Origin: France, described 1947.
Parentage: Unknown.
Flowering: Mid-season.
Other name: Pourprée.

Note: Trees do best in a sheltered site in well-drained soil. The fruits are good for cider making.

Rose de Bénauge

The flattened, slightly uneven fruits, around 7cm (2¾in) across, are bright yellow-green with a strong red flush. The yellowish white flesh is firm and fairly tender with a sweet subacid flavour.

Type: Dessert.
Origin: ?Bordeaux, France, recorded 1872.
Parentage: Unknown.
Flowering: Late.
Other names: Bonne de Mai, Cadillac, de Cadillac, Dieu, Dieudonne, Pomme de Cadillac, Rose (de Knoop), Rose d'Hollande, Rose de Dropt, Rose de Hollande, Rose de la Bénauge, Rose de Mai, Rose du Dropt, Rose Tendre, Rosenapfel aus Benauge and Rozovka iz Benozha.

Note: The fruits are also used in cooking. Late flowering makes this a suitable variety for areas where spring frosts are likely.

Rose de Bouchetière

Type: Dessert.
Origin: France, 1948.
Parentage: Unknown.
Flowering: Early.

Note: This variety is nowadays rare in cultivation.

The flattened fruits, up to around 7cm (2¾ in) across or more, are bright green with a netting of russeting. The greenish white flesh is fine but a little tough with a sweet flavour.

Rose Double

Type: Dessert.
Origin: France, 1948.
Parentage: Unknown.
Flowering: Very late.

The slightly flattened and irregular fruits, around 6cm (2¼ in) across, are bright yellowish green with a pinkish red flush and some russeting. The pale cream flesh is firm with a nutty flavour.

Note: Trees are very wind-resistant and are generally free from disease. Young trees may not crop freely.

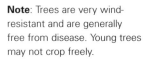
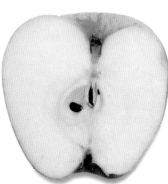

Rose Rouge

Type: Dessert.
Origin: France, 1950.
Parentage: Unknown.
Flowering: Mid-season.

The somewhat flattened, slightly irregular fruits, around 6cm (2¼ in) across, are yellow-green with a pinkish red flush and some russeting. The whitish flesh is firm and coarse with a subacid flavour.

Note: This variety is rare in cultivation. Trees are moderately vigorous.

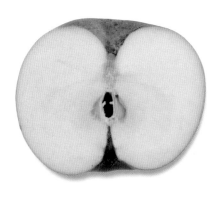

Rosemary Russet

The somewhat conical, irregular fruits, up to around 7cm (2¾in) across or more, are yellow-green with a red flush and some pale brown russeting. The creamy white flesh is firm, fine-textured and juicy with a rather acid and good flavour.

Type: Dessert.
Origin: England, UK, first described 1831.
Parentage: Unknown.
Flowering: Mid-season.
Other names: Benskin's Russet, Buzzan, Rosemary and Rosemary Apple.

Note: The fruits can be stored for two to three months. Trees are moderately vigorous.

Ross Nonpareil

The rounded fruits, around 6cm (2¼in) across, are green with a light flush and a netting of russeting. The creamy white to greenish flesh is firm and rather dry with a rich, aromatic flavour.

Left: Fruits of this variety are generally russeted.

Type: Dessert.
Origin: Ireland, UK, recorded 1802, introduced to England 1819.
Parentage: Unknown.
Flowering: Early.
Other names: French Pippin, Lawson Pearmain, Non-Pareille de Ross, Nonpareil Ross and Nonpareille de Ross.

Note: The trees are very hardy and are tolerant of most soils. They bear freely. The fruits can be stored for two to three months.

Rossie Pippin

The flattened, irregular fruits, up to around 7cm (2¾in) across or more, are an even bright green. The greenish white flesh is fine with an acid flavour.

Type: Culinary.
Origin: Maidstone, Kent, UK, catalogued 1890.
Parentage: Unknown.
Flowering: Mid-season.

Note: This variety is rare in cultivation.

Right: The fruits retain an even green colouring.

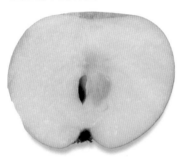

Roter Eiserapfel

Type: Dessert.
Origin: Germany, early 1700s.
Parentage: Unknown.
Flowering: Mid-season.
Other names: Arsapple,
Bamberger, Cristapfel,
Durable Trois Ans, Eiser
Rouge, Fragone, Hunt's Royal
Red, Jarnapple, Kloster Apfel,
Mohrenkopf, Nagelsapfel,
Red Eisen, Roter Bach,Roter
Jahrapfel, Roter Krieger,
Roter Paradiesapfel, Rother
Backapfel, Rother Eiser, Rott
Jarnapple, Rouge Ravée,
Schorsteinfeger, Tartos Piros
Alma, Treckhletnee, Zelezne
jablko and Zelezniac.

The rounded to conical fruits, around 7cm (2¾in)
across, are yellow-green with a strong dark red flush.
The creamy white flesh is very hard and fine with a
sweet, subacid flavour.

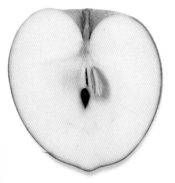

Note: These vigorous trees crop
heavily but are prone to biennial
bearing. The flowers are resistant
to frost. The fruits are also
suitable for cooking.

Roter Münsterländer Borsdorfer

Type: Dessert.
Origin: Germany, 1951.
Parentage: Unknown.
Flowering: Mid-season.

The rounded, slightly irregular fruits, around 6cm (2¼in)
across or more, are bright green with a strong dark red flush
and some russeting. The greenish white flesh is firm and
somewhat coarse with a subacid and slightly sweet flavour.

Note: Fruits can be stored for
two to three months. Trees are
generally disease resistant.

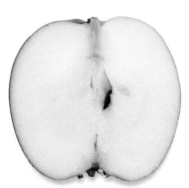

Roter Sauergrauech

Type: Dessert.
Origin: Switzerland, 1947.
Parentage: Unknown.
Flowering: Early.
Other name:
Sauergrauech Rouge.

The rounded to slightly conical fruits, around 6cm (2¼in)
across, are bright yellow-green with a strong red flush and
some streaking and striping. The greenish white flesh is fine
and soft with a slightly sweet, vinous, aromatic flavour.

Note: This variety is a
more highly coloured
sport of Sauergrauech.

Roter Stettiner

The irregular fruits, sometimes slightly flattened, around 6cm (2¼in) across or more, are bright yellow-green with a deep pink to red flush. The greenish white flesh is firm and fine with a subacid, sweet flavour.

Note: Trees are moderately vigorous. This variety does well in cool areas. The flowers are frost resistant. The fruits can be stored for several months.

Type: Dessert.
Origin: Germany, first described 1598.
Parentage: Unknown.
Flowering: Early.
Other names: Adam, Annaberger, Belle Hervey, Botzen, Butter-Apfel, Calviller, d'Hiver, Eisenapfel, Guly-Muly, Herrenapfel, Kack, Kohl, Mahler, Matapfel, Paradies Apfel, Pomme de Fer Vineuse, Rouge de Stettin, Rubiner, Schuller, Schwer, Shchetinka, Stetting Rouge, Tragamoner, Vejlimek chocholaty, Vineuse Rouge, Winter Sussapfel, Wintersuss, Wittlaboth and Zwiebelapfel.

Roxbury Russet

The very irregular fruits, up to around 7cm (2¾in) across or more, are bright yellowish green and greenish bronze with some spotting. The creamy white flesh is somewhat coarse and fairly tender with a subacid flavour.

Note: This is possibly the oldest American variety. The fruits store well.

Type: Dessert.
Origin: Roxbury, MA, USA, early 1600s.
Parentage: Unknown.
Flowering: Mid-season.
Other names: Belper Russet, Boston Russet, English Russet, Hewe's Russet, Howe's Russet, Jusset, Marietta Russet, Pitman's Russet, Pomme Russet, Putman Russet, Putnam Russet, Putnam Russet of Ohio, Renet Bostonskii, Rox, Rox Russet, Roxburg Russet, Roxbury Russeting, Shippen's Russet, Sylvan Russet and Warner's Russet.

Royal Gala

The rounded fruits, around 7cm (2¾in) across, are green with a pinkish red flush. The creamy white flesh is firm, crisp, fine-textured and juicy with a sweet and good aromatic flavour.

Type: Dessert.
Origin: A cultigen made from a sport of Gala, 1970s.
Parentage: Kidd's Orange Red (female) x Golden Delicious (male).
Flowering: Early.

Note: This is a very important commercial variety. Trees are moderately vigorous.

Runse

Type: Dessert.
Origin: Italy, 1958.
Parentage: Unknown.
Flowering: Mid-season.

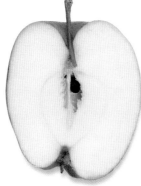

The rounded to slightly conical fruits, around 6cm (2¼in) across, are bright yellow-green with a strong red flush and some striping. The yellowish white flesh is soft and coarse with a subacid flavour.

Note: This variety is rare in cultivation.

Left: *Fruits develop red striping on the side facing the sun.*

Sacramentsappel

Type: Dessert.
Origin: Plant Breeding Institute, Wageningen, Netherlands, 1955.
Parentage: Unknown.
Flowering: Very late.

The very irregular fruits, around 7cm (2¾in) across, are yellow with a strong red flush. The creamy white flesh is fine and tender with a subacid and slightly rich flavour.

Note: Late flowering makes this variety suitable for areas where late spring frosts are likely.

Saint Edmund's Pippin

Type: Dessert.
Origin: Bury St Edmunds, Suffolk, UK, recorded 1875.
Parentage: Unknown.
Flowering: Early.
Other names: Early Golden Russet, St Edmonds, St Edmund's Pippin, St Edmund's Russet and St Edmunds.

The rounded fruits, up to around 7cm (2¾in) across or more, are bright green with extensive greenish brown russeting that makes the skins very rough. The creamy yellow flesh is moderately firm, juicy and slightly acid with a good flavour.

Note: This variety tolerates a range of growing conditions, is neat growing and shows good disease resistance. The fruits, which tend to shrivel in storage, are particularly good for juicing and cider making.

Right: *Fruits develop a rough, sandpaper-like skin that is typical of russet apples.*

Salome

The rounded to conical, slightly uneven fruits, around 6cm (2¼in) across, are yellow-green with a light pinkish red mottled flush and flecking. The greenish white flesh is firm and fine with a subacid flavour.

Type: Dessert.
Origin: Ottawa, IL, USA, introduced 1884.
Parentage: Unknown.
Flowering: Early.

Note: The fruits can be ribbed. Trees are moderately vigorous. They are hardy and crop abundantly.

Sam Young

The flattened fruits, around 5cm (2in) across, are bright green with a bright red flush and are almost covered with grey russeting. The greenish white flesh is firm and rather tough with a subacid flavour.

Type: Dessert.
Origin: Ireland, brought to notice in England, UK, 1818.
Parentage: Unknown.
Flowering: Early.
Other names: Irish Russet, Irlandischer Rothling and Irlandischer Rotling.

Note: Trees are moderately vigorous. The fruits can be stored for two to three months.

Sandlin Duchess

The flattened fruits, often more than 7cm (2¾in) across, are bright green with some flushing and russeting. The creamy green flesh is fine and tender with a subacid and slightly sweet flavour.

Type: Dessert.
Origin: Sandlin, Malvern, Worcestershire, UK, 1880.
Parentage: Unknown.
Flowering: Mid-season.

Note: Fruits store well for around four months. Newton Wonder has been claimed to be in its parentage.

Sandow

Type: Dessert.
Origin: Central Experiment Farm, Ottawa, Canada, selected 1912, introduced 1935.
Parentage: Northern Spy (female) x Unknown.
Flowering: Mid-season.

The rounded, slightly flattened fruits, more than 6cm (2¼in) across, are bright yellow-green with a strong dark red flush and striping. The creamy white flesh is coarse and tender with a sweet to fairly acid, and sometimes raspberry-like, flavour.

Note: This variety is similar to its parent Northern Spy but is hardier and less prone to scab. The fruits have a fuller flavour.

Sanspareil

Type: Dessert.
Origin: Known in England, UK, since the late 1800s.
Parentage: Unknown.
Flowering: Early.

The rounded to slightly flattened fruits, around 6cm (2¼in) across, are bright green with a pinkish red flush and a small amount of russeting. The yellow flesh is crisp with a sweet, aromatic flavour.

Note: The fruits can be stored for several months. Trees are moderately vigorous.

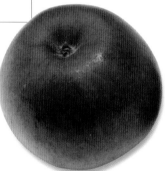

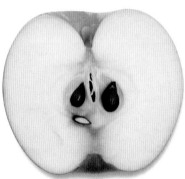

Schöner aus Herrnhut

Type: Dessert.
Origin: Herrnhut, Germany.
Parentage: Unknown.
Flowering: Early.
Other names: Herrnhutsk and Piekna z Herrnhut.

Note: This variety is moderately susceptible to scab and mildew. Biennial bearing can be a problem. Fruits are good for juicing.

The rounded to irregular fruits, up to around 7cm (2¾in) across or more, are bright yellow-green with a strong red flush and some striping and spotting. The yellowish white flesh is juicy with a sweet but tart flavour.

Above: The fruits of this variety can vary in shape, and develop their red colouring on the side facing the sun.

Schweizer Orange

The flattened, uneven fruits, around 7cm (2¾in) across or more, are bright yellow-green with a strong red flush. The creamy white flesh is firm with a subacid flavour.

Note: This variety has a tendency to produce quantities of small fruits.

Type: Dessert.
Origin: Swiss Federal Agricultural Research Station, Wädenswil, Switzerland, 1935, released 1955.
Parentage: Ontario (female) x Cox's Orange Pippin (male).
Flowering: Mid-season.
Other names: Schweizer Orangenapfel and Suisse Orange.

September Beauty

The rounded, slightly irregular fruits, around 7cm (2¾in) across, are bright green with a bright red flush and some russeting. The creamy white flesh is coarse and loose with a fairly sweet flavour.

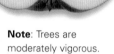

Type: Dessert.
Origin: Bedford, UK, 1885.
Parentage: Unknown.
Flowering: Mid-season.

Note: Trees are moderately vigorous.

Right: This variety was raised by Laxtons, a noted Victorian grower.

Sharon

The rounded fruits, around 6cm (2¼in) across, are bright green with a strong red flush and some flecking and striping. The whitish green flesh is juicy, fine and tender with a sweet flavour.

Note: The flavour is similar to McIntosh but sweeter and firmer.

Type: Dessert.
Origin: Iowa State Agricultural Experiment Station, Ames, USA, 1906, introduced 1922.
Parentage: McIntosh (female) x Longfield (male).
Flowering: Early.

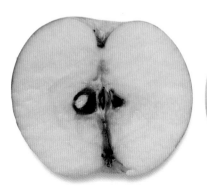

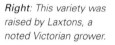

Shin Indo

Type: Dessert.
Origin: Aomori Apple Experiment Station, Japan, raised 1930, named 1948.
Parentage: Indo (female) x Golden Delicious (male).
Flowering: Mid-season.

The conical fruits, around 7cm (2¾in) across or more, are bright green with a pinkish red flush. The cream flesh, tinged green, is firm and dry with a sweet flavour.

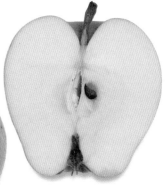

Note: Trees are very vigorous, so should be grown on dwarfing rootstocks.

Siddington Russet

Type: Culinary and dessert.
Origin: Siddington, Gloucestershire, UK, 1923.
Parentage: Unknown.
Flowering: Mid-season.

Note: This variety, currently endangered, is a russeted sport of Galloway Pippin.

The flattened fruits, around 6cm (2¼in) across, are bright green with a netting of russeting. The creamy white flesh is firm, crisp and juicy with a subacid flavour.

Signe Tillisch

Type: Culinary and dessert.
Origin: ?Denmark, *c.*1866, first described 1889.
Parentage: ?Calville Blanc D'Hiver (female) x Unknown.
Flowering: Mid-season.
Other names: Signe Tillish and Sini Tillis.

The rounded fruits are bright green with a bright red flush and some striping. The creamy white flesh is loose and soft with a sweet, subacid, aromatic flavour.

Note: This variety was raised by Councillor Tillisch and named after his daughter. Trees are moderately vigorous.

Sikulai-alma

Note: This variety is resistant to fireblight. It is self-sterile, so a suitable pollinator is required for good fruiting.

The irregular, somewhat flattened fruits, around 7cm (2¾in) across, are bright green with a strong dark red flush. The greenish white to cream flesh is firm and fine with a subacid flavour.

Type: Dessert.
Origin: Hungary, first recorded 1875.
Parentage: Unknown.
Flowering: Mid-season.
Other names: de Sikula, Seklerapfel, Siculane, Sikula, Sikulaer Apfel, Sikulaerapfel, Sikulai Alma, Sikulaske, Szekely-alma and Szekelyalma.

Simonffy Piros

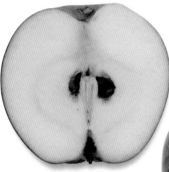

Note: This variety is resistant to fireblight.

The rounded fruits, around 7cm (2¾in) across or more, are bright yellow-green with a strong dark red flush and some russeting. The greenish white flesh is firm and fine with a very sweet, subacid, perfumed, strawberry-like taste.

Type: Dessert.
Origin: Hungary, recorded 1876.
Parentage: Unknown.
Flowering: Early.
Other name: Simonffy Roth.

Sir John Thornycroft

The flattened fruits, around 7cm (2¾in) across, are bright yellow-green with a red flesh, some red flecking and some russeting. The creamy white flesh is hard, tough and coarse with a slightly sweet flavour.

Note: This variety is now rare in cultivation but is often included in heritage plantings.

Type: Dessert.
Origin: Bembridge, Isle of Wight, UK, introduced 1913.
Parentage: Unknown.
Flowering: Mid-season.
Other name: Sir John Thorneycroft.

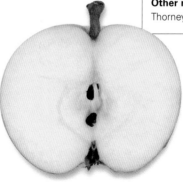

Sisson's Worksop Newton

Type: Dessert.
Origin: Worksop, Nottinghamshire, UK, 1910.
Parentage: Newtown Pippin (female) x Unknown.
Flowering: Mid-season.

The irregular, somewhat flattened-to-square fruits, up to around 7cm (2¾in) across, are pale greenish-yellow with a light orange-brown flush and some light spotting. The greenish white flesh is coarse, with a subacid to acid flavour.

Note: This variety needs a sunny location in order for the flavour to develop its full pineapple-like aroma.

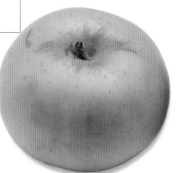  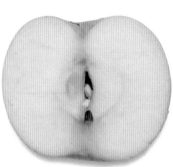

Slavyanka

Type: Dessert.
Origin: Russia, 1899.
Parentage: Antonovka (female) x Ananas Reinette (male).
Flowering: Mid-season.
Other names: Slavianka and Slavjanka.

The rounded, irregular fruits, around 6cm (2¼in) across, are an even bright yellow-green. The white flesh is fine with a sweet, subacid, aromatic flavour.

Note: This variety is a partial tip-bearer.

 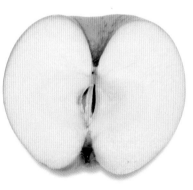

South Park

Type: Dessert.
Origin: South Park, Penshurst, Kent, UK, 1940.
Parentage: Cox's Orange Pippin (female) x Winter Queening (male).
Flowering: Mid-season.

The rounded fruits, around 6cm (2¼in) across or more, are bright yellow-green with a strong red flush and some russeting. The cream flesh, tinged green, is crisp with an acid flavour.

Note: Trees are moderately vigorous.

Spencer Seedless

The rounded or slightly flattened fruits, around 6cm (2¼in) across, are dull yellowish green with a red flush and russeting. The creamy white flesh has poor flavour.

Type: Dessert.
Origin: Long Ashton Research Station, Bristol, UK, 1970.
Parentage: Unknown.
Flowering: Late.

Note: The fruits of this variety rarely set any seed.

Stark's Late Delicious

The conical, irregular fruits, around 7cm (2¾in) across, are bright yellow-green with a pinkish red flush and some striping. The cream flesh, tinged green, is very sweet.

Type: Dessert.
Origin: Scotland, UK, 1967.
Parentage: Unknown.
Flowering: Mid-season.

Note: Trees are moderately vigorous.

Right: Fruits of this variety taper sharply towards the blossom end.

Starkrimson Delicious

The conical fruits, around 6cm (2¼in) across, are bright green with a strong dark red flush. The creamy white flesh is firm, very sweet and juicy with a highly aromatic flavour.

Type: Dessert.
Origin: Hood River, OR, USA, c.1953, introduced 1956.
Parentage: Unknown.
Flowering: Mid-season.
Other names: Bisbee Red Delicious and Starkrimson.

Note: This variety, which can be weak-growing, is a more highly coloured and taller-fruited clone of Starking. Trees bear well and are resistant to fungal diseases.

Stearns

Type: Dessert.
Origin: North Syracuse, NY, USA, recorded 1900.
Parentage: Esopus Spitzenburg (female) x Unknown.
Flowering: Mid-season.

The slightly irregular fruits, up to 8cm (3in) across, are bright green with a pinkish red flush and some striping.
The creamy white flesh is crisp yet melts in the mouth with a sweet, subacid flavour.

Note: Trees are very vigorous, so are suitable for growing on dwarfing rootstocks.

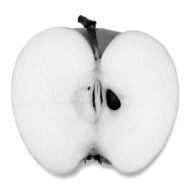

Steyne Seedling

Type: Dessert.
Origin: Steyne, Isle of Wight, UK, c.1893.
Parentage: Unknown.
Flowering: Early.
Other name:
Steyne's Seedling.

The flattened fruits, around 6cm (2¼in) across or more, are bright yellow-green with a pinkish red flush and some streaking. The creamy white flesh is soft, tender and juicy with a subacid flavour.

Note: This is one of several notable varieties raised in the gardens of Sir John Thornycroft on the Isle of Wight. The flavour is similar to Cox's Orange Pippin.

Stina Lohmann

Type: Dessert.
Origin: Germany, 1951.
Parentage: Unknown.
Flowering: Mid-season.

The rounded but irregular fruits, around 6cm (2¼in) across, are bright green with a red flush and some russeting and streaking. The yellowish white flesh is firm and fine with a slightly sweet, subacid, somewhat rich flavour.

Note: Trees are vigorous and tolerant of a range of soil types. Fruits can be stored for up to six months or even longer.

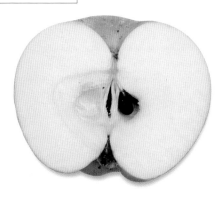

Stoke Edith Pippin

The rounded, slightly irregular fruits, around 6cm (2¼ in) across or more, are bright yellow-green, tinged orange, with some grey russeting and spotting. The yellow flesh is firm and crisp with a subacid, sweet and perfumed flavour.

Type: Dessert.
Origin: ?Stoke Edith, Herefordshire, UK, recorded 1872.
Parentage: Unknown.
Flowering: Mid-season.
Other name: Stock-Edith Pippin.

Note: The fruits can be stored for two to three months. For the best flavour, fruits should be allowed to ripen fully on the tree.

Stonetosh

The rounded, slightly irregular fruits, around 7cm (2¾ in) across, are yellowish green with a dark red flush and some streaking. The white flesh is rather soft with a moderately sweet and slightly acid flavour.

Type: Dessert.
Origin: Horticulture Division, Experimental Farm, Ottawa, Canada, 1909, introduced 1923.
Parentage: Stone (female) x McIntosh (male).
Flowering: Mid-season.
Other name: Stontosh.

Note: This variety shows some resistance to bitter pit. Trees are very vigorous.

Storey's Seedling

The rounded, slightly conical fruits, around 7cm (2¾ in) across, are bright green with a strong red flush and some russeting. The white flesh is somewhat soft with a sweet and slightly subacid flavour.

Type: Dessert.
Origin: Northolt Park, Middlesex, UK, 1927.
Parentage: Newtown Pippin (female) x Unknown.
Flowering: Mid-season.

Note: Fruits can be stored throughout the winter. Trees are self-sterile so need a suitable pollination partner.

Sturmer Pippin

Type: Dessert.
Origin: Sturmer, Suffolk, UK, first recorded 1831.
Parentage: ?Ribston Pippin (female) x ?Nonpareil (male).
Flowering: Mid-season.
Other names: Apple Royal, Creech Pearmain, Moxhay, Pearmain de Sturmer, Pepin de Sturmer, Pepin iz Shturmera, Royal, Sturmer's Pepping, Sturmer, Sturmer Pepping, Sturmer's Pippin and Sturmers Pepping.

The rounded fruits, around 6cm (2¼ in) across, are bright yellow-green with a red flush and brown russeting. The creamy white to yellow flesh is very firm, fine-textured and juicy with a little subacid and rich aromatic flavour.

Note: Trees are very hardy and crop freely. The fruits have exceptional keeping qualities. The flavour improves in storage and can be at its best in late winter. It was taken to Australia in the 19th century, as its keeping capacity makes it useful for exporting.

Sunburn

Type: Dessert.
Origin: Hornchurch, Essex, UK, 1925.
Parentage: Cox's Orange Pippin (female) x Unknown.
Flowering: Mid-season.

The rounded fruits, around 6cm (2¼ in) across, are bright yellow-green with a strong red flush. The creamy white flesh is soft with a sweet, subacid, aromatic flavour.

Note: The fruits can be stored for two to three months.

Right: The red flush develops on the side facing the sun.

Sunset

Type: Dessert.
Origin: Ightham, Kent, UK, c.1918, named 1933.
Parentage: Cox's Orange Pippin (female) x Unknown.
Flowering: Early.

The rounded, slightly flattened fruits, around 6cm (2¼ in) across, are bright yellow-green with an orange-red flush and some streaking. The creamy white flesh is firm, crisp and fine-textured with a good aromatic flavour.

Note: Trees are self-fertile, show good disease resistance and crop reliably. The flavour, though variable and sometimes disappointing, is similar to Cox's Orange Pippin. The fruits can be small.

Suntan

The somewhat flattened fruits, around 6cm (2¼in) across, are bright yellow-green with a strong red flush and some streaking and patches of russeting. The creamy yellow flesh is slightly coarse-textured and moderately juicy with an aromatic, pineapple-like but acid flavour.

Note: This variety is prone to bitter pit. It is a triploid. Fruits are best around eight weeks after picking and can be stored for a further three months.

Type: Dessert.
Origin: East Malling Research Station, Maidstone, Kent, UK, 1956.
Parentage: Cox's Orange Pippin (female) x Court Pendu Plat (male).
Flowering: Late.

Swaar

The rounded, uneven fruits, around 6cm (2¼in) across, are dull yellow with russeting and spotting. The creamy white flesh is firm and fine with a sweet, aromatic, nutty flavour.

Note: The best flavour develops in storage.

Type: Dessert.
Origin: Nr Esopus, Hudson River, NY, USA (allegedly), recorded 1804.
Parentage: Unknown.
Flowering: Mid-season.
  Other names: Der Schwere Apfel, Hardwich, Hardwick, Schwere Apfel, Schwerer Apfel, Suaar, Swaar Appel, Swaar Apple and Zwaar.

Sweet-Tart

The rounded, slightly irregular fruits, around 6cm (2¼in) across, are yellow-green with a deep pinkish red flush. The creamy white flesh is soft and juicy with a very sweet flavour.

Note: Early flowering makes this variety unsuitable for growing in areas where late frosts are likely.

Type: Dessert.
Origin: Gordon Apple Trees, Whittier, CA, USA, date unknown.
Parentage: Unknown.
  Flowering: Very early.

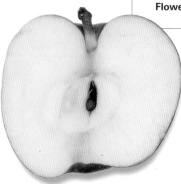

Szabadkai Szercsika

Type: Dessert.
Origin: Hungary, 1948.
Parentage: Unknown.
Flowering: Early.

The rounded, somewhat irregular fruits, up to around 7cm (2¾in) across, are bright green with a pinkish red flush. The creamy white flesh is firm with a slightly sweet, subacid flavour.

Note: Early flowering makes this variety unsuitable for growing in frost-prone areas.

Left: Exposure to the sun brings out the characteristic pinkish flush of this variety.

Tellina

Type: Dessert.
Origin: Italy, 1958.
Parentage: Unknown.
Flowering: Mid-season.

The conical, somewhat irregular fruits, around 6cm (2¼in) across, are bright yellow-green with a red flush and some striping and streaking. The greenish white flesh is firm and fine with a subacid flavour.

Note: Trees are moderately vigorous.

Far left: The fruits of this variety can develop an uneven shape.

Telstar

Type: Dessert.
Origin: Greytown, Wairarapa, New Zealand, 1943, named 1965.
Parentage: Golden Delicious (female) x Kidd's Orange Red (male).
Flowering: Mid-season.

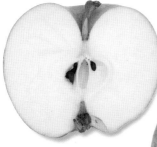

The rounded fruits, around 6cm (2¼in) across or more, are dull yellow-green with a red flush and some streaking. The creamy white flesh is firm and coarse with a sweet, slightly acid and rich, complex flavour.

Note: This variety has the same parentage as Gala. Trees do not grow vigorously but crop freely.

Tenroy

The rounded fruits, around 6cm (2¼in) across or more, are bright yellow-green with a strong red flush and some flecking. The creamy white flesh is sweet, crisp and juicy with an aromatic flavour.

Type: Dessert.
Origin: New Zealand, discovered 1971, introduced 1974.
Parentage: Kidd's Orange Red (female) x Golden Delicious (male).
Flowering: Early.

Note: This variety is a more highly coloured clone of Gala. Trees do not do well at high altitude or in dry soil. Leaves are susceptible to spotting.

Tentation

The rounded fruits, similar to Golden Delicious, are golden yellow with an orange flush. The creamy white flesh is firm, crisp and juicy, with a pleasant, refreshing, sweet, nutty flavour.

Type: Dessert.
Origin: France, 1990 or 1979
Parentage: Golden Delicious (female) and Grifier (male).
Flowering: Mid-season.
Other name: Delblush.

Note: This variety is potentially important commercially owing to the appeal of its colouring, which develops best in the southern hemisphere. Trees are of average vigour and set fruit at a young age.

Texola

The rounded, sometimes almost square, fruits, around 7cm (2¾in) across, are bright yellow-green with a red flush. The white flesh, tinged green, is soft with a subacid flavour.

Type: Dessert.
Origin: Utah, USA, 1930.
Parentage: Ben Davies (female) x Unknown.
Flowering: Early.

Note: Trees can be weak growing so may not be suitable for the most dwarfing rootstocks.

Far right: The flushing develops on the side of the fruit nearest the sun.

Tillington Court

Type: Culinary and dessert.
Origin: Burghill, Herefordshire, UK, recorded 1988 but much older.
Parentage: Unknown.
Flowering: Very early.

The rounded, slightly irregular fruits, around 7cm (2¾in) across, are bright yellow-green with a red flush which is sometimes patchy. The yellow flesh is juicy with an acid taste.

Note: Early flowering makes this variety unsuitable for growing in areas where late frosts are likely.

Tom Putt

Type: Culinary.
Origin: Trent, Somerset, UK, late 1700s.
Parentage: Unknown.
Flowering: Mid-season.
Other names: Coalbrook, Devonshire Nine Square, Izod's Kernel, January Tom Putt, Jeffrey's Seedling, Marrow Bone, Ploughman, Thomas Jeffreys, Tom Potter and Tom Put.

The uneven fruits, up to around 7cm (2¾in) across or more, are clear yellow-green with a strong crimson red flush. The creamy white flesh, stained red beneath the skin, is crisp and juicy with an acid flavour.

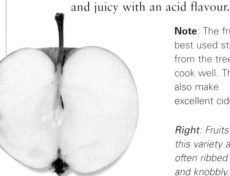

Note: The fruits, best used straight from the tree, cook well. They also make excellent cider.

Right: Fruits of this variety are often ribbed and knobbly.

Twenty Ounce

Type: Culinary and dessert.
Origin: ?New York or Connecticut, USA, 1844.
Parentage: Unknown.
Flowering: Mid-season.
Other names: Aurora, Cayuga Red Streak, Coleman, de Dix-huit Onces, de Vin du Connecticut, Dix-huit Onces, Eighteen Ounce, Gov. Seward's, Lima, Morgan's Favourite, Pomme de Vin du Connecticut, Pomme de Vingt-onces, Pomme rayée de Cayuga, Reinette de Vingt-Onces, Twenty Ounce Apple, Twenty Ounce Pippin, Wine, Wine of Connecticut and Zwanzig Unzen.

The somewhat irregular fruits, around 7cm (2¾in) across or more, are bright yellow-green with a red flush that can appear in flecks and stripes. The creamy white flesh is coarse, juicy and moderately tender with a subacid flavour.

Note: This variety is a triploid. Trees are moderately vigorous and crop well.

Tydeman's Early Worcester

Above: The bright red flush makes the Tydeman's Early Worcester a very appealing variety.

The rounded, often irregular fruits have a strong bright red flush. The white flesh is crisp, fine-textured and juicy with a good vinous flavour.

Note: Leaf spots can be a problem.

Type: Dessert.
Origin: East Malling Research Station, Maidstone, Kent, UK, raised 1929 and introduced 1945.
Parentage: McIntosh (female) x Worcester Pearmain (male).
Flowering: Mid-season.
Other names: Early Worcester, Tydeman Early, Tydeman's Early, Tydeman's Red and Tydemans Early Worcester.

Tydeman's Late Orange

Note: The fruits store well, until early spring. The flavour is similar to a Cox but is sharper.

The rounded to conical fruits, around 6cm (2¼ in) across, are golden green with a strong red flush and some russeting. The cream flesh is very firm, crisp and fairly juicy with a rich, aromatic flavour.

Type: Dessert.
Origin: East Malling Research Station, Maidstone, Kent, UK, 1930, introduced 1949.
Parentage: Laxton's Superb (female) x Cox's Orange Pippin (male).
Flowering: Mid-season.
Other name: Tydeman's Late Cox.

Underleaf

The rounded, slightly flattened fruits, around 6cm (2¼ in) across, are bright yellow-green with some russeting. The creamy white flesh is sweet, with a flavour similar to Blenheim.

Type: Dessert.
Origin: Long Ashton Research Station, Bristol, UK, 1967.
Parentage: Unknown.
Flowering: Late.
Other name: Gloucestershire Underleaf.

Note: Trees bear heavily. The fruits are suitable for cider making.

Upton Pyne

Type: Culinary and dessert.
Origin: Topsham, Devon, UK, introduced 1910.
Parentage: Unknown.
Flowering: Mid-season.

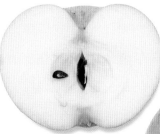

The rounded fruits, around 6cm (2¼in) across or more, are bright yellow-green with a red flush and some flecking. The creamy white flesh is firm, rather coarse-textured and juicy with a somewhat acid and fair flavour.

Note: The fruit cooks to a purée. The flavour is like that of a pineapple. Trees show good disease resistance.

Left: *Upton Pyne is a versatile, dual-purpose apple.*

Venus Pippin

The rounded to slightly conical or rectangular fruits, around 6cm (2¼in) across, are clear bright green with a faint pinkish brown flush and some spotting. The creamy white flesh is tender, soft and coarse with a slightly sweet, slightly acid flavour.

Type: Culinary.
Origin: Thought to be Devon, UK, *c.*1800.
Parentage: Unknown.
Flowering: Mid-season.
Other names: Plumderity and Venus' Pippin.

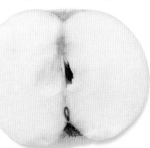

Note: Trees are very vigorous so are best grown on very dwarfing rootstocks.

Right: *The clear, almost yellowish, colouring of the ripe fruits is unusual.*

Verallot

Type: Culinary.
Origin: France, 1948.
Parentage: Unknown.
Flowering: Very late.

The flattened fruits, around 6cm (2¼in) across, are bright yellow-green with a bright red flush and some russeting. The greenish white flesh is firm with an acid flavour.

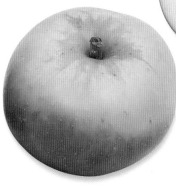

Note: Late flowering makes this a very useful variety for growing in areas where late frosts are likely to occur.

Vérité

The somewhat flattened fruits, around 6cm (2¼in) across, are bright yellow-green with a strong red flush. The greenish white flesh is firm with a slightly sweet, subacid flavour.

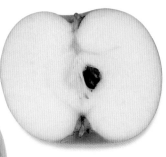

Type: Dessert.
Origin: France, recorded 1876.
Parentage: Unknown.
Flowering: Very late.

Note: Fruits, which store well, can also be used in cooking and are good for juicing and cider making. Trees are very hardy.

Vernajoux

The rounded, occasionally somewhat flattened fruits, around 6cm (2¼in) across, are bright yellow-green with a light red flush and some russeting. The white flesh, tinged green, is firm and tough with a slightly sweet flavour.

Type: Dessert.
Origin: France, described 1947.
Parentage: Unknown.
Flowering: Late.

Note: Fruits can be stored for around four months, sometimes longer. They show some resistance to bruising.

Victory

The rounded to slightly conical fruits are around 6cm (2¼in) across. They are green with a pinkish red flush and some darker flecking. The creamy white flesh is firm with an acid flavour.

Note: This variety should not be confused with the American Victory, normally styled as Victory (USA).

Type: Culinary.
Origin: Unknown.
Parentage: Bismarck (female) x Blenheim Orange (male).
Flowering: Mid-season.
Other name: Carpenter.

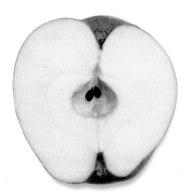

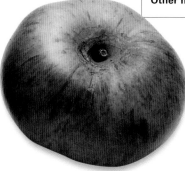

Vincent

Type: Dessert.
Origin: France,
described 1947.
Parentage: Unknown.
Flowering: Late.
Other name: Saint-Vincent.

The slightly flattened fruits, around 6cm (2¼in) across,
are yellowish green with a red flush and russeting. The
creamy white flesh is firm and crisp with a subacid and
slightly sweet flavour.

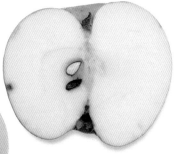

Note: Trees are
moderately vigorous.
Late flowering makes this
a suitable variety for areas
where late frosts are likely.

Violetta

Type: Dessert.
Origin: Italy, 1958.
Parentage: Unknown.
Flowering: Mid-season.

The rounded fruits, around 5cm (2in) across, are bright
yellow-green with a bright red flush and some flecking.
The creamy white flesh is firm and fine with a subacid
and slightly sweet flavour.

Note: This variety is unusual
in commerce outside its
country of origin.

Far left: *The flush on the
skins deepens on the area
nearest the sun.*

Violette

Type: Dessert.
Origin: France, known
early 1600s.
Parentage: Unknown.
Flowering: Early.
Other names: Black Apple,
Calville Rayée d'Automne,
De Quatre-Goûts, de Violette,
Des Quatre-Goûts,
Framboise, Framboox Apple,
Grosse Pomme Noire
d'Amérique, Pomme Violette,
Quatre Goûts, Reinette des
Quatre-Goûts, Reinette
Violette, Violet, Violette de
Mars, Violette de Quatre
Goûts, Violetter Apfel and
Winter Veilchen.

The conical to oblong, somewhat irregular fruits, around
6cm (2¼in) across, are bright yellow-green with a
pinkish to very dark, almost bluish to blackish, red flush.
The yellowish white flesh, tinged red under the skin, is
firm and fine with a subacid and slightly aromatic flavour.

Note: This variety shows
some resistance to black
spot. Trees are very vigorous.
The fruits are also suitable
for cooking.

Wagener

The rounded, very slightly flattened, fruits, around 6cm (2¼ in) across, are bright green with a strong red flush. The creamy white flesh is firm and moderately juicy with a pleasant flavour.

Note: Trees are hardy, scab-resistant and bear heavily. Thinning may be necessary. The fruits can also be used for apple sauce and in cider making. They do not shrivel in storage.

Type: Dessert.
Origin: Penn Yann, NY, USA, 1791.
Parentage: Unknown.
Flowering: Early.
Other names: Pomme Wagener, Vagner, Vagnera Premirovannoe, Vagnera Prizovoe, Wagener Premiat, Wagener Price Apple, Wagener's, Wagenerapfel, Wageners Preisapfel, Waggoner, Wagner, Wagner Dijas, Wagner Preiss Apfel, Wagner Premiat, Wagnera Prizovoe and Wegenerovo.

Wang Young

The rounded fruits, around 6cm (2¼ in) across, are bright green with a pinkish to dark red flush. The creamy white flesh is soft, juicy and sweet.

Note: Trees are moderately vigorous. This is one of the few South Korean apples in commerce outside its country of origin.

Type: Dessert.
Origin: South Korea, 1967.
Parentage: Unknown.
Flowering: Mid-season.

Warden

The rounded fruits, around 6cm (2¼ in) across, are bright yellow with a strong dark red flush and flecking. The white flesh is soft and juicy with a fairly sweet flavour.

Note: Trees are moderately vigorous. Warden is an old English term for a pear.

Type: Dessert.
Origin: Scotland, UK, 1967.
Parentage: Unknown.
Flowering: Mid-season.

Wealthy

Type: Dessert.
Origin: Excelsior, MN, USA, first recorded 1860.
Parentage: Cherry Crab (female) x Unknown.
Flowering: Mid-season.
Other names: Lelsy, Plodovodnoe and Uelsi.

The flattened fruits, around 6cm (2¼in) across, are bright yellow-green with a pinkish red flush and some streaking. The creamy white flesh is rather soft, coarse-textured and juicy with a sweet and faintly vinous flavour.

Note: Trees bear heavily, even when young, but are prone to biennial bearing. A long flowering period makes this a good pollinator for many other varieties.

Right: This was the first apple variety of commercial quality to be grown in Minnesota and eventually became one of the five most-produced apples in the USA.

Wellington Bloomless

Type: Dessert.
Origin: USA, 1966.
Parentage: Unknown.
Flowering: Mid-season.

The irregular, quince-like fruits, around 7cm (2¾in) across, are yellow-green with a strong red flush and some spotting. The creamy white flesh has a sweet and pleasant flavour.

Above: No two fruits of this variety are likely to show the same shape.

Note: A unique feature of this variety is that its flowers have no petals – hence the name.

Wellspur Delicious

Type: Dessert.
Origin: Azwell Orchard of the Wells and Wade Fruit Company, Wenatchee, WA, USA, discovered 1952, introduced 1958.
Parentage: Unknown.
Flowering: Mid-season.
Other name: Wellspur.

The rounded but irregular fruits, around 6cm (2¼in) across, are bright green with a strong pinkish to dark red, sometimes patchy, flush. The creamy white flesh is very firm, very sweet and juicy with a highly aromatic flavour.

Note: This variety is a sport of Starking with a more solid red flush.

Wheeler's Russet

The flattened, irregular fruits, around 6cm (2¼in) across, are mid-green with yellowish grey to reddish brown russeting and some freckling. The greenish white flesh is a little soft with a subacid, slightly sweet and slightly aromatic flavour.

Type: Dessert.
Origin: England, UK, known in 1717.
Parentage: Unknown.
Flowering: Mid-season.
Other name: Reinette Grise de Wheeler.

Note: Trees are very hardy and bear well. The fruits can be stored for four to five months. They retain a good flavour even as they begin to shrivel.

White Winter Pearmain

The irregular fruits, around 6cm (2¼in) across, are yellowish green with a red flush and some dotting. The creamy white flesh is firm, crisp, tender and fine with a subacid and aromatic flavour.

Type: Dessert.
Origin: Thought to have originated in the eastern states, USA, 1867.
Parentage: Unknown.
Flowering: Mid-season.

Note: Trees are moderately vigorous. This variety makes an excellent pollinator for other apple trees.

Widdup

The rounded fruits, up to around 7cm (2¾in) across, are bright green with a red flush and some flecking. The greenish white flesh is firm, fine and crisp with a subacid and slightly sweet flavour.

Note: This variety is increasingly rare in cultivation.

Type: Dessert.
Origin: New Zealand, 1961.
Parentage: Unknown.
Flowering: Early.

William Crump

Type: Dessert.
Origin: Rowe's Nurseries, Worcester, UK, 1908.
Parentage: Cox's Orange Pippin (female) x Worcester Pearmain (male).
Flowering: Mid-season.

The rounded, slightly irregular fruits, around 6cm (2¼in) across or more, are yellow-green with a strong red flush. The creamy white flesh is firm, fine-textured and juicy with a sweet and rich, aromatic flavour.

Note: Trees are very vigorous. The fruits can be stored for two to three months.

Right: *The regular flecking on the skins makes this a very appealing apple.*

Winesap

Type: Culinary.
Origin: USA, first described 1817.
Parentage: Unknown.
Flowering: Mid-season.
Other names: American Winesop, Banana, Henrick's Sweet, Holland's Red Winter, Pot Pie Apple, Red Sweet Wine Sop, Royal Red, Royal Red of Kentucky, Texan Red, Virginia Winesaps, Winesopa and Winter Winesap.

The rounded fruits, up to around 7cm (2¾in) across, are dull yellow-green with a pinkish red flush. The yellowish white flesh is firm, tender and coarse with a sweet, subacid flavour.

Note: The fruits store well. They are suitable for cider making. The skins can be tough.

Winston

Type: Dessert.
Origin: Welford Park, Berkshire, UK, introduced 1935 as Winter King, renamed 1944.
Parentage: Cox's Orange Pippin (female) x Worcester Pearmain (male).
Flowering: Mid-season.
Other names: Cox d'Hiver, Winter King and Wintercheer.

The rounded to slightly conical fruits, around 6cm (2¼in) across, are bright yellow-green with a strong red flush and some russeting. The creamy white flesh is firm, fine-textured and juicy with a sweet and good aromatic flavour.

Note: Trees are resistant to most diseases and crop reliably.

Right: *Fruits of this variety tend to taper towards the blossom end.*

Winter Banana

The irregular fruits, up to around 7cm (2¾in) across or more, are pale yellow-green with a red flush. The creamy white flesh is rather soft, rather coarse-textured and moderately juicy with a sweet and pleasant aromatic flavour.

Note: This variety is suitable for training, especially as an espalier. Trees, which are vigorous, are resistant to nearly all diseases. The flavour is similar to that of a banana. The fruits can also be cooked.

Type: Dessert.
Origin: Cross County, IN, USA, introduced 1890.
Parentage: Unknown.
Flowering: Mid-season.
Other names: Banan zimnii, Banana, Banana de Iarna, Banane, Banane d'Hiver, Bananove zimni, Bananovoe, Flory, Teli banan and Zimna bananova.

Winter Peach

The flattened, somewhat irregular fruits, up to around 7cm (2¾in) across or more, are pale green with a red flush. The yellowish flesh is crisp, tender and juicy with an acid and slightly spicy flavour.

Type: Dessert.
Origin: ?USA, known in England, UK, 1853.
Parentage: Unknown.
Flowering: Mid-season.
Other names: Peach Bloom and Pêche d'Hiver.

Note: The fruits can be stored for up to six months or even longer. They are also suitable for cooking.

Winter Pearmain

The rounded to conical fruits, up to around 7cm (2¾in) across, are bright green with a strong red flush and some russeting and dotting. The yellowish flesh is firm and crisp with a pleasant, sweet, subacid flavour.

Note: Trees are very hardy and bear freely. The fruits can be stored for three to four months.

Type: Culinary and dessert.
Origin: Thought to be an old English variety, date unknown.
Parentage: Unknown.
Flowering: Early.
Other names: Duck's Bill, English Winter Pearmain, Grange's Pearmain, Grauwe of Blanke Pepping van der Laan, Great Pearmain, Hertfordshire Pearmain, Old Winter Pearmain, Pepin Pearmain d'Angleterre, Pepin Pearmain d'Hiver, Reinette très tardive, Somerset Apple Royal, Striped Winter, Sussex Scarlet Pearmain, Sussex Winter Pearmain and Winter Queening.

Woolbrook Pippin

Type: Dessert.
Origin: Sidmouth, Devon, UK, 1903.
Parentage: Cox's Orange Pippin (female) x Unknown.
Flowering: Mid-season.

The irregular fruits, up to around 7cm (2¾ in) across, are bright yellow-green with a pinkish red flush and some striping. The creamy white flesh is firm, crisp and tender with a sweet, slightly acid and aromatic flavour.

Note: This variety shows some resistance to scab and canker. Trees are vigorous and upright.

Right: This attractive variety is widely used in heritage plantings of older varieties.

Worcester Pearmain

Type: Dessert.
Origin: Swan Pool, near Worcester, UK, introduced 1874.
Parentage: ?Devonshire Quarrenden (female) x Unknown.
Flowering: Early.
Other names: Pearmain de Worcester, Worcester, Worcester Parmaene, Worcester Parman, Worcester Parmane, Worcester-Parman and Worchester Parmane.

Note: This variety is often used in breeding programmes to develop new varieties. It makes a good garden tree, bearing freely. Fruits ripen early in the season but for the best flavour should be left as long on the tree as possible.

The rounded to conical, slightly irregular fruits, around 6cm (2¼ in) across, are bright yellow-green with an intense red-crimson flush and some spotting, flecking and russeting. The white flesh is firm and a little juicy with a sweet and pleasant, sometimes strawberry-like flavour.

Wyken Pippin

Type: Dessert.
Origin: ?Wyken, nr Coventry, UK; also said to have been introduced from Holland, early 1700s.
Parentage: Unknown.
Flowering: Mid-season.
Other names: Airley, Alford Prize, Arley, Gerkin Pippin, German Nonpareil, Girkin Pippin, Pepin de Warwickshire, Pepin du Warwick, Pepping aus Warwickshire, Pepping von Wyken, Pheasant's Eye, Pippin du Warwick, Warwick Pippin, Warwickshire Pippin and White Moloscha.

The rounded to flattened fruits, around 6cm (2¼ in) across, are bright yellow-green with a dull orange flush and russeting that appears in spots. The creamy white flesh, tinged with green, is moderately firm, fine-textured and very juicy with a sweet and good aromatic flavour.

Note: Trees are generally healthy and crop freely. The fruits can be stored for two to three months.

Yellow Bellflower

The conical, somewhat irregular fruits, around 6cm (2¼in) across or more, are bright yellow-green with an orange-red flush and some spotting. The creamy white flesh is moderately firm and crisp with a sweet, slightly subacid flavour.

Note: Trees, which are vigorous and quick-growing, are suitable for training. They are resistant to leaf spots.

Type: Culinary and dessert.
Origin: Burlington County, NJ, USA, by 1817.
Parentage: Unknown.
Flowering: Early.
Other names: Belfiore giallo, Belfler zheltyi, Bell Flower, Belle Fleur jaune, Belle Flavoise, Belle Fleur, Belle Flower, Belle-Flavoise, Belle-Fleur Yellow, Belle-Flower, Bellefleur Yellow, Bellflower, Bishop's Pippin, Bishop's Pippin of Nova Scotia, Calville Metzger, Connecticut Seek-no-Further, Frumos galben, Gelber Bellefleur and Gelber Englischer Schönblühender.

Yellow Ingestrie

The rounded to square fruits, around 6cm (2¼in) across, are bright yellow-green sometimes tinged with a deeper yellow. The greenish yellow flesh is fine and tender with a rich and subacid vinous flavour.

Note: Trees are large and spreading and crop abundantly.

Left: This old English variety has very distinctive coloration.

Type: Dessert.
Origin: Wormsley Grange, Herefordshire, UK, *c.*1800.
Parentage: Orange Pippin (female) x Golden Pippin (male).
Flowering: Early.
Other names: d'Ingestrie jaune, Early Pippin, Early Yellow, Gelber Pepping von Ingestrie, Ingestrie, Ingestrie Jaune, Ingestrie Yellow, Little Golden Knob, Pomme d'Ingestrie Jaune, Summer Golden Pippin, White Pippin and Yellow Ingestrie Pippin.

Yorkshire Greening

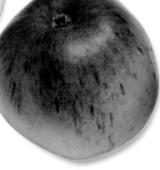

The flattened, very irregular fruits, up to around 7cm (2¾in) across or more, are bright green with a red flush and some striping. The creamy white flesh is firm, rather coarse-textured and somewhat dry with a very acid flavour.

Note: Trees are very hardy, performing well in difficult locations, and crop reliably. The fruits, which can be stored for up to two or three months, cook to a purée.

Type: Culinary.
Origin: ?Yorkshire, UK, recorded 1803.
Parentage: Unknown.
Flowering: Early.
Other names: Coate's, Coates, Coates', Coates' Greening, Goose Sauce, Grünling von Yorkshire, Seek-no-Farther, Seek-no-Further, Verte du Comte d'York, Yorkshire Goose Sauce and Yorkshire Greeting.

Zabergäu Renette

Type: Dessert.
Origin: Hausen an der Zaber, Baden-Württemberg, Germany, from seed sown in 1885.
Parentage: Unknown.
Flowering: Mid-season.
Other names: Graue Renette von Zabergäu, Hausener Graue Renette, Zabergäu, Zabergäu-Renette and Zabergäurenette.

The rounded fruits, around 6cm (2¼in) across, are bright yellow-green with heavy russeting over the whole surface. The creamy white flesh is firm, moderately fine-textured and fairly juicy with a rich, nutty flavour.

Note: This variety is a triploid. Fruits eaten straight from the tree taste of nettles. They can be stored for three months or more. Trees show good disease resistance.

Right: Fruits of this variety are notable for their uniform shape.

Zelyonka Kharkovskaya

Type: Dessert.
Origin: Russia, first half of the 1800s.
Parentage: Unknown.
Flowering: Mid-season.
Other names: Kharkovskaya zelyonka, Kharkowskaia zelenka, Zelenka, Zelenka Kharkovskaya and Zelyonka.

The rounded fruits, around 7cm (2¾in) across or more, are bright yellow-green with a red flush. The greenish white flesh is rather soft.

Note: This variety is not widely grown outside its country of origin but has been used in research programmes.

Zoete Ermgaard

Type: Dessert.
Origin: Netherlands, known since 1864.
Parentage: Unknown.
Flowering: Late.

Note: This variety is very hardy, so is suitable for growing in areas that experience hard frosts.

The slightly conical, rather uneven fruits, around 6cm (2¼in) across or more, are pale yellow-green with a strong pinkish red flush. The creamy white flesh is firm, crisp, coarse and dry with a sweet, slightly subacid flavour.

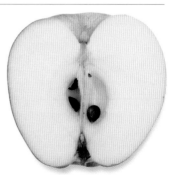

APPLE RECIPES

Apples come in a wide range of shapes, colours, flavours and textures so there's bound to be a fruit to suit your taste or need. Whether it's a tart, savoury appetizer or main course or an indulgently sweet dessert or after-dinner treat that you are after, the versatile apple is the perfect ingredient for so many tasty recipes. Some varieties such as Winesap or Bramley's Seedling are suitable for cooking with, while other crisp eating varieties such as Cortland or Granny Smith are ideal for juicing or eating raw grated in salads.

The apple recipes in this section are accompanied by clear, simple instructions. To start your meal, you could try a warming Curried Apple Soup or light Poached Apples with Berry Compote. There are a great variety of appley main dishes to choose from including Pumpkin and Apple Risotto, Spiced Pork Roast with Apple and Thyme Cream Sauce and Roast Goose with Apples, and delicious desserts range from Apple and Blackberry Crumble to Crunchy Apple and Almond Flan.

Above left: Apple fritters with fruit compote.
Above right: Apple-stuffed crêpes.
Left: Orchards provide the perfect shade for a picnic.

APPETIZERS, SALADS AND SIDES

The humble and inexpensive apple can be used to create all manner of mouth-watering hot or cold appetizers, salads and side dishes. From colourful and refreshing fruit soups to tart and tangy salads and accompaniments, there's a recipe to suit all tastes and occasions.

Apple and juniper soup

This is an excellent example of the delicious savoury fruit soups that are popular throughout northern Europe. The contrasting apple and juniper flavours in this recipe are particularly popular in Norway.

Serves 4
15ml/1 tbsp juniper berries
4 cardamom pods
3 whole allspice
1 small cinnamon stick
a bunch of fresh parsley
30ml/2 tbsp olive oil
3 cooking apples, peeled,
   cored and diced
2 celery sticks, finely chopped
2 shallots, chopped
2.5cm/1in piece fresh root ginger,
   finely chopped
1 litre/1¾ pints/4 cups light
   chicken stock
250ml/8fl oz/1 cup (hard) cider
250ml/8fl oz/1 cup double
   (heavy) cream
75ml/5 tbsp Armagnac (optional)
salt and ground black pepper
chopped fresh parsley, to garnish

1 Put the juniper berries, cardamom pods, allspice and cinnamon in a piece of muslin (cheesecloth) and tie together with string. Tie the parsley together.

2 Heat the oil in a pan, add the apples, celery, shallots and ginger, and season with salt and pepper. Place a piece of dampened baking parchment on top, cover the pan and cook gently for 10 minutes. Discard the parchment.

3 Add the stock and cider and stir well. Add the spices and parsley. Bring slowly to the boil, then lower the heat and simmer for 40 minutes. Remove the spices and parsley.

4 Pour the soup into a blender and blend until smooth, then sieve (strain) into a clean pan. Bring to the boil and add the cream and Armagnac, if using. Add salt and pepper if necessary. Serve hot, garnished with parsley.

Per portion Energy 406kcal/1677kJ; Protein 1.4g; Carbohydrate 8.5g, of which sugars 8.1g; Fat 39.2g, of which saturates 21.7g; Cholesterol 86mg; Calcium 48mg; Fibre 1.2g; Sodium 29mg.

Curried apple soup

Coconut milk replaces cream in this spicy soup for a smooth, rich texture.

Serves 4
50g/2oz/4 tbsp butter
2 shallots, finely chopped
1 cooking apple, peeled and chopped
10ml/2 tsp curry paste
30ml/2 tbsp plain (all-purpose) flour
1.25 litres/2¼ pints/5½ cups chicken stock
400ml/14fl oz can unsweetened
   coconut milk
salt and ground black pepper

To garnish
60ml/4 tbsp double (heavy) cream
chopped fresh parsley

1 Melt the butter in a pan, add the shallots and cook for about 5 minutes until soft. Add the apple and seasoning and cook for another 2 minutes.

2 Stir in the curry paste and flour and cook for 1–2 minutes. Remove from the heat and gradually stir in the stock. Return to the heat and, stirring all the time, cook until the sauce thickens. Simmer for 10 minutes.

3 Stir in the coconut milk and heat gently. Pour into bowls and garnish.

Per portion Energy 195kcal/812kJ; Protein 1.7g; Carbohydrate 14.3g, of which sugars 7.6g; Fat 15g, of which saturates 9.2g; Cholesterol 37mg; Calcium 66mg; Fibre 1.3g; Sodium 200mg.

Parsnip and apple soup

The Romans introduced apple orchards to England. Since then the country has been proud of its wonderful range of apples, and many fine apple juices are now available, often made from single varieties. For this soup, choose a fairly sharp-tasting juice – it will complement the sweetness of the parsnips and the warmth of the spices.

Serves 4–6
25g/1oz/2 tbsp butter
1 medium onion, finely chopped
1 garlic clove, finely chopped
500g/1¼lb parsnips, peeled and
    thinly sliced
5ml/1 tsp curry paste or powder
300ml/½ pint/1¼ cups apple juice
600ml/1 pint/2½ cups vegetable stock
300ml/½ pint/1¼ cups milk
salt and ground black pepper
thick natural (plain) yogurt, and chopped
    fresh herbs such as mint or parsley,
    to garnish

1 Melt the butter in a large pan and add the onion, garlic and parsnips. Cook gently, without browning, for about 10 minutes, stirring often to avoid sticking.

2 Add the curry paste or powder and cook, stirring, for 1 minute.

3 Add the juice and stock, bring to the boil, cover and simmer gently for about 20 minutes until the parsnips are soft.

4 Process or blend the mixture until smooth and return it to the pan.

5 Add the milk and season to taste with salt and pepper.

6 Reheat the soup gently and serve topped with a spoonful of yogurt and a sprinkling of herbs.

Per portion Energy 130kcal/548kJ; Protein 3.4g; Carbohydrate 18.5g, of which sugars 12.6g; Fat 5.3g, of which saturates 2.9g; Cholesterol 12mg; Calcium 101mg; Fibre 4g; Sodium 56mg.

Carrot and apple soup

Combining the sweetness of carrots with the fruity taste of apples creates a wonderful soup that you can enjoy all year round.

Serves 4
50g/2oz/¼ cup butter
1 onion, roughly chopped
1 garlic clove, roughly chopped
500g/1¼lb carrots, roughly chopped
1 large cooking apple, peeled, cored
    and roughly chopped
100ml/3½fl oz/scant ½ cup white wine
500ml/17fl oz/generous 2 cups
    vegetable stock
100ml/3½fl oz/scant ½ cup apple juice
salt and ground white pepper
200ml/7fl oz/scant 1 cup single
    (light) cream
100ml/3½fl oz/scant ½ cup crème fraîche
15ml/1 tbsp dry-fried pumpkin seeds
    and 5ml/1 tsp fresh chives, to garnish

1 Melt the butter in a pan. Add the onion and cook for 5 minutes until softened. Add the garlic and cook for a few minutes more. Stir in the carrots and the apple.

2 Add the wine, stock and apple juice. Season with salt and pepper. Bring to the boil, then simmer for 15 minutes. Add the cream and the crème fraîche and bring to the boil again.

3 Blend the soup with a hand blender. If it seems too thick, add some more stock. Serve with a sprinkling of pumpkin seeds and chopped chives.

Per portion Energy 341kcal/1412kJ; Protein 3g; Carbohydrate 18.2g, of which sugars 16.5g; Fat 27.2g, of which saturates 16.8g; Cholesterol 71mg; Calcium 84mg; Fibre 3.7g; Sodium 150mg.

Apple and cranberry soup

Fruit soups are mostly summer dishes, made with berries that are in season then. This tasty soup, however, is better suited to later in the year when cranberries are readily available, and it is perfect for festive meals around Christmas and New Year.

Serves 6
600g/1lb 6oz/5¼ cups cranberries
200ml/7fl oz/ scant 1 cup water
115g/4oz/generous ½ cup caster (superfine) sugar
350g/12oz cooking apples, peeled and finely grated
15ml/1 tbsp cornflour (cornstarch)
100ml/3½ fl oz/scant ½ cup sour cream

1 Put the cranberries in a large pan, add the water and bring to the boil. Simmer gently for 10 minutes, or until the cranberries are soft. Allow the cranberries to cool a little.

2 Transfer the cranberries and liquid to a food processor or blender and pulse to a purée. Pass the purée through a sieve (strainer), pressing down with the back of a spoon. Discard the fruit pulp and keep the strained fruit and juices. Add the sugar, put back in the pan and gently bring back to a simmer.

3 Add the grated apples to the cranberry mixture. Mix the cornflour with 30ml/2 tbsp water to make a smooth paste, then stir into the soup. Simmer, stirring, for 5 minutes. Allow the soup to cool, then transfer to a bowl and chill. Ladle the cold soup into bowls and add a dollop of sour cream to each serving. Swirl the sour cream with a skewer to decorate.

Per portion Energy 130kcal/552kJ; Protein 1.2g; Carbohydrate 25.1g, of which sugars 22.8g; Fat 3.5g, of which saturates 2.1g; Cholesterol 10mg; Calcium 35mg; Fibre 2.4g; Sodium 12mg.

Apple, kohlrabi and caraway soup

This chunky apple and kohlrabi soup is absolutely delicious, having a delightfully sweet edge.

Serves 4–6
10g/¼oz/½ tbsp butter
1 kohlrabi, diced
2 carrots, diced
2 celery sticks, diced
1 yellow (bell) pepper, seeded and diced
1 tomato, diced
1.5 litres/2½ pints/6¼ cups vegetable stock
800g/1¾lb crisp, tart eating apples, peeled
15ml/1 tbsp sugar
2.5ml/½ tsp ground caraway seeds
salt and ground black pepper
45ml/3 tbsp sour cream
a small bunch of parsley, leaves chopped

1 Put the butter in a large pan and melt over medium heat. Add the diced vegetables and sauté for 3–4 minutes, or until soft. Season to taste.

2 Add the vegetable stock and bring to the boil, then reduce the heat to low and simmer for 1 hour.

3 Grate the apples and add to the simmering soup, followed by the sugar and the caraway seeds. Cook for a further 15 minutes and adjust the seasoning.

4 Stir in the sour cream and sprinkle with the parsley to garnish. Serve hot.

Per portion Energy 104kcal/442kJ; Protein 1.6g; Carbohydrate 18.1g, of which sugars 17.9g; Fat 3.4g, of which saturates 1.9g; Cholesterol 8mg; Calcium 69mg; Fibre 4.6g; Sodium 44mg.

Apples with bacon

In this classic Danish open sandwich, the sweet combination of apples and onions mixed with crisp, salty bacon is both rich and satisfying. Apples appear in many savoury dishes in Denmark, from the classic pork loin stuffed with prunes and apples, to poached apple halves filled with currant jelly, served as a side dish with roast pork.

Serves 4

8 unsmoked streaky (fatty) bacon rashers (strips)
75g/3oz/1 cup finely chopped onion
2 firm apples, peeled and chopped
25g/1oz/2 tbsp salted butter, softened
2 slices rye bread
2 leaves round (butterhead) lettuce
4 parsley sprigs, to garnish

Cook's tip
Choosing crisp, tart eating apples for this recipe will give the best results.

1 Fry the bacon rashers over a medium-high heat until they crispen; drain the bacon on kitchen paper, leaving the fat in the pan.

2 Cook the finely chopped onion in the reserved bacon fat for about 5–7 minutes, until transparent but not browned.

3 Add the chopped apples, and continue cooking for a further 5 minutes, until tender.

4 Crumble half the bacon into the apple mixture.

5 Butter the slices of bread to the edges, top with the lettuce leaves and cut each slice in half. Leaving one curl of lettuce visible on each piece, spoon the apple and bacon mixture on to the lettuce, dividing it evenly among the sandwiches.

6 Break the four reserved bacon rashers in half, and place two pieces on each sandwich. Garnish with parsley sprigs, and serve warm.

Per portion Energy 215kcal/895kJ; Protein 9.8g; Carbohydrate 13.9g, of which sugars 8g; Fat 13.7g, of which saturates 6.4g; Cholesterol 40mg; Calcium 21mg; Fibre 2g; Sodium 883mg.

Black pudding with apple and potato

Black pudding has come a long way from its humble origins. Traditionally grilled or fried and served as part of a full English breakfast, black pudding now features on many a contemporary restaurant menu. Made in West Cork, Ireland, and widely available, Clonakilty black pudding is especially popular.

Serves 4

4 large potatoes, peeled
45ml/3 tbsp olive oil
8 slices black pudding (blood sausage), such as Clonakilty
115g/4oz cultivated mushrooms, such as oyster or shiitake
2 eating apples, peeled, cored and cut into wedges
15ml/1 tbsp sherry vinegar or wine vinegar
15g/1oz/2 tbsp butter
salt and ground black pepper

1 Grate the potatoes, putting them straight into a bowl of water as you grate them. Drain and squeeze out the excess moisture.

2 Heat 30ml/2 tbsp olive oil in a large non-stick frying pan, add the grated potatoes and season. Press the potatoes into the pan with your hands.

3 Cook the potatoes until browned, then turn over and cook the other side. Slide the cooked potatoes on to a warm plate.

4 Heat the remaining oil and sauté the black pudding and mushrooms together for a few minutes. Remove from the pan and keep warm.

5 Add the apple wedges to the frying pan and gently sauté to colour them golden brown. Add the sherry or wine vinegar to the apples, and boil up the juices. Add the butter, stir with a wooden spatula until it has melted and season to taste with salt and ground black pepper.

6 Cut the potato cake into wedges and divide among four warmed plates. Arrange the black pudding and cooked mushrooms on the bed of potato cake, pour over the apples and the warm juices and serve immediately.

> **Variation**
> If you are not keen on black pudding, you could try replacing it with mini burgers made from minced (ground) pork, or some sliced spicy sausages.

Per portion Energy 247kcal/1034kJ; Protein 4.2g; Carbohydrate 28.8g, of which sugars 5.4g; Fat 13.6g, of which saturates 4g; Cholesterol 13mg; Calcium 16mg; Fibre 2.4g; Sodium 132mg.

Beetroot, apple and potato salad

This attractive salad is from Finland, where it is served on Christmas Eve, just as the festive excitement mounts.

Serves 4
1 eating apple
3 cooked potatoes, finely diced
2 large gherkins, finely diced
3 cooked beetroot (beets), finely diced
3 cooked carrots, finely diced
1 onion, finely chopped
500ml/17fl oz/generous 2 cups double (heavy) cream
3 hard-boiled eggs, roughly chopped
15ml/1 tbsp chopped fresh parsley
salt and ground white pepper

1 Cut the apple into small dice. Put in a bowl and add the potatoes, gherkins, beetroot, carrots and onion and season with salt and pepper. Carefully mix together and spoon into individual serving glasses or bowls.

2 Mix any beetroot juice into the cream to flavour and give it a pinkish colour, then spoon over the vegetables and apple. Sprinkle the chopped eggs and parsley on top before serving.

Variation

Stir in ½ finely chopped salted herring fillet or 2 finely chopped anchovy fillets to the mixture with the parsley to add an extra dimension to the dish. Omit the added salt.

Per portion Energy 717kcal/2959kJ; Protein 8.5g; Carbohydrate 11g, of which sugars 10.2g; Fat 71.5g, of which saturates 42.9g; Cholesterol 314mg; Calcium 114mg; Fibre 2.3g; Sodium 132mg.

Beetroot and apple salad

These two typically English ingredients complement each other well to make a pretty salad, with the apple pieces turning pink on contact with the beetroot juices. The crispness of the apple contrasts well with the soft texture of the cooked beetroot.

Serves 4
6 beetroot (beets)
30ml/2 tbsp mayonnaise
30ml/2 tbsp thick natural (plain) yogurt
2 crisp eating apples
a small handful of chopped fresh chives
salt and ground black pepper
salad leaves and/or watercress sprigs, to serve

1 Wash the beetroot gently, without breaking their skins. Trim the stalks until very short but do not remove them completely. Put into a pan and cover well with water. Bring to the boil and simmer gently for 1–2 hours, depending on their size, or until soft throughout (check by inserting a sharp knife into the centre). Drain and leave to cool. When cold, remove the skins and cut into small cubes.

2 In a large bowl, stir together the mayonnaise and yogurt.

3 Peel the apples, remove their cores and cut into small cubes.

4 Add the beetroot, apples and two-thirds of the chives to the mayonnaise mixture and toss until well coated, seasoning to taste with salt and pepper. Leave to stand for 10–20 minutes.

5 Pile on to a serving dish. Add salad leaves and/or watercress sprigs and sprinkle with the remaining chives.

Per portion Energy 191kcal/793kJ; Protein 4.1g; Carbohydrate 9.5g, of which sugars 8.8g; Fat 15.5g, of which saturates 1.6g; Cholesterol 0mg; Calcium 54mg; Fibre 2.7g; Sodium 58mg.

Apple and leek salad

Fresh and tangy, this simple salad of sliced leeks and apples with a lemon and honey dressing can be served with a range of cold meats as part of a summer meal. For the best result, make sure you use slim young leeks and tart, crisp apples.

Serves 4

2 slim leeks, white part only,
    washed thoroughly
2 large eating apples
15ml/1 tbsp chopped fresh parsley
juice of 1 lemon
15ml/1 tbsp clear honey
salt and ground black pepper

1 Thinly slice the leeks. Peel and core the apples, then slice thinly.

2 Put in a large serving bowl and add the parsley, lemon juice, honey and seasoning to taste.

3 Toss well, then leave to stand in a cool place for about an hour, to allow the flavours to blend together.

Per portion Energy 59kcal/252kJ; Protein 1.9g; Carbohydrate 12.5g, of which sugars 11.8g; Fat 0.6g, of which saturates 0.1g; Cholesterol 0mg; Calcium 27mg; Fibre 3.4g; Sodium 4mg.

Sauerkraut salad with apple and cranberries

This sauerkraut salad is a Russian classic. Cabbage is a staple ingredient in Russia and the best soured cabbage can be bought in the market halls, where you are invited to taste both the cabbage and the brine. It is not unusual for a customer to taste up to ten different kinds before making a decision.

Serves 4–6

500g/1¼lb sauerkraut
2 red apples
100–200g/3¾–7oz/scant 1–1¾ cups
    fresh cranberries or lingonberries
30ml/2 tbsp sugar
60–75ml/4–5 tbsp sunflower oil
2–3 sprigs fresh parsley, to garnish

1 Put the sauerkraut in a colander and drain thoroughly. Taste, and if you find it is too sour, rinse it under cold running water then drain well.

2 Put the sauerkraut in a large bowl. Slice the apples or cut into wedges. Add the apples and the cranberries or lingonberries to the sauerkraut. Sprinkle over the sugar, pour the oil on top and mix all the ingredients well together.

3 To serve, turn the sauerkraut into a serving bowl and garnish with the parsley sprigs.

> **Cook's Tip**
> Cover the salad and chill for a few hours to allow the flavours to develop.

Per portion Energy 105kcal/437kJ; Protein 1.3g; Carbohydrate 8.8g, of which sugars 8.8g; Fat 7.4g, of which saturates 0.9g; Cholesterol 0mg; Calcium 49mg; Fibre 3.1g; Sodium 493mg.

Herring, ham, apple and beetroot salad

This colourful salad looks stunning and makes a perfect light snack.

Serves 4
2 fillets of pickled herring, drained
    and diced
1 large potato, boiled and diced
2 large cooked beetroot (beets),
    peeled and diced
1 small onion, grated
2 medium tart apples, cored and
    cut into thin wedges
2 gherkins, chopped
200g/7oz thick piece of ham, diced
2 thinly sliced hard-boiled eggs
salt and ground black pepper
30ml/2 tbsp finely chopped fresh dill,
    to garnish

For the dressing
100ml/3½fl oz/scant ½ cup sour cream
15ml/1 tbsp vinegar (any kind)
15ml/1 tbsp wholegrain mustard
1 medium beetroot (beet), finely grated
5ml/1 tsp creamed horseradish

Variation
Add a small amount of freshly grated
horseradish root for a little extra heat.

1 To make the dressing, put the sour cream in a bowl and add the vinegar, mustard, grated beetroot and horseradish. Season to taste and combine well. Set aside.

2 Put the herring in a large bowl with the potato, beetroot, onion, apples, gherkins and ham. Season and mix together gently.

3 Add the dressing to the mixed salad and gently toss together to combine.

4 Transfer the salad to serving bowls, top each with the sliced hard-boiled eggs and garnish with dill, then serve.

Per portion Energy 355kcal/1495kJ; Protein 25g; Carbohydrate 30.8g, of which sugars 22.2g; Fat 15.4g, of which saturates 4.5g; Cholesterol 160mg; Calcium 84mg; Fibre 4.2g; Sodium 1169mg.

Carrot and apple salad

This refreshingly sweet and fragrant salad looks colourful and tastes good. Adding the lemon juice will help the grated carrot, apple and ginger to keep their natural brightness.

Serves 1
90g/3½oz carrots, peeled and
    coarsely grated
2 eating apples, coarsely grated
2.5cm/1in piece fresh root ginger,
    peeled and finely grated
juice of ½ lemon or 15ml/1 tbsp
    cider vinegar
5ml/1 tsp clear honey
a handful of alfalfa sprouts or other
    beansprouts
5ml/1 tsp sesame seeds, to garnish

1 In a large bowl, mix together the carrots, apples, ginger, lemon juice or cider vinegar and honey.

2 Place in a small bowl and press down, then turn out on to a plate to make a neat 'castle'. Top this with the alfalfa sprouts and sprinkle with sesame seeds to garnish.

Variation
Try replacing the apples with pears, and the carrots with grated courgette (zucchini). This cooling choice will give extra vitamin C.

Per portion Energy 194kcal/818kJ; Protein 3g; Carbohydrate 41g of which sugars 39g; Fat 3g of which saturates 0g; Cholesterol 0mg; Calcium 70mg; Fibre 6.6g; Sodium 36mg.

Courgettes and apples with hazelnut sauce

This recipe originates from Turkey, where steamed, fried, grilled or roasted vegetables are often served with a nut sauce, *tarator*. In this recipe the courgettes and apples are roasted, but they could be cooked by any method, such as grilling or steaming. This dish can be served as a side dish to grilled and roasted meats, or as a hot *meze* dish.

Serves 4
2 firm, fat courgettes (zucchini)
2 sweet, firm red, pink, or yellow apples
30–45ml/2–3 tbsp olive oil
15–30ml/1–2 tbsp chopped roasted
   hazelnuts, to garnish

For the nut sauce
115g/4oz/⅔ cup hazelnuts
1–2 garlic cloves
30ml/2 tbsp olive oil
juice of 1 lemon
15ml/1 tbsp clear honey
salt and ground black pepper

1 Preheat the oven to 180°C/350°F/ Gas 4.

2 Using a vegetable peeler, partially peel the courgettes in stripes. Slice them on the diagonal. Quarter and core the apples then cut each quarter into two or three segments.

3 Place the courgette and apple slices in an ovenproof dish and pour over the olive oil.

4 Put into the oven and roast for 35–40 minutes, or until golden brown.

5 Meanwhile, make the nut sauce. Using a mortar and pestle, or a food processor, pound the hazelnuts with the garlic to form a thick paste.

6 Gradually beat in the oil and lemon juice, until the mixture is quite creamy. Sweeten with the clear honey, and season to taste.

7 Arrange the roasted courgettes and apples on a serving dish and drizzle the nut sauce over them. Sprinkle the roasted hazelnuts over the top and serve while still warm.

Variations
You can serve other vegetables this way, including whole Mediterranean (bell) peppers, sliced aubergine (eggplant), pumpkin and squash, as well as fruits, such as plums.

Per portion Energy 365kcal/1513kJ; Protein 6.6g; Carbohydrate 13.3g, of which sugars 12.6g; Fat 32.1g, of which saturates 3.2g; Cholesterol 0mg; Calcium 74mg; Fibre 4.2g; Sodium 5mg.

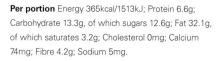

Poached apples with cranberry compote

The small trailing cranberries that grow in Europe are paler than their more robust American cousins and have a slightly different flavour. Here, combined with poached apples, they make a unique starter or side dish.

Serves 4
2 firm, sharp eating apples
45ml/3 tbsp sugar
500ml/17fl oz/generous
  2 cups water
juice of ½ lemon

For the berry compote
250g/9oz/2½ cups cranberries
60–90ml/4–6 tbsp water
150g/5oz/¾ cup sugar, or to taste
5–10ml/1–2 tsp lemon juice

1 Peel the apples and cut them in half. Cut away the stem and core from each with a paring knife and use a spoon to enlarge the core space and create a cavity.

2 In a pan large enough to hold the apple halves in a single layer, heat the sugar with the water. Gradually bring to the boil, stirring occasionally, to make a syrup.

3 Stir in the lemon juice. Reduce the heat and place the apple halves in the pan, so they are covered with syrup.

4 Cover and simmer for about 20 minutes or until they are tender but still hold their shape.

5 Lift out the apples with a slotted spoon and drain on a wire rack over a baking sheet.

6 To make the berry compote, rinse the berries and place them in a pan with the water. Add the sugar and bring to the boil. Reduce the heat, cover and simmer for 10 minutes or until the berries have softened. Stir occasionally and skim off any foam that rises to the surface.

7 Add 5ml/1 tsp of the lemon juice, taste and adjust for sweetness. If necessary, add more sugar, heating until it dissolves.

8 Transfer the apples to a platter, with the cavities uppermost. Fill them with the berry compote. To serve warm, reheat the apples in a shallow pan for about 5 minutes. Offer any remaining berry compote in a separate bowl.

Per portion Energy 250kcal/1069kJ; Protein 0.8g; Carbohydrate 65.6g, of which sugars 65.6g; Fat 0.2g, of which saturates 0g; Cholesterol 0mg; Calcium 33mg; Fibre 2.7g; Sodium 6mg.

MAIN DISHES

Apples make a fantastically diverse contribution to numerous main courses and are often used in savoury cooking to add flavour and texture. A popular accompaniment to pork, apples also go surprisingly well with duck and game birds, as well as many fish and vegetarian dishes.

Pilaff stuffed apples

Vegetables and fruit stuffed with an aromatic pilaff are a great favourite in the summer months. This recipe is for stuffed apples, but you can easily use it to make an impressive medley of different stuffed fruit and vegetables for a buffet or a summer lunch.

Serves 4
4 cooking apples, or any firm,
    sour apple of your choice
30ml/2 tbsp olive oil
juice of ½ lemon
10ml/2 tsp sugar
salt and ground black pepper

For the filling
30ml/2 tbsp olive oil
a little butter
1 onion, finely chopped
2 garlic cloves
30ml/2 tbsp pine nuts
30ml/2 tbsp currants, soaked in
    warm water for 5–10 minutes
    and drained
5–10ml/1–2 tsp ground cinnamon
5–10ml/1–2 tsp ground allspice
5ml/1 tsp sugar
175g/6oz/scant 1 cup short grain rice,
    thoroughly rinsed and drained
1 bunch each of fresh flat leaf parsley
    and dill, finely chopped
1 lemon and a few fresh mint or basil
    leaves, to serve

1 Make the filling. Heat the oil and butter in a heavy pan, stir in the chopped onion and garlic and cook until they soften. Add the pine nuts and currants and cook until the nuts turn golden.

2 Stir in the spices, sugar and rice, and stir to combine thoroughly. Pour in enough water to cover the rice – roughly 1–2cm/½–¾in above the grains – and bring to the boil.

3 Taste, then season the mixture with salt and pepper to taste and stir to combine. Lower the heat and simmer for about 10–12 minutes, until almost all the water has been absorbed.

4 Toss in the chopped herbs, stir to combine and remove from the heat. Cover the pan with a dry, clean dish towel and the lid, and leave the rice to steam for 5 minutes.

5 Preheat the oven to 200°C/400°F/ Gas 6. Using a knife, cut the stalk ends off the apples and set them aside to use as lids.

6 Carefully core each apple, removing some of the flesh to create a cavity that is large enough to stuff.

7 Take spoonfuls of the rice and pack it into the apples. Replace the lids and stand the apples, upright and tightly packed, in a small baking dish.

8 In a jug (pitcher), mix together 100ml/3½fl oz/scant ½ cup water with the oil, lemon juice and sugar. Pour over and around the apples, then bake for 30–40 minutes, until the apples are tender and the juices are caramelized.

9 Serve the baked apples with lemon wedges and a sprinkling of mint or basil leaves to garnish.

Per portion Energy 382kcal/1595kJ; Protein 5g; Carbohydrate 54.1g, of which sugars 18.8g; Fat 16.5g, of which saturates 1.9g; Cholesterol 0mg; Calcium 26mg; Fibre 2.1g; Sodium 4mg.

Pumpkin and apple risotto

Pumpkin and other squash are very popular in the winter months. If pumpkins are out of season, use butternut or onion squash – the flavours will be slightly different, but they both work well.

Serves 3–4
225g/8oz pumpkin flesh or
    butternut squash
1 cooking apple
120ml/4fl oz/½ cup water
25g/1oz/2 tbsp butter
25ml/1½ tbsp olive oil
1 onion, finely chopped
1 garlic clove, crushed
275g/10oz/1½ cups risotto rice,
    such as Vialone Nano
175ml/6fl oz/¾ cup fruity white wine
900ml–1 litre/1½–1¾ pints/3¾–4 cups
    simmering vegetable stock
75g/3oz/1 cup freshly grated
    Parmesan cheese
salt and ground black pepper

1 Cut the pumpkin into small pieces. Peel, core and roughly chop the apple. Place the pumpkin and apple chunks in a pan and pour in the water. Bring to the boil, then simmer for about 15–20 minutes until the pumpkin is very tender. Drain, return the pumpkin mixture to the pan and add half the butter.

2 Mash the mixture roughly with a fork to break up any overly large pieces, but keep the mixture quite chunky. Heat the oil and remaining butter in a pan and fry the onion and garlic until the onion is soft.

3 Add the rice. Cook, stirring constantly, over a medium heat for 2 minutes until it is coated in oil and the grains are slightly translucent.

4 Add the wine and stir into the rice. When all the liquid has been absorbed, begin to add the stock one ladleful at a time, making sure each addition has been absorbed before adding the next ladleful. This should take approximately 20 minutes.

5 When roughly two ladlefuls of stock are left, add the pumpkin and apple mixture together with another addition of stock. Continue to cook, stirring well and adding the rest of the stock, until the risotto is very creamy.

6 Stir in the Parmesan cheese, adjust the seasoning and serve immediately.

Per portion Energy 439kcal/1831kJ; Protein 13.2g; Carbohydrate 59.1g, of which sugars 3.6g; Fat 13.3g, of which saturates 7.4g; Cholesterol 32mg; Calcium 264mg; Fibre 1.1g; Sodium 245mg.

Herring fillets in oatmeal with apples

Although traditionally herrings were eaten salted or smoked, herrings are now more likely to be eaten fresh. The tartness of the apple rings in this dish is a perfect accompaniment to the oily fish.

Serves 4
8 herring fillets
seasoned flour, for coating
1 egg, beaten
115g/4oz/1 cup fine pinhead
    oatmeal or oatflakes
vegetable oil, for frying
2 eating apples
25g/1oz/2 tbsp butter

1 Wash the fish and pat dry with kitchen paper. Check that all bones have been removed.

2 Toss the herring fillets in the seasoned flour, and then dip them in the beaten egg and coat them evenly with the oatmeal or oatflakes.

3 Heat a little oil in a heavy frying pan and fry the fillets, a few at a time, until golden brown. Drain on kitchen paper and keep warm.

4 Core the apples, but do not peel. Slice them thinly. In another pan, melt the butter and fry the apple slices until softened, then serve the herring fillets with the apple slices.

Per portion Energy 420kcal/1754kJ; Protein 26.5g; Carbohydrate 24.3g, of which sugars 3.4g; Fat 24.8g, of which saturates 7.6g; Cholesterol 120mg; Calcium 97mg; Fibre 2.6g; Sodium 209mg.

Smoked haddock with apple and vegetables

This light recipe is full of the fresh flavours of sautéed apples, leeks and root vegetables to complement the poached smoked haddock. Smoked cod could be used instead.

Serves 4

5ml/1 tsp caraway seeds
5ml/1 tsp butter
2 leeks, finely sliced lengthways
3–4 thin carrots, finely sliced
1 parsnip, finely sliced lengthways
2 cooking apples, peeled and sliced in wedges
250ml/8fl oz/1 cup vegetable stock
4 fillets smoked haddock, 250g/9oz each, bones removed
salt and ground black pepper
30ml/2 tbsp finely chopped fresh parsley, to garnish

> **Cook's Tip**
> A light horseradish cream is a delicious accompaniment to this dish.

1 Put the caraway seeds in a dry pan over a medium-high heat and toast them for 1 minute, or until they release their aroma. Heat the butter in a deep pan over a medium-high heat and add the leeks, carrots, parsnip and apples. Season to taste and add the caraway seeds. Turn the heat to medium and cook, stirring gently, for 3–5 minutes.

2 Add the stock and reduce the heat to low. Cook for 10–12 more minutes. Add the fish fillets to the stock, making sure that they are covered by the stock and vegetables. Cook for a further 5 minutes.

3 Remove the fish, using a slotted spoon, and arrange in a deep serving plate. Spoon over some of the cooked vegetables and cooking liquid. Sprinkle with the chopped parsley and serve.

Per portion Energy 323kcal/1368kJ; Protein 51.1g; Carbohydrate 21.8g, of which sugars 17.2g; Fat 4.1g, of which saturates 1.2g; Cholesterol 93mg; Calcium 152mg; Fibre 8.3g; Sodium 1947mg.

Haggis, potato and apple pie

Haggis is traditionally served with 'neeps and tatties' (mashed swede and mashed potatoes), but here is another way to serve your haggis, with just a little refinement and the extra sumptuousness of puff pastry. Apple combines very well with haggis as its tart and sweet taste cuts through the richness of the meat.

Serves 4
450g/1lb potatoes
1 garlic clove, crushed with 1 tsp salt
freshly grated nutmeg
400g/14oz ready-made puff pastry
300g/11oz haggis
2 cooking apples, peeled and cored
1 egg, beaten
salt and ground black pepper

1 Preheat the oven to 220°C/425°F/ Gas 7. Peel and slice the potatoes and mix with the crushed garlic. Season with a little freshly grated nutmeg and salt and ground black pepper.

2 Roll out the puff pastry into two discs, one about 25cm/10in in diameter and the other a little larger.

3 Place the smaller pastry disc on a baking tray and spread half the potatoes over it, leaving a rim of about 2cm/¾in all the way round.

4 Cut the haggis open and crumble the meat in a layer to cover the top of the sliced potatoes. Finely slice the apples into circles and spread all over the haggis. Then top the apples with the rest of the potatoes.

5 Brush the egg all around the exposed pastry rim, then place the other pastry circle on top, pushing down on the rim to seal. Use a fork to tidy up the edges and then press down around the edge again to create a firm seal. Leave to rest for 10 minutes.

6 Brush over with more egg and bake the pie in the preheated oven for 10 minutes to set the pastry. Then reduce the oven temperature to 200°C/400°F/ Gas 6 and bake for a further 40 minutes until evenly browned and cooked. Serve in slices with broccoli and mustard.

Variation
You could also use a tart variety of eating apple, such as Granny Smith.

Per portion Energy 698kcal/2919kJ; Protein 15.8g; Carbohydrate 72.9g, of which sugars 6.1g; Fat 41.2g, of which saturates 5.8g; Cholesterol 68mg; Calcium 88mg; Fibre 1.9g; Sodium 901mg.

German sausages with apple sauerkraut

These finger-length Bratwurst sausages taste delicious with sauerkraut and sourdough bread.

Serves 4
25g/1oz/2 tbsp butter
50g/2oz bacon, diced
1 onion, chopped
500g/1¼lb canned sauerkraut
3 allspice berries
3 bay leaves
2.5ml/½ tsp caraway seeds
200ml/7fl oz/scant 1 cup apple juice
1 apple, peeled, cored and diced
2 carrots, grated
5ml/1 tsp potato flour (potato starch)
30ml/2 tbsp vegetable oil
24 bratwurst sausages
salt, ground white pepper and sugar
chopped fresh parsley, to garnish
medium-hot mustard and sourdough
   bread, to serve

1 Heat the butter in a large pan over medium heat and gently fry the bacon and onion for about 3 minutes. Add the sauerkraut, the spices and the apple juice. Cook for 30 minutes, stirring occasionally and adding more apple juice if needed. Add the diced apple and grated carrots and cook for a further 5 minutes.

2 Blend the potato flour to a smooth paste with a little apple juice or water and stir it into the sauerkraut. As it comes back to the boil, the remaining juices will thicken and the sauerkraut will become shiny. Season to taste with salt, pepper and sugar, then spoon into a serving dish and keep warm.

3 Heat the oil in a frying pan over high heat, and fry the sausages for 6–10 minutes, turning frequently, until they are browned on all sides and cooked through. Arrange the sausages on top of the sauerkraut and garnish with chopped parsley. Serve with mustard and slices of sourdough bread.

Per portion Energy 644kcal/2675kJ; Protein 18.6g; Carbohydrate 34g, of which sugars 17.5g; Fat 49.1g, of which saturates 19.8g; Cholesterol 81mg; Calcium 159mg; Fibre 5.2g; Sodium 2207mg.

Braised sausages with onions, celeriac and apple

For this recipe, choose your favourite good-quality sausages, such as classic pork, Cumberland, duck or wild boar.

Serves 4
30ml/2 tbsp vegetable oil
8 meaty sausages
2 onions, sliced
15ml/1 tbsp plain (all-purpose) flour
400ml/14fl oz/1⅔ cups dry (hard) cider
350g/12oz celeriac, cut into chunks
15ml/1 tbsp chopped fresh sage
15ml/1 tbsp Worcestershire sauce
2 small cooking apples, cored
salt and ground black pepper

1 Preheat the oven to 180°C/350°F/ Gas 4. Heat the oil in a frying pan, add the sausages and fry for 5 minutes. Transfer the sausages to an ovenproof dish and drain any excess oil from the pan to leave 15ml/1 tbsp. Add the onions and cook for a few minutes, stirring occasionally, until softened and turning golden.

2 Stir in the flour, then gradually add the cider and bring to the boil, stirring. Add the celeriac and stir in the sage, Worcestershire sauce and seasoning. Pour the cider and celeriac mixture over the sausages. Cover, put into the hot oven and cook for 30 minutes, or until the celeriac is soft.

3 Slice the apples, then stir into the casserole. Cover and cook for a further 10–15 minutes. Serve hot.

Per portion Energy 508kcal/2114kJ; Protein 12.7g; Carbohydrate 29.3g, of which sugars 13.6g; Fat 35.8g, of which saturates 12.3g; Cholesterol 45mg; Calcium 131mg; Fibre 3.3g; Sodium 1019mg.

Bacon chops with apple and cider sauce

Thick bacon or pork chops can be used in this recipe, which tastes great with lots of creamy mashed potatoes.

Serves 4
15ml/1 tbsp vegetable oil
4 bacon chops
1 or 2 cooking apples
a knob (pat) of butter
1 or 2 garlic cloves, finely chopped
5ml/1 tsp sugar
150ml/¼ pint/⅔ cup dry (hard) cider
5ml/1 tsp cider vinegar
15ml/1 tbsp wholegrain mustard
10ml/2 tsp chopped fresh thyme
salt and ground black pepper
sprigs of thyme, to garnish

1 Heat the oil in a large heavy frying pan, over a medium heat, and cook the chops for 10–15 minutes, browning well on both sides.

2 Peel, core and slice the apples. Remove the chops from the pan and keep warm. Add the butter and apples to the pan and cook until the juices begin to brown.

3 Add the finely chopped garlic and sugar, and cook for 1 minute, then stir in the cider, cider vinegar, mustard and chopped thyme. Boil for a few minutes until reduced to a saucy consistency.

4 Season to taste and place the chops on warmed serving plates. Garnish with the thyme sprigs and serve.

Per portion Energy 285kcal/1190kJ; Protein 26.4g; Carbohydrate 6.5g, of which sugars 6.5g; Fat 16.1g, of which saturates 5.4g; Cholesterol 40mg; Calcium 17mg; Fibre 0.8g; Sodium 1.34g

Noisettes of pork with creamy Calvados sauce

This dish gives the impression of being far more difficult to prepare than it really is, so it is ideal as part of a formal menu for entertaining guests.

Serves 4
30ml/2 tbsp plain (all-purpose) flour
4 noisettes of pork, about 175g/6oz each, firmly tied
25g/1oz/2 tbsp butter
4 baby leeks, finely sliced
5ml/1 tsp mustard seeds, coarsely crushed
30ml/2 tbsp Calvados
150ml/¼ pint/⅔ cup dry white wine
2 Golden Delicious apples, peeled, cored and sliced
150ml/¼ pint/⅔ cup double (heavy) cream
30ml/2 tbsp chopped fresh parsley
salt and ground black pepper

1 Place the flour in a bowl and add plenty of seasoning. Turn the noisettes in the flour to coat them lightly.

2 Melt the butter in a heavy frying pan and cook the noisettes until golden on both sides. Remove from the pan and set aside.

3 Add the leeks to the fat remaining in the pan and cook for 5 minutes. Stir in the mustard seeds and pour in the Calvados, then carefully ignite it to burn off the alcohol. When the flames have died down pour in the wine and replace the pork. Cook gently for 10 minutes, turning the pork frequently.

4 Add the sliced apples and double cream and simmer for 5 minutes, or until the apples are tender and the sauce is thick, rich and creamy. Taste for seasoning, then stir in the chopped parsley and serve immediately.

Per portion Energy 553kcal/2304kJ; Protein 40.6g; Carbohydrate 14.3g, of which sugars 6.1g; Fat 32.9g, of which saturates 18.3g; Cholesterol 175mg; Calcium 72mg; Fibre 2.8g; Sodium 173mg.

Pork escalopes baked with apple and potato rösti

The juices from the pork cook into the apples and potatoes giving them a wonderful flavour as well as making a delicious sauce.

Serves 4
2 large potatoes, finely grated
2 medium Bramley apples, one grated
and one cut into thin wedges
2 garlic cloves, crushed
1 egg, beaten
butter, for greasing
15ml/1 tbsp olive oil
4 large slices Parma ham
4 pork escalopes (US scallops),
about 175g/6oz each
4 sage leaves
25g/1oz/2 tbsp butter, diced
salt and ground black pepper
caramelized apple wedges, to serve

1 Preheat the oven to 200°C/400°F/ Gas 6. Squeeze out all the excess liquid from the grated potatoes and apple. Mix the grated ingredients together with the garlic, egg and seasoning.

2 Divide the potatoes into four portions and spoon each quarter on to a baking sheet that has been lined with foil and greased. Form a circle with the potatoes and flatten out slightly with the back of a spoon. Drizzle with a little olive oil. Bake for 10 minutes.

3 Meanwhile, lay the Parma ham on a clean surface and place a pork escalope on top. Lay a sage leaf and apple wedges over each escalope and top each piece with the butter. Wrap the Parma ham around each piece of meat, making sure it is covered completely.

4 Remove the potatoes from the oven, place each pork parcel on top and return to the oven for 20 minutes. Do not be tempted to overcook the pork as it will start to dry out.

5 Carefully lift the pork and potatoes off the foil and serve with caramelized wedges of apple and any cooking juices on the side.

Per portion Energy 396kcal/1659kJ; Protein 42.7g; Carbohydrate 19.2g, of which sugars 4.4g; Fat 16.9g, of which saturates 6.7g; Cholesterol 177mg; Calcium 29mg; Fibre 1.5g; Sodium 310mg.

Roast pork with apple and redcurrant jelly

Roasted apples with redcurrant jelly provides the perfect foil for roast pork and crackling.

Serves 8–10
1 bone-in pork loin, weighing about 2.25kg/5lb
10ml/2 tsp mustard powder
15 whole cloves
2 bay leaves
900ml/1½ pints/3¾ cups water
175ml/6fl oz/¾ cup single (light) cream (optional)
salt and ground white pepper
braised red cabbage, to serve

For the glazed potatoes
900g/2lb small potatoes
50g/2oz/¼ cup caster (superfine) sugar
65g/2½oz/5 tbsp butter

For the apples with redcurrant jelly
750ml/1¼ pints/3 cups water
115g/4oz/generous ½ cup soft light brown sugar
5ml/1 tsp lemon juice
4–5 tart apples, peeled, cored and halved
60–75ml/4–5 tbsp redcurrant jelly

1 Preheat the oven to 200°C/400°F/ Gas 6.

2 Use a sharp knife to score the pork skin with diagonal cuts to make a diamond pattern. Rub the rind with the salt, pepper and mustard powder. Push the cloves and bay leaves into the skin.

3 Place the pork loin, skin side up, on a rack in a roasting pan and cook for about 1 hour, until the skin is crisp and golden.

4 Pour the water into the bottom of the roasting pan and cook for a further 30 minutes.

5 For the glazed potatoes, boil the potatoes in salted water for 15–20 minutes, or until soft. Drain, peel and keep warm. Melt the sugar in a frying pan over a low heat until it turns light brown. Add the potatoes and butter, stirring to coat the potatoes, and cook for about 6–8 minutes, until the potatoes are a rich golden brown. Keep warm.

6 To cook the apples, bring the water to the boil in a large pan and stir in the brown sugar. Add the lemon juice and apple halves, lower the heat and poach gently until the apples are just tender. Remove the apples from the pan. Spoon 7.5ml/1½ tsp redcurrant jelly into the hollow of each apple half and keep warm.

7 When the pork is cooked, transfer it to a serving dish and leave it in a warm place to rest for 15 minutes before carving. Meanwhile, make the gravy. Transfer the roasting pan juices into a pan and reduce over a medium heat. Whisk in a little cream if you wish, and season with salt and pepper to taste.

8 Remove the crackling from the pork, and serve it separately, warm. Serve the pork with the gravy, caramelized potatoes, poached apple halves and braised red cabbage.

Per portion Energy 654kcal/2735kJ; Protein 36.9g; Carbohydrate 39.5g, of which sugars 26.2g; Fat 39.9g, of which saturates 16.1g; Cholesterol 124mg; Calcium 36mg; Fibre 1.5g; Sodium 152mg.

Spiced pork roast with apple and thyme cream sauce

Belly of pork (sometimes called 'lap' of pork) makes a tasty and tender roasting joint. In this unusual dish, the pork is boned and skinned for stuffing and rolling.

Serves 6

1 medium onion, finely chopped
3 garlic cloves, crushed
75g/3oz/6 tbsp butter
a bunch of mixed fresh herbs, leaves
  finely chopped
225g/8oz/4 cups fine fresh breadcrumbs
1 egg, beaten
1 piece of pork belly, about 1.3kg/3lb
15ml/1 tbsp vegetable oil
salt and ground black pepper
steamed green vegetables, to serve

For the spicy paste

25g/1oz/2 tbsp butter, melted
30ml/2 tbsp chutney
15ml/1 tbsp lemon juice
2 garlic cloves, crushed
30ml/2 tbsp mild wholegrain mustard

For the sauce

2 large cooking apples, peeled, cored
  and chopped
1 medium onion, chopped
2 garlic cloves, crushed
1 or 2 thyme sprigs
150ml/¼ pint/⅔ cup medium (hard) cider
about 150ml/¼ pint/⅔ cup chicken
  stock
300ml/½ pint/1¼ cups single
  (light) cream

1 Cook the onion and garlic in the butter until soft, then add the herbs and breadcrumbs. Cool a little before mixing in the egg, and season well with salt and ground pepper. Preheat the oven to 150°C/300°F/Gas 2.

2 Meanwhile, trim off any fat from the meat and prick the centre with a fork. Combine all the spicy paste ingredients together and brush the meat with this. Spread the stuffing all over the meat, then roll it up and secure it with cotton string.

3 Brown the meat in the oil in a hot roasting pan and cook in the oven for 3 hours. Halfway through cooking remove the joint from the oven and brush liberally with the remainder of the spicy paste; turn over, return the pan to the oven, and continue cooking.

4 To make the apple and thyme cream sauce, put the cooking apples, onion and garlic in a large pan and add the thyme sprigs, cider and stock. Bring to the boil and simmer gently for 15 minutes, then discard the thyme. Add the cream. Blend the mixture, strain and season to taste. If the sauce is too thick, add extra stock. Serve the sliced meat on heated plates with steamed green vegetables and the sauce.

Per portion Energy 814kcal/3409kJ; Protein 73.2g; Carbohydrate 41.9g, of which sugars 12.6g; Fat 39.8g, of which saturates 20.2g; Cholesterol 264mg; Calcium 145mg; Fibre 2.4g; Sodium 581mg.

Roast duck with apples and prunes

For a special family occasion, serve this classic roast dish with roast potatoes and braised white cabbage.

Serves 4
1 duck, about 1.8–2.5kg/4–5½lb, with giblets
150g/5oz stoned (pitted) prunes, sliced
2 medium dessert apples, peeled and chopped
20g/¾oz/⅓ cup fine breadcrumbs
475ml/16fl oz/2 cups chicken stock
a small bay leaf
30ml/2 tbsp plain (all-purpose) flour
15ml/1 tbsp single (light) cream
salt and ground white pepper

1 Preheat the oven to 240°C/475°F/Gas 9. Rinse the duck and pat dry with kitchen paper. Score the breast with a crosshatch pattern. Season well.

2 Toss the prunes and apples with the breadcrumbs in a bowl and spoon this mixture into the duck cavity, packing it firmly. Close the opening with skewers or sew up with fine string.

3 Pour 250ml/8fl oz/1 cup of the chicken stock into a roasting pan. Place the duck on a rack in the roasting pan, breast side down, and cook for 20 minutes.

4 Put the giblets in a pan with 475ml/16fl oz/2 cups water and the bay leaf. Bring to a rolling boil for 20–30 minutes until reduced. Strain and set aside.

5 Lower the oven heat to 180°C/350°F/Gas 4. Remove the roasting pan from the oven and turn the duck breast side up. Pour the remaining stock into the pan. Continue to cook for 20 minutes per 450g/lb, until the juices run clear when the thickest part of the leg is pierced. Transfer the duck to a serving dish and leave in a warm place to rest for 10 minutes before carving.

Per portion Energy 663kcal/2757kJ; Protein 31.6g; Carbohydrate 24g, of which sugars 14.6g; Fat 49.6g, of which saturates 14g; Cholesterol 100mg; Calcium 55mg; Fibre 2.8g; Sodium 222mg.

6 To make the gravy, pour off the fat from the roasting pan and whisk the flour into the remaining juices. Cook over a medium heat for 2–3 minutes until light brown. Gradually whisk in the giblet stock and stir in the cream. Cook the gravy, stirring, for 3 minutes more, pour into a sauceboat and serve.

Variations
• Serve the duck with lingonberry or cherry sauce.
• Add a few sultanas (golden raisins) to the prune stuffing mixture.

Roast farmyard duck with apples and cider

Sharp fruit flavours offset the richness of duck: orange is the classic, but cooking apples work just as well and are used here with cider. Serve with a selection of vegetables, including roast potatoes and, perhaps, some braised red cabbage.

Serves 4
2kg/4½lb oven-ready duck or duckling
300ml/½ pint/1¼ cups dry (hard) cider
60ml/4 tbsp double (heavy) cream
salt and ground black pepper

For the stuffing
75g/3oz/6 tbsp butter
115g/4oz/2 cups fresh white
    breadcrumbs
450g/1lb cooking apples, peeled, cored
    and diced
15ml/1 tbsp sugar, or to taste
freshly grated nutmeg

1 Preheat the oven to 200°C/400°F/ Gas 6.

2 To make the stuffing, melt the butter in a pan and fry the breadcrumbs until golden brown. Add the apples to the breadcrumbs with salt, pepper, the sugar and a pinch of nutmeg. Mix well.

3 Wipe the duck out with a clean, damp cloth, and remove any obvious excess fat (including the flaps just inside the vent). Rub the skin with salt. Stuff the duck with the prepared mixture, then secure the vent with a small skewer.

4 Weigh the stuffed duck and calculate the cooking time, allowing 20 minutes per 450g/1lb.

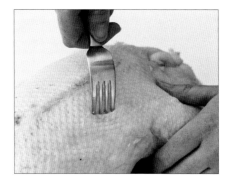

5 Prick the skin all over with a fork to allow the fat to run out during the cooking time, then lay it on top of a wire rack in a roasting pan, sprinkle with freshly ground black pepper and put it into the preheated oven to roast.

Cook's tip
The giblets aren't needed for this recipe but can be used later, with the duck carcass, to make a delicious stock for soup.

6 About 20 minutes before the end of the estimated cooking time, remove the duck from the oven and pour off all the fat that has accumulated under the rack (reserve it for frying). Slide the duck off the rack into the roasting pan and pour the cider over it. Return the duck to the oven and finish cooking, basting occasionally.

7 When the duck is cooked, remove it from the pan and keep it warm while you make the sauce. Set the roasting pan over a medium heat and boil the cider to reduce it by half. Stir in the cream, heat through and season. Meanwhile, remove the stuffing from the duck. Carve the duck into slices or quarter it using poultry shears. Serve with a portion of stuffing and the cider sauce.

Per portion Energy 572kcal/2397kJ; Protein 31.5g; Carbohydrate 34.6g, of which sugars 13.1g; Fat 33.1g, of which saturates 17.8g; Cholesterol 211mg; Calcium 74mg; Fibre 2.4g; Sodium 498mg.

Roast goose with apples

In Russia it is traditional to serve your guests roast goose with apples on New Year's Eve. The goose is served on a silver plate and carved at the table.

Serves 4–6
1 goose
8–10 Granny Smith apples, peeled, cored and cut into wedges
65g/2½oz/5 tbsp butter
200ml/7fl oz/scant 1 cup water
salt and ground black pepper
boiled or roasted potatoes with fresh dill, and boiled buckwheat, to serve

1 Preheat the oven to 180°C/350°F/Gas 4. Season the goose inside and out. Peel, core and quarter four of the apples and stuff them inside the neck end of the goose. Fold the neck skin over then truss the goose, making sure that the legs are close to the body.

2 Weigh the goose to work out the cooking time, and calculate 15 minutes per 450g/1lb, plus a further 15 minutes.

3 Grease a roasting pan with 25g/1oz/2 tbsp of the butter. Put the goose in the pan. Melt the rest of the butter and brush over the goose. Pour the water around the goose. Cook for 1½ hours.

4 Remove the cores from the remaining apples.

5 Put the whole apples around the goose and bake for the remainder of the cooking time. The goose is cooked when a skewer is pierced into the thickest part of a leg and the juices come out clear.

6 Transfer the goose to a platter. Remove the stuffing, carve, and serve with the potatoes and boiled buckwheat.

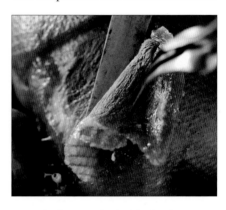

Per portion Energy 822kcal/3437kJ; Protein 54.8g; Carbohydrate 44.1g, of which sugars 21.8g; Fat 48.7g, of which saturates 0.9g; Cholesterol 0mg; Calcium 87mg; Fibre 3.1g; Sodium 486mg.

Grouse with orchard fruit stuffing

Tart apples, plums and pears, with a hint of spice, make a fabulous orchard fruit stuffing that complements the rich gamey flavour of grouse perfectly.

Serves 2
juice of ½ lemon
2 young grouse
50g/2oz/¼ cup butter
4 Swiss chard leaves
50ml/2fl oz/¼ cup Marsala
salt and ground black pepper

For the stuffing
2 shallots, finely chopped
1 cooking apple, peeled, cored
    and chopped
1 pear, peeled, cored and chopped
2 plums, halved, stoned (pitted)
    and chopped
a large pinch of mixed
    (apple pie) spice

1 Sprinkle the lemon juice over the grouse and season them with salt and freshly ground black pepper.

2 Melt half the butter in a large flameproof casserole, add the grouse and cook for 10 minutes, or until browned, turning occasionally. Use tongs to remove the grouse from the casserole and set aside.

Cook's tip
There isn't a lot of liquid in the casserole for cooking the birds – they are steamed rather than boiled, so it is very important that the casserole is heavy with a tight-fitting lid, otherwise the liquid may evaporate and the chard burn on the base of the pan.

3 Add the shallots to the fat remaining in the casserole and cook until they are softened but not coloured.

4 Add the apple, pear, plums and a generous pinch of mixed spice and cook for approximately 5 minutes, or until the fruits are just beginning to soften.

5 Remove the casserole from the heat and spoon the hot fruit mixture into the body cavities of the birds.

6 Truss the grouse neatly with string. Smear the remaining butter over the birds and wrap them in the chard leaves. Replace them in the casserole.

7 Pour in the Marsala and heat until simmering. Cover tightly and simmer for 20 minutes, or until the birds are tender, taking care not to overcook them. Leave to rest in a warm place for about 10 minutes before serving.

Per portion: Energy 521kcal/2191kJ; Protein 76.5g; Carbohydrate 17.5g, of which sugars 17.3g; Fat 13.5g, of which saturates 2.9g; Cholesterol 0mg; Calcium 302mg; Fibre 5.8g; Sodium 404mg.

Slow-roast belly of wild boar with apple

There are those who love fat and those who do not. This recipe can be enjoyed by both, as wild boar is much less fatty than its domestic cousins and this slow-cooked method renders much of what fat there is, basting the flesh as it cooks to leave a soft-textured meat with a lip-smacking stickiness. The tart apple complements the rich pork.

Serves 4

1.3kg/3lb wild boar belly, skin scored
15ml/1 tbsp olive oil
4 firm, tart green apples
50g/2oz/¼ cup butter
50g/2oz/¼ cup demerara (raw) sugar
a sprig of thyme, plus extra for garnish
3 heads chicory (Belgian endive),
   2 white, 1 red, outer leaves and
   stems removed, leaves separated

For the salad dressing

10ml/2 tsp Dijon mustard
10ml/2 tsp maple syrup
5ml/1 tsp cider vinegar
30ml/2 tbsp light olive oil
salt and ground black pepper

1 Preheat the oven to 150°C/300°F/ Gas 2. Rub the pork all over with the olive oil and salt and pepper, rubbing it into the scores in the skin.

2 Place the pork, skin side up, in a sturdy roasting pan. Sprinkle the skin with extra salt. Place in the oven for 3½–4 hours, until the meat is cooked.

3 To make the salad dressing, put the mustard, maple syrup and vinegar in a bowl and whisk together. Gently drizzle in the light olive oil, whisking as you go to emulsify the ingredients. Season with salt and pepper.

4 When the meat has been cooking for 3 hours, prepare the apples. Halve them horizontally, remove the cores and pips (seeds) with a spoon, and set aside.

5 In a heavy frying pan, gently heat the butter, sugar and thyme leaves, stirring, until the sugar and butter have melted.

6 Place the apples cut side down in the mixture and cook gently for 5 minutes, moving them in the pan occasionally. Turn the apples, cover, and cook for a further 10–15 minutes, until softening. Remove from the pan and keep warm.

7 When the belly is cooked, remove from the oven and leave to rest for 10 minutes. Carve into eight slices, two for each serving.

8 Arrange the meat on warm plates with two halves of apple each and some chicory leaves. Drizzle the chicory with the maple and mustard dressing and garnish with thyme.

Per portion Energy 1499kcal/6203kJ; Protein 50.6g; Carbohydrate 24.1g, of which sugars 22.4g; Fat 134.6g, of which saturates 50.7g; Cholesterol 263mg; Calcium 56mg; Fibre 1.9g; Sodium 415mg.

Quail with apples

These tiny birds have very short cooking times, and increasingly appear in restaurants and domestic kitchens.

Serves 2 as a main course
  or 4 as a first course
2 firm eating apples
4 oven-ready quail
120ml/4fl oz/½ cup olive oil
115g/4oz/½ cup butter
4 slices white bread
salt and ground black pepper

1 Preheat the oven to 220°C/425°F/ Gas 7. Core the apples and slice them thickly (leave the peel on if it is pretty and not too tough).

2 Brush the quail with half the olive oil and roast them in a pan in the oven for 10 minutes, or until brown and tender.

3 Meanwhile, heat half the butter in a frying pan and sauté the apple slices for about 3 minutes until they are golden but not mushy. Season with pepper, cover and keep warm until required.

4 Remove the crusts from the bread. Heat the remaining olive oil and the butter in a frying pan and fry the bread on both sides until brown and crisp.

5 Lay the fried bread on heated plates and place the quail on top. Arrange the fried apple slices around them, and serve immediately.

Per portion Energy 814kcal/3389kJ; Protein 53.3g; Carbohydrate 33.3g, of which sugars 10.5g; Fat 43.6g, of which saturates 23.4g; Cholesterol 69mg; Calcium 169mg; Fibre 2.4g; Sodium 644mg.

Pheasant breast with apples

This classic French recipe contains apples, Calvados and rich cream.

Serves 2
2 boneless pheasant breasts
30g/1oz/2 tbsp butter
1 onion, thinly sliced
1 eating apple, peeled and quartered
10ml/2 tsp sugar
60ml/4 tbsp Calvados
60ml/4 tbsp chicken stock
1.5ml/¼ tsp dried thyme
1.5ml/¼ tsp white pepper
125ml/4fl oz/½ cup whipping cream
salt
sautéed potatoes, to serve

1 With a sharp knife, score the thick end of each pheasant breast. In a heavy frying pan melt half the butter over a medium heat. Add the onion and cook for 8–10 minutes until golden, stirring occasionally. Using a slotted spoon, transfer the onion to a plate.

2 Cut each apple quarter crossways into thin slices. Melt half of the remaining butter in the pan and add the apple slices. Sprinkle with the sugar and cook the apple slices slowly for 5–7 minutes until golden and caramelized, turning occasionally. Transfer the apples to the plate with the onion, then wipe out the pan.

3 Add the remaining butter to the pan and increase the heat to medium-high. Add the pheasant breasts, skin side down, and cook for 3–4 minutes until golden. Turn and cook for a further 1–2 minutes until the juices run slightly pink when the thickest part of the meat is pierced with a knife. Transfer to a board and cover to keep warm.

4 Add the Calvados to the pan and boil over a high heat until reduced by half. Add the stock, thyme, a little salt and the white pepper and reduce by half again. Stir in the cream, bring to the boil and cook for 1 minute. Add the reserved onion and apple slices to the pan and cook for 1 minute.

5 Slice each pheasant breast diagonally and arrange on warmed plates. Spoon over a little sauce with the onion and apples.

> **Cook's tip**
> If you can't find Calvados, substitute Cognac, cider or apple juice instead.

Per portion Energy 629kcal/2611kJ; Protein 19g; Carbohydrate 29g, of which sugars 27g; Fat 45g, of which saturates 26g; Cholesterol 230mg; Calcium 81mg; Fibre 2g; Sodium 387mg.

DESSERTS

Sweet and juicy or tart and crunchy, apples are a wonderfully versatile and healthy option for many hot or cold desserts. Choose from traditional favourites such as Apple and Blackberry Crumble or Eve's Pudding, or more unusual desserts such as Apple Snow or Apple and Lemon Risotto with Poached Plums.

Frozen apple and blackberry terrine

This pretty autumn fruit terrine is frozen so that you can enjoy a healthy dessert at any time of the year.

Serves 6
450g/1lb cooking or eating apples
300ml/½ pint/1¼ cups sweet
    (hard) cider
15ml/1 tbsp clear honey
5ml/1 tsp vanilla extract
200g/7oz/scant 2 cups fresh or frozen
    and thawed blackberries
15ml/1 tbsp powdered gelatine
2 egg whites
fresh apple slices and blackberries,
    to decorate

1 Peel, core and chop the apples and place them in a pan with half the cider. Bring the cider to the boil, then lower the heat, cover the pan and let the apples simmer gently until tender.

2 Transfer the apples to a food processor and process them to a smooth purée. Stir in the honey and vanilla extract. Add half the blackberries to half the apple purée, and process again. Press through a sieve (strainer) to remove the seeds.

3 Heat the remaining cider until almost boiling, then sprinkle the gelatine over and stir until the gelatine has dissolved completely.

4 Add half the gelatine mixture to the apple purée and half to the blackberry and apple purée. Leave both purées to cool until almost set. Whisk the egg whites until stiff. Quickly fold them into the apple purée.

5 Stir the remaining whole blackberries into half the apple purée, and then transfer this to a 1.75 litre/3 pint/7½ cup loaf tin (pan), packing it in firmly.

6 Top with the blackberry purée and spread it evenly. Finally, add a layer of the plain apple purée and smooth it evenly. If necessary, freeze each layer until firm before adding the next.

7 Freeze until firm. To serve, remove from the freezer and allow to stand at room temperature for 20 minutes to soften. Serve in slices, decorated with apples slices and blackberries.

Per portion Energy 67kcal/283kJ; Protein 1.5g; Carbohydrate 12.4g, of which sugars 12.4g; Fat 0.2g, of which saturates 0g; Cholesterol 0mg; Calcium 21mg; Fibre 2.2g; Sodium 26mg.

Apple ice cream with cinnamon bread

Cooking apples with butter, lemon and spice accentuates their flavour and makes a marvellous ice cream.

Serves 2
675g/1½lb cooking apples
50g/2oz/¼ cup unsalted butter
1.5ml/¼ tsp mixed (apple pie) spice
finely grated rind and juice of 1 lemon
90g/3½oz/scant ½ cup cream cheese
2 egg whites, beaten
150ml/¼ pint/⅔ cup double (heavy) cream
mint sprigs, to decorate

For the cinnamon bread
6 thick slices of white bread
1 egg, beaten
1 egg yolk
2.5ml/½ tsp vanilla extract
150ml/¼ pint/⅔ cup single (light) cream
65g/2½oz/5 tbsp caster (superfine) sugar
2.5ml/½ tsp ground cinnamon
25g/1oz/2 tbsp unsalted butter
45ml/3 tbsp vegetable oil

1 Peel, core and slice the apples. Melt the butter in a pan. Add the apple slices, mixed spice and lemon rind. Cover and cook gently for 10 minutes until the apples are soft. Leave to cool.

2 Put the apples into a food processor. Add the lemon juice and cream cheese. Blend until smooth. In separate bowls, whisk the egg whites until stiff and the cream until it forms soft peaks.

3 Scrape the purée into a bowl. Fold in the cream, then the egg whites. Spoon into a plastic tub and freeze overnight.

4 Make the cinnamon bread about 20 minutes before serving. Cut the crusts off the bread slices, then cut each slice diagonally in half. Beat together the egg, egg yolk, vanilla extract, cream and 15ml/1 tbsp of the sugar.

5 Arrange the bread triangles in a single layer on a large, shallow plate or tray. Pour the cream mixture over the bread triangles and leave for about 10 minutes until the mixture has been thoroughly absorbed.

6 Mix the remaining sugar with the cinnamon on a plate. Melt the butter with the oil in a large frying pan. When it is hot, add half the bread and fry until golden underneath. Turn the slices with a metal spatula and fry the other side.

7 Drain the slices lightly on kitchen paper, then coat them on both sides in the cinnamon sugar and keep them hot. Cook the remaining slices in the same way. Serve at once, topped with scoops of the apple ice cream and decorated with the mint sprigs.

Per portion Energy 535kcal/2227kJ; Protein 5.7g; Carbohydrate 34.7g, of which sugars 23g; Fat 42.6g, of which saturates 23.3g; Cholesterol 123mg; Calcium 94mg; Fibre 2.2g; Sodium 288mg.

Apple and cider water ice

This very English combination has a subtle apple flavour with just a hint of cider. As the apple purée is very pale, almost white, add a few drops of green food colouring to echo the pale green skin of the Granny Smith apples.

Serves 6
500g/1¼lb Granny Smith apples
150g/5oz/¾ cup caster (superfine) sugar
300ml/½ pint/1¼ cups water
250ml/8fl oz/1 cup strong dry (hard) cider
few drops of green food colouring (optional)
strips of thinly pared lime rind, to decorate

1 Quarter, core and roughly chop the apples. Put them into a pan. Add the caster sugar and half the water. Cover and simmer for 10 minutes or until the apples are soft.

2 Press the mixture through a sieve (strainer) placed over a bowl. Discard the apple skins. Stir the cider and the remaining water into the apple purée and add a little colouring, if you like.

3 Pour into a shallow plastic container and freeze for 6 hours, beating with a fork once or twice to break up the ice crystals.

4 Scoop into dishes and decorate with twists of thinly pared lime rind.

Per portion Energy 143kcal/610kJ; Protein 0.4g; Carbohydrate 34.6g, of which sugars 34.6g; Fat 0.1g, of which saturates 0g; Cholesterol 0mg; Calcium 20mg; Fibre 1.3g; Sodium 6mg.

Apple and blueberry fool

Using dessert apples instead of cooking apples introduces a naturally sweet flavour, so no added sugar is needed.

Serves 6–8
450g/1lb sweet eating apples
450g/1lb/4 cups blueberries or bilberries
juice of 1 lemon
1 sachet powdered gelatine
2 egg whites
60ml/4 tbsp double (heavy) cream,
    whipped to serve

1 Peel, core and slice the apples. Put them in a large pan with the bilberries and 150ml/¼ pint/⅔ cup water. Cook the fruit for 15 minutes. Remove from the heat.

2 Strain the lemon juice into a cup, sprinkle the gelatine over and leave it to soak. When the gelatine has dissolved mix it into the fruit.

3 Turn the fruit mixture into a nylon sieve (strainer) over a large mixing bowl and press the fruit through it to make a purée; discard anything that is left in the sieve. Leave the purée to stand until it is cool and beginning to set.

4 Whisk the egg whites until they are standing in soft peaks.

5 Using a metal spoon, fold the whites gently into the fruit purée to make a smooth mousse. Turn into serving glasses and chill until set. Serve topped with the whipped cream.

Per portion Energy 92kcal/385kJ; Protein 1.6g; Carbohydrate 13g, of which sugars 10.8g; Fat 4.1g, of which saturates 2.5g; Cholesterol 10mg; Calcium 6mg; Fibre 2g; Sodium 18mg.

Apple snow

This fluffy nursery dish is as simple as it is delicious – and best made with late-cropping Bramley's Seedling cooking apples, which grow abundantly in Britain and 'fall' when cooked, to make a fluffy purée. Serve with crisp cookies, or sponge fingers.

Serves 6
675g/1½lb cooking apples, preferably
    Bramley's Seedling
a little thinly peeled lemon rind
about 115g/4oz/generous ½ cup caster
    (superfine) sugar
3 egg whites

1 Peel, core and slice the apples. Place in a pan with 45ml/3 tbsp water and the lemon rind. Cover and simmer gently for 15 minutes, or until the apples become fluffy. Remove from the heat, take out the lemon rind and sweeten to taste with caster sugar.

2 Beat the apples well with a wooden spoon to make a purée, or rub through a sieve (strainer) if a smoother texture is preferred. Leave to cool.

3 When the purée is cold, whisk the egg whites until stiff.

4 Fold the egg whites into the apple using a metal spoon. Whisk together until the mixture is thick and light.

5 Turn into a serving bowl, or divide between six individual dishes, and chill until required.

Per portion Energy 121kcal/516kJ; Protein 1.8g; Carbohydrate 30.1g, of which sugars 30.1g; Fat 0.1g, of which saturates 0g; Cholesterol 0mg; Calcium 7mg; Fibre 1.8g; Sodium 34mg.

Brandied apple Charlotte

Loosely based on a traditional Apple Charlotte recipe, this iced version combines brandy-steeped dried apple with a spicy ricotta cream to make an unusual and inspiring dessert.

Serves 8–10

130g/4½oz/¾ cup dried apples
75ml/5 tbsp brandy
50g/2oz/¼ cup unsalted butter
115g/4oz/½ cup light muscovado (brown) sugar
2.5ml/½ tsp mixed (apple pie) spice
60ml/4 tbsp water
75g/3oz/½ cup sultanas (golden raisins)
300g/11oz Madeira cake, cut into 1cm/½in slices
250g/9oz/generous 1 cup ricotta cheese
30ml/2 tbsp lemon juice
150ml/¼ pint/⅔ cup double (heavy) or whipping cream
icing (confectioners') sugar and fresh mint sprigs, to decorate

1 Roughly chop the dried apples, then transfer them to a clean bowl. Pour over the brandy and set aside for about 1 hour or until most of the brandy has been absorbed.

2 Melt the butter in a frying pan. Add the sugar and stir over a low heat for 1 minute.

3 Add the mixed spice, water and soaked apples, with any remaining brandy. Heat until just simmering, reduce the heat slightly, if necessary, and then cook gently for about 5 minutes or until the apples are tender. Stir in the sultanas, take off the heat and leave the mixture to cool completely.

4 Use the Madeira cake slices to line the sides of a 20cm/8in square or 20cm/8in round springform or loose-based cake tin (pan). Place in the freezer while you make the filling.

5 Beat the ricotta in a bowl until it has softened, then stir in the apple mixture and lemon juice. Whip the cream in a separate bowl and fold it in. Spoon the mixture into the lined tin and level the surface. Cover and freeze overnight.

6 Transfer the apple Charlotte to the refrigerator 1 hour before serving. Invert it on to a serving plate, dust with sugar, and decorate with mint sprigs.

> **Cook's tip**
> Line the tin with clear film (plastic wrap) before placing the cake in it to help the dessert turn out more easily,

Per portion Energy 446kcal/1869kJ; Protein 6g; Carbohydrate 54.4g, of which sugars 46.2g; Fat 21.9g, of which saturates 13.3g; Cholesterol 49mg; Calcium 119mg; Fibre 2.1g; Sodium 222mg.

Apple and almond cheesecake

This isn't a typical cheesecake, more of a cheese and apple pie. It has plenty of flavour and is perfect served with a summer berry coulis.

Serves 8

250g/9oz/generous 1 cup cream cheese
250g/9oz/generous 1 cup ricotta cheese
4 eggs, separated
75g/3oz/⅔ cup semolina flour
30ml/2 tbsp ground almonds
200ml/7fl oz/scant 1 cup sour cream
115g/4oz/generous ½ cup caster (superfine) sugar
5 eating apples, peeled, cored and thinly sliced
grated rind and juice of 1 lemon
115g/4oz/1 cup flaked (sliced) almonds
250g/9oz/generous 2 cups berries (any that are in season)
10ml/2 tsp sugar

1 Preheat the oven to 180°C/350°F/ Gas 4. Butter and line a 20 × 30cm/ 8 × 12in cake tin (pan).

2 Put the cream cheese and ricotta cheese in a large bowl and mix well. Add the egg yolks one at a time, stirring each into the cheese mixture.

3 Sprinkle the semolina flour over the top and stir in, then add the ground almonds, followed by the sour cream and sugar.

4 Put the egg whites into a clean, grease-free bowl and whisk until they form stiff peaks. Stir two large spoonfuls into the cheese mixture, then fold in the remainder.

5 Put the apples into a large bowl. Add the lemon juice and rind, and mix well to coat. (The juice will protect the apples from discoloration and add flavour.) Add the apples to the cheese mixture and fold in. Transfer to the prepared tin and sprinkle with the flaked almonds. Bake for 40 minutes, or until the top is golden brown.

6 While the cheesecake is baking in the oven, put the berries in a small pan with the sugar and 15–30ml/1–2 tbsp water. Simmer the fruit for 5–6 minutes, or until just softened. Purée the berries in a blender, then pass through a fine sieve (strainer) and leave to cool. Serve the cheesecake warm topped with a generous dollop of the berry coulis.

Per portion Energy 500kcal/2080kJ; Protein 12.8g; Carbohydrate 30.1g, of which sugars 22.3g; Fat 37.5g, of which saturates 16.9g; Cholesterol 153mg; Calcium 124mg; Fibre 2.4g; Sodium 145mg.

Apple-stuffed crêpes

Light, fluffy crêpes, filled with sweet, sugary apple slices, combine to make a delicious summertime dessert.

Serves 4
115g/4oz/1 cup plain (all-purpose) flour
a pinch of salt
2 large (US extra large) eggs
175ml/6fl oz/¾ cup milk
120ml/4fl oz/½ cup sweet (hard) cider
butter, for frying
4 eating apples
60ml/4 tbsp caster (superfine) sugar
120ml/8 tbsp clear honey, and 150ml/
    ¼ pint/⅔ cup double (heavy) cream,
    to serve

1 Make the batter. Sift the flour and salt into a large bowl. Add the eggs and milk and beat until smooth. Stir in the cider. Leave to stand for 30 minutes.

2 Heat a small heavy non-stick frying pan. Add a little butter and ladle in enough batter to coat the pan thinly.

3 Cook the crêpe for about 1 minute until it is golden underneath, then flip it over and cook the other side until golden. Slide the crêpe on to a plate, then repeat with the remaining batter to make seven more. Set the crêpes aside and keep warm.

4 Make the apple filling. Core the apples and cut them into thick slices. Heat 15g/½oz butter in a large frying pan. Add the apples to the pan and cook until golden on both sides. Transfer the slices to a bowl with a slotted spoon and sprinkle with sugar.

5 Fold each pancake in half, then fold in half again to form a cone. Fill each with some of the fried apples. Place two filled pancakes on each dessert plate. Drizzle with a little honey and serve at once, accompanied by cream.

Cook's tip
For the best results, use full-fat (whole) milk in the batter.

Per portion Energy 489kcal/2057kJ; Protein 8.2g; Carbohydrate 71.5g, of which sugars 49.6g; Fat 20.1g, of which saturates 11.3g; Cholesterol 139mg; Calcium 137mg; Fibre 2.1g; Sodium 69mg.

Baked apple dumplings

A treat good enough for any special occasion. The sharpness of the fruit contrasts perfectly with the maple syrup drizzled over this delightful pastry parcel.

Serves 8

8 firm cooking apples, peeled
1 egg white
130g/4½oz/⅔ cup caster (superfine) sugar
45ml/3 tbsp double (heavy) cream, plus extra whipped cream, to serve
2.5m/½ tsp vanilla extract
250ml/8fl oz/1 cup maple syrup

For the pastry

475g/1lb 2oz/4½ cups plain (all-purpose) flour
2.5ml/½ tsp salt
350g/12oz/1½ cups butter or white vegetable fat, diced
175–250ml/6–8fl oz/¾–1 cup chilled water

1 To make the pastry, sift the flour and salt into a large bowl. Rub or cut in the butter or fat until the mixture resembles fine breadcrumbs.

2 Sprinkle over 175ml/6fl oz/¾ cup water and mix until the dough holds together, adding a little more water if necessary. Gather into a ball. Wrap the dough in clear film (plastic wrap) and chill for at least 20 minutes. Preheat the oven to 220°C/425°F/Gas 7.

3 Cutting from the stem end, core the apples without cutting through the base. Roll out the pastry thinly. Cut squares almost large enough to enclose the apples; brush with egg white and set an apple in the centre of each. Cut pastry rounds to cover the tops of the apples. Reserve the trimmings. Combine the sugar, cream and vanilla extract in a small bowl. Spoon into the hollow of each apple.

4 Place a pastry circle on top of each apple, then bring up the sides of the pastry square to enclose it, pleating the larger piece of pastry to make a snug fit around the apple. Moisten the joins where they overlap.

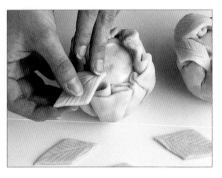

5 Make apple stalks and leaves from the pastry trimmings and decorate the tops of the dumplings.

6 Set them in a large greased baking dish, at least 2cm/¾in apart. Bake for 30 minutes, then lower the oven temperature to 180°C/350°F/Gas 4 and continue baking for 20 minutes more until the pastry is golden brown and the apples are tender.

7 Transfer the dumplings to a serving dish. Mix the maple syrup with the juices in the baking dish and drizzle over the dumplings. Serve hot.

> **Cook's tip**
> Egg yolk glaze brushed on to the pastry gives it a nice golden sheen.

Per portion Energy 713kcal/2988kJ; Protein 6.6g; Carbohydrate 94.7g, of which sugars 49.5g; Fat 36.8g, of which saturates 22.9g; Cholesterol 93mg; Calcium 108mg; Fibre 3g; Sodium 361mg.

Baked apples with marzipan

This is a traditional recipe for the winter, when apples were once the only fresh fruits available and cooks needed to be really creative to find different ways to serve them. It's a comforting hot dessert: when you eat it you won't mind at all that the range of local fruit is so small at this time of year.

Serves 4
25g/1oz/¼ cup raisins
10ml/2 tsp brandy
4 large, crisp eating apples,
    such as Braeburn
75g/3oz marzipan, chopped
juice of ½ lemon
20g/¾oz/¼ cup chopped pistachio nuts
single (light) cream, to serve

1 Preheat the oven to 160°C/325°F/ Gas 3. Soak the raisins in the brandy for 20 minutes. Meanwhile, core the apples. Cut a small slice off the bottom of each one, if necessary, so that they will stand up. Score the skin around the apple in three places to prevent it rolling up during baking.

2 Mix the marzipan with the lemon juice, chopped pistachio nuts and raisins, and push the filling into the centre of the apples. Put the apples on a baking tray lined with baking parchment, and bake them for 20–25 minutes, until tender. Serve the apples warm with a splash of cream.

Per portion Energy 150kcal/631kJ; Protein 2.2g; Carbohydrate 22.9g, of which sugars 22.7g; Fat 5.3g, of which saturates 0.6g; Cholesterol 0mg; Calcium 23mg; Fibre 2.3g; Sodium 33mg.

Caramel apples

These delicious treats are popular at fairs and fêtes around the world. The buttery, chewy caramel contrasts wonderfully with the crisp apple.

Serves 8
8 small or medium eating apples
115g/4oz/½ cup unsalted butter
200g/7oz/1 cup granulated (white) sugar
150ml/¼ pint/⅔ cup double (heavy) cream
15ml/1 tbsp soft light brown sugar
125g/4¼oz/⅓ cup golden (light corn) syrup
2.5ml/½ tsp vanilla extract
1.5ml/¼ tsp salt

1 Wash and dry the apples. Push lollipop sticks or wooden dowels into the stem-end of the apples.

2 Prepare an ice-water bath and line a shallow baking tray with a sheet of baking parchment.

3 Place all of the remaining ingredients in a large, heavy pan and heat them gently over a medium heat. Stir to dissolve everything together into an emulsified mass.

4 Once the sugar has completely dissolved, bring the mixture to the boil and cook until it reaches the soft-ball stage (114°C/238°F).

5 Remove the caramel from the heat and arrest the cooking by placing the pan over the ice-water bath.

6 Leave the mixture to cool to 82°C/180°F before dipping the apples into the caramel, holding them by their sticks.

7 Place the caramel-covered apples on the parchment-lined baking sheet, stick- or dowel-end up, and allow them to cool.

8 If the caramel slips off the apple at all, leave it to cool slightly and dip again. Eat immediately or store in an airtight container at room temperature for up to 3 days.

Per portion Energy 366kcal/1534kJ; Protein 0.8g; Carbohydrate 46.9g, of which sugars 46.9g; Fat 21.9g, of which saturates 13.4g; Cholesterol 57mg; Calcium 33mg; Fibre 1.1g; Sodium 160mg.

Apple and blackberry crumble

Autumn heralds the harvest of apples and succulent soft fruits. The pinhead oatmeal in the topping makes this traditional hot dessert especially crunchy and flavoursome.

Serves 6–8
900g/2lb cooking apples
450g/1lb/4 cups blackberries
a squeeze of lemon juice (optional)
175g/6oz/scant 1 cup sugar

For the topping
115g/4oz/½ cup butter
115g/4oz/1 cup wholemeal (whole-wheat) flour
50g/2oz/½ cup fine or medium pinhead oatmeal
50g/2oz/¼ cup soft light brown sugar
a little grated lemon rind (optional)

1 Preheat the oven to 200°C/400°F/Gas 6.

2 Rub the butter into the flour, and then add the oatmeal and brown sugar. Continue to rub in until the mixture begins to stick together, forming large crumbs. Mix in the grated lemon rind.

3 Peel, core and slice the cooking apples into wedges.

4 Put the fruit, lemon juice (if using), 30ml/2 tbsp water and the sugar into a shallow ovenproof dish.

5 Cover the fruit with the topping. Sprinkle with a little cold water. Bake in the oven for 15 minutes, then reduce the heat to 190°C/375°F/Gas 5 and cook for another 15–20 minutes until crunchy and brown on top. Serve hot with chilled crème fraîche or ice cream.

Per portion Energy 470kcal/1974kJ; Protein 5.1g; Carbohydrate 78.2g, of which sugars 60.3g; Fat 17.2g, of which saturates 10g; Cholesterol 41mg; Calcium 71mg; Fibre 7g; Sodium 128mg.

Baked apples with cinnamon and nuts

This cinnamon-sweet light dessert is one for the health conscious.

Serves 4
4 large, firm cooking apples
15g/½oz/1 tbsp butter
vanilla ice cream, to serve

For the filling
25g/1oz/2 tbsp butter
90ml/6 tbsp blanched almonds
30ml/2 tbsp sugar
5ml/1 tsp ground cinnamon

1 Preheat the oven to 220°C/425°F/Gas 7.

2 To make the filling, melt the butter. Grind or finely chop the almonds and put in a bowl. Using a wooden spoon, add the sugar, cinnamon and melted butter and mix together.

3 Peel the apples and remove the cores, leaving the apples intact at the bottom so that the filling will not run out. Put the apples in an ovenproof dish.

4 Stuff the apples evenly. Melt the butter in a small pan and pour over the apples to coat.

5 Bake the apples in the oven for about 20 minutes, until the apples are soft, but before they collapse. Serve hot, with vanilla ice cream.

Per portion Energy 294kcal/1229kJ; Protein 5.3g; Carbohydrate 22.8g, of which sugars 22.2g; Fat 20.9g, of which saturates 6.2g; Cholesterol 21mg; Calcium 66mg; Fibre 4.1g; Sodium 67mg.

Hot blackberry and apple soufflés

As the blackberry season is so short and the apple season so long, it's always worth freezing a bag of blackberries to have on hand for making treats like this one.

Serves 6
butter, for greasing
150g/5oz/⅔ cup caster (superfine) sugar, plus extra for dusting
350g/12oz/3 cups blackberries
1 large cooking apple, peeled, cored and finely diced
grated rind and juice of 1 orange
3 egg whites
icing (confectioner's) sugar, for dusting

1 Preheat the oven to 200°C/400°F/ Gas 6. Put a baking sheet in the oven to heat. Generously grease six 150ml/ ¼ pint/⅔ cup individual soufflé dishes with butter and dust with caster sugar, shaking out the excess sugar.

2 Put the blackberries and diced apple in a pan with the orange rind. Squeeze the juice from the orange into the pan and cook for 10 minutes or until the apple has pulped down well.

3 Press through a sieve (strainer) into a bowl. Stir in 50g/2oz/¼ cup of the caster sugar. Set aside to cool.

4 Put a spoonful of the fruit purée into each prepared dish and smooth the surface. Set the dishes aside.

5 Whisk the egg whites in a large grease-free bowl until they form stiff peaks. Very gradually whisk in the remaining caster sugar to make a stiff, glossy meringue mixture.

6 Fold in the remaining fruit purée and spoon the flavoured meringue into the prepared dishes. Level the tops with a palette knife, and run a table knife around the edge of each dish.

7 Place the dishes on the hot baking sheet and bake for 10–15 minutes until the soufflés have risen well and are lightly browned. Dust the tops with icing sugar and serve immediately.

Per portion Energy 123kcal/522kJ; Protein 2.1g; Carbohydrate 30.1g, of which sugars 30.1g; Fat 0.1g, of which saturates 0g; Cholesterol 0mg; Calcium 38mg; Fibre 2g; Sodium 33mg.

Apple fritters with fruit compote

Hot fruit fritters are a popular dessert and are very quick and easy to make.

Serves 4
200g/7oz/1¾ cups self-raising (self-rising) flour
100ml/3½ fl oz/scant ½ cup milk
5ml/1 tsp baking powder
40g/1½oz/3 tbsp caster (superfine) sugar
a pinch of salt
5ml/1 tsp butter
2 eating apples
vegetable oil, for deep-frying
icing (confectioners') sugar, to dust
mixed berry compote, to serve

1 Mix the flour and milk in a bowl and add the baking powder, sugar and salt. Melt the butter in a small pan until it starts to brown, then mix it into the batter.

2 Heat the oil in a deep-fryer to 180°C/350°F.

3 Peel and core the apples and cut them into thick rings. Dip them in the batter, making sure that they are completely covered, then drop them straight into the hot oil and deep-fry for approximately 2–3 minutes, until the batter is crisp and golden brown.

4 Drain the fritters on kitchen paper, dust with icing sugar and serve immediately with the berry compote.

Per portion Energy 391kcal/1644kJ; Protein 5.5g; Carbohydrate 54g, of which sugars 16.8g; Fat 18.6g, of which saturates 2.8g; Cholesterol 4mg; Calcium 213mg; Fibre 2.4g; Sodium 205mg.

Apple pudding

3 Put the milk, butter and flour in a pan. Stirring continuously with a whisk, cook over medium heat until the sauce thickens and comes to the boil. Let it bubble gently for 1–2 minutes, stirring well to make sure it does not stick and burn on the bottom of the pan.

4 Pour into a bowl, add the sugar and vanilla extract, and then whisk in the egg yolks.

5 In a separate bowl, whisk the egg whites until stiff peaks form. With a large metal spoon, fold the egg whites into the custard. Pour the custard mixture over the apples in the dish.

6 Put into the hot oven and cook for about 40 minutes until puffed up, deep golden brown and firm to the touch. Serve straight out of the oven, before the soufflé-like topping begins to fall.

Per portion Energy 240kcal/1006kJ; Protein 7g; Carbohydrate 26.8g, of which sugars 19.2g; Fat 12.5g, of which saturates 6.8g; Cholesterol 121mg; Calcium 127mg; Fibre 1.9g; Sodium 131mg.

This deliciously light soufflé-like dessert is made here with an apple base, but there are plenty of other fruits you could choose from.

Serves 4
4 crisp eating apples
a little lemon juice
300ml/½ pint/1¼ cups milk
40g/1½oz/3 tbsp butter
40g/1½oz/⅓ cup plain (all-purpose) flour
25g/1oz/2 tbsp caster (superfine) sugar
2.5ml/½ tsp vanilla extract
2 eggs, separated

Variations
Stewed fruit, such as plums, rhubarb or gooseberries sweetened with honey or sugar would also make a good base.

---

1 Preheat the oven to 200°C/400°F/Gas 6. Butter an ovenproof dish that is 20–23cm/8–9in in diameter and 5cm/2in deep.

2 Peel, core and slice the apples. Toss them with the lemon juice and cover the bottom of the buttered ovenproof dish.

Apple and kumquat sponge puddings

The intense flavour of kumquats makes these dainty puddings special. Served with more kumquats in a creamy sauce, this is a dessert that is sure to please.

Serves 8
150g/5oz/10 tbsp butter, at room temperature, plus extra for greasing
175g/6oz cooking apples, peeled and thinly sliced
75g/3oz kumquats, thinly sliced
150g/5oz/¾ cup golden caster (superfine) sugar
2 eggs
115g/4oz/1 cup self-raising (self-rising) flour

For the sauce
75g/3oz kumquats, thinly sliced
75g/3oz/6 tbsp caster (superfine) sugar
250ml/8fl oz/1 cup water
150ml/¼ pint/⅔ cup crème fraîche
5ml/1 tsp cornflour (cornstarch) mixed with 10ml/2 tsp water
lemon juice, to taste

1 Prepare a steamer. Butter eight 150ml/¼ pint/⅔ cup dariole moulds or ramekins and put a disc of buttered baking parchment on the base of each.

2 Melt 25g/1oz/2 tbsp butter in a frying pan. Add the apples, kumquats and 25g/1oz/2 tbsp sugar and cook over medium heat for 5–8 minutes, or until the apples start to soften and the sugar begins to caramelize. Remove from the heat and leave to cool.

3 Cream the remaining butter with the remaining sugar until pale and fluffy. Add the eggs, one at a time, beating after each addition. Fold in the flour.

4 Evenly divide the apple and kumquat mixture among the prepared moulds. Top with the sponge mixture. Cover the moulds and place in the steamer. Steam for 45 minutes.

5 Meanwhile, make the sauce. Place the kumquats, sugar and water in a pan and bring to the boil, stirring to dissolve the sugar. Simmer gently for 5 minutes.

6 Stir in the crème fraîche and bring back to the boil, stirring. Remove the pan from the heat and gradually whisk in the cornflour mixture. Simmer very gently for 2 minutes, stirring constantly. Add lemon juice to taste. Turn out the puddings and serve hot, with the sauce.

Per portion Energy 402kcal/1680kJ; Protein 3.7g; Carbohydrate 44.4g, of which sugars 33.7g; Fat 24.5g, of which saturates 15.3g; Cholesterol 109mg; Calcium 93mg; Fibre 1g; Sodium 190mg.

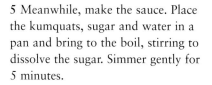

Autumn pudding

Although summer pudding is made more often, autumn pudding is equally easy to make, using seasonal fruit that is in abundant supply during the autumn months, instead of the soft fruits of summer. This juicy dessert is very simple to make, but it looks superb. Serve with lightly whipped chilled cream, or crème fraîche.

Serves 6–8

1 loaf white bread, 2 or 3 days old
675g/1½lb/6 cups mixed soft fruit, such as blackberries, autumn raspberries, late strawberries, and peeled and chopped eating apples
115g/4oz/generous ½ cup caster (superfine) sugar or 75ml/5 tbsp honey

1 Remove the crusts from the loaf and slice the bread thinly. Use several slices of the bread to line the base and sides of a 900ml–1.2 litres/1½–2 pints/3¾–5 cup pudding bowl or soufflé dish, cutting them into shape so that the pieces fit closely together leaving no gaps.

2 Put all the fruit into a wide, heavy pan, sprinkle the sugar or honey over and bring very gently to the boil. Cook for 2–3 minutes, or until the sugar has dissolved and the juices run.

3 Remove the pan from the heat and set aside 30–45ml/2–3 tbsp of the juices. Spoon the fruit and the remaining juices into the prepared bread-lined dish and cover the top closely with the remaining slices of bread. Put a plate that fits neatly inside the top of the dish on top of the pudding and weigh it down with a heavy tin or jar. Leave in the refrigerator for at least 8 hours, or overnight.

4 Before serving the dish, remove the weight and plate, cover the bowl with a serving plate and turn upside down to unmould the pudding.

5 Use the reserved fruit juice to pour over any patches of the bread that have not been completely soaked and coloured by the fruit juices. Serve cold cut into wedges with lightly whipped chilled cream or crème fraîche.

Per portion Energy 261kcal/1112kJ; Protein 7.7g; Carbohydrate 57.5g, of which sugars 27.1g; Fat 1.7g, of which saturates 0.4g; Cholesterol 0mg; Calcium 153mg; Fibre 4.2g; Sodium 398mg.

Eve's pudding

The name 'Mother Eve's pudding', from the biblical Eve, was first used in the 19th century for a boiled suet dessert.

Serves 4–6
115g/4oz/½ cup butter
115g/4oz/generous ½ cup caster (superfine) sugar
2 eggs, beaten
grated rind and juice of 1 lemon
90g/3¼oz/scant 1 cup self-raising (self-rising) flour
40g/1½oz/⅓ cup ground almonds
115g/4oz/½ cup light muscavado (brown) sugar
550–675g/1¼–1½lb cooking apples, cored and thinly sliced
25g/1oz/¼ cup flaked (sliced) almonds

1 Preheat the oven to 180°C/350°F/ Gas 4. Beat together the butter and caster sugar in a large mixing bowl until the mixture is light and fluffy.

2 Gradually beat the eggs into the butter mixture, beating well after each addition, then fold in the lemon rind, flour and ground almonds.

3 Mix together the brown sugar, apples and lemon juice and put the mixture into an ovenproof dish, spreading it out evenly.

4 Spoon the sponge mixture over the top in an even layer and right to the edges. Sprinkle the almonds over.

5 Put into the hot oven and cook for 40–45 minutes until risen and golden brown. Serve hot.

Per portion Energy 507kcal/2128kJ; Protein 6.9g; Carbohydrate 65.5g, of which sugars 52.7g; Fat 26.1g, of which saturates 12g; Cholesterol 114mg; Calcium 91mg; Fibre 2.8g; Sodium 159mg.

Apple batter pudding

Quick and simple to make, this pudding is also good made with pears, plums or cherries. Serve with cream.

Serves 4
30ml/2 tbsp sunflower oil
450g/1lb eating apples, peeled, cored and thickly sliced
115g/4oz/1 cup plain (all-purpose) flour
a pinch of salt
5ml/1 tsp ground cinnamon
50g/2oz/¼ cup caster (superfine) sugar
1 egg, beaten
300ml/½ pint/1¼ cups milk
15ml/1 tbsp icing (confectioners') sugar

1 Preheat the oven to 220°C/425°F/ Gas 7. Pour the oil in a roasting pan, about 25 × 30cm/10 × 12in, and swirl around the base and up the sides to coat evenly. Add the apple slices, spreading them out evenly. Put the pan in the oven for 10 minutes.

2 To make the batter, sift the flour, salt and cinnamon into a bowl. Stir in the sugar, then make a well in the middle. Add the egg and gradually whisk in the milk to make a smooth batter.

3 Remove the pan from the oven and pour the batter over the apples. Return to the oven and bake for 25–30 minutes, until well-risen and dark golden-brown. Dust with icing sugar. Serve immediately.

Per portion Energy 304kcal/1286kJ; Protein 7.2g; Carbohydrate 53.1g, of which sugars 31.2g; Fat 8.7g, of which saturates 1.9g; Cholesterol 52mg; Calcium 151mg; Fibre 2.7g; Sodium 63mg.

CAKES AND BAKING

The addition of apples in baking gives a wonderfully sweet, moist texture to a host of home-baked treats. From crunchy, crumbly cookies and sharp, spongy muffins to spicy cakes and juicy pastries, there is something to suit all tastes and occasions.

Apple crumble and custard slices

These luscious apple slices are easy to make using ready-made sweet pastry and custard. Just think, all the ingredients of one of the world's most popular desserts – in a cookie.

Makes 16
350g/12oz ready-made sweet pastry
1 large cooking apple, about 250g/9oz
30ml/2 tbsp caster (superfine) sugar
60ml/4 tbsp ready-made thick custard

For the crumble topping
115g/4oz/1 cup plain (all-purpose) flour
2.5ml/½ tsp ground cinnamon
60ml/4 tbsp sugar
90g/3½oz/7 tbsp unsalted butter, melted

1 Preheat the oven to 190°C/375°F/ Gas 5. Roll out the pastry and use to line the base of a 28 × 18cm/11 × 7in shallow cake tin (pan). Prick the pastry with a fork, line with foil and baking beans and bake blind for about 10–15 minutes.

2 Remove the foil and baking beans and return the pastry to the oven for a further 5 minutes until cooked and golden brown.

> **Cook's tip**
> For best results, buy the best quality custard you can find.

3 Meanwhile, peel, core and chop the apple evenly. Place in a pan with the sugar. Heat gently until the sugar dissolves, then cover with a lid and cook gently for 5–7 minutes until a thick purée is formed. Beat with a wooden spoon and set aside to cool.

4 Mix the cold apple with the custard. Spread over the pastry. To make the crumble topping, put the flour, cinnamon and sugar into a bowl and pour over the melted butter. Stir thoroughly until the mixture forms small clumps. Sprinkle the crumble over the filling.

5 Return to the oven and bake for about 10–15 minutes until the crumble topping is cooked and a golden brown. Leave to cool in the tin, then slice into bars to serve.

Per portion Energy 196kcal/822kJ; Protein 2.1g; Carbohydrate 23.7g, of which sugars 8.1g; Fat 11g, of which saturates 4.9g; Cholesterol 15mg; Calcium 37mg; Fibre 0.9g; Sodium 124mg.

Toffee apple and oat crunchies

An unashamedly addictive mixture of chewy oats, soft apple and wonderfully crunchy toffee, this cookie won't win large prizes in the looks department but is top of the class for flavour.

Makes about 16

150g/5oz/10 tbsp unsalted butter
175g/6oz/¾ cup light muscovado (brown) sugar
90g/3½oz/½ cup white sugar
1 large (US extra large) egg, beaten
75g/3oz/⅔ cup plain (all-purpose) flour
2.5ml/½ tsp bicarbonate of soda (baking soda)
a pinch of salt
250g/9oz/2½ cups rolled oats
50g/2oz/scant ½ cup sultanas (golden raisins)
50g/2oz dried apple rings, coarsely chopped
50g/2oz chewy toffees, coarsely chopped

1 Preheat the oven to 180°C/350°F/Gas 4. Line two or three baking sheets with baking parchment. Beat together the butter and both sugars until creamy. Add the beaten egg and stir well until thoroughly combined.

2 Sift together the flour, bicarbonate of soda and salt. Add to the egg mixture and mix in well. Finally add the oats, sultanas, chopped apple rings and toffee and stir until just combined.

3 Using a small ice cream scoop or large tablespoon, place heaps of the mixture well apart on the prepared baking sheets. Bake for about 10–12 minutes, or until lightly set in the centre and just beginning to brown at the edges.

4 Remove from the oven and leave to cool on the baking sheets for a few minutes. Using a palette knife or metal spatula, transfer the cookies to a wire rack to cool completely.

Per portion Energy 249kcal/1047kJ; Protein 3.1g; Carbohydrate 38.8g, of which sugars 23.2g; Fat 10.1g, of which saturates 5.3g; Cholesterol 32mg; Calcium 34mg; Fibre 1.3g; Sodium 79mg.

Variation
Ripe, juicy pears will also work very well in this recipe.

Apple and elderflower stars

These delicious, crumbly apple cookies are topped with a sweet yet very sharp icing. Packaged in a pretty box, they would make a delightfully festive gift for someone special.

Makes 18

115g/4oz/½ cup unsalted butter, at room
    temperature, diced
75g/3oz/scant ½ cup caster (superfine)
    sugar
2.5ml/½ tsp mixed (apple pie) spice
1 large (US extra large) egg yolk
25g/1oz dried apple rings,
    finely chopped
200g/7oz/1¾ cups self-raising
    (self-rising) flour
5–10ml/1–2 tsp milk, if necessary

For the topping

200g/7oz/1¾ cups icing (confectioners')
    sugar, sifted
60–90ml/4–6 tbsp elderflower cordial
sugar, for sprinkling

1 Preheat the oven to 190°C/375°F/
Gas 5.

2 Cream together the butter and sugar until light and fluffy. Beat in the mixed spice and egg yolk.

3 Add the chopped apple and flour and stir together well. The mixture should form a stiff dough but if it is too dry, add some milk.

4 Roll the dough out on a floured surface to 5mm/¼in thick. Draw a five-pointed star on cardboard. Cut out and use as a template for the cookies. Alternatively, use a star biscuit (cookie) cutter.

5 Place the cookies on non-stick baking sheets and bake for about 10–15 minutes, or until just beginning to brown around the edges.

6 Using a palette knife or metal spatula, carefully transfer the cookies to a wire rack to cool.

7 To make the topping, sift the icing sugar into a bowl and add just enough elderflower cordial to mix to a fairly thick but still pourable consistency.

Cook's tip

Try to buy the darker dried apple rings as these have no added preservatives.

8 When the cookies are completely cool, trickle the icing randomly over the stars. Immediately sprinkle with sugar and leave to set.

Per portion Energy 157kcal/659kJ; Protein 1.4g;
Carbohydrate 26.6g, of which sugars 18.1g; Fat 5.7g,
of which saturates 3.4g; Cholesterol 25mg; Calcium
27mg; Fibre 0.4g; Sodium 42mg.

Apple and cranberry muffins

Sweet, sharp and moreish, these spiced muffins are packed with of fruit.

Makes 12
1 egg
50g/2oz/¼ cup butter, melted
100g/4oz/generous ½ cup caster (superfine) sugar
grated rind of 1 large orange
120ml/4fl oz/½ cup freshly squeezed orange juice
140g/5oz/1¼ cups plain (all-purpose) flour
5ml/1 tsp baking powder
2.5ml/½ tsp ground cinnamon
2.5ml/½ tsp freshly grated nutmeg
2.5ml/½ tsp ground allspice
a pinch of ground ginger
a pinch of salt
2 small eating apples
170g/6oz/1½ cups cranberries
55g/2oz/1⅓ cups walnuts, chopped
icing (confectioners') sugar, for dusting

Variation
Try replacing the cranberries with blackberries or blackcurrants.

---

1 Preheat the oven to 180°C/350°F/ Gas 4. Lightly grease the cups of a muffin tin (pan) or line them with paper cases.

2 In a bowl, whisk the egg with the melted butter to combine.

3 Add the sugar, grated orange rind and juice. Whisk to blend. Set aside.

4 In a large bowl, sift together the flour, baking powder, cinnamon, nutmeg, allspice, ginger and salt.

5 Make a well in the dry ingredients and pour in the egg mixture. With a spoon, stir until just blended.

6 Peel, core and quarter the apples. Chop the apple flesh coarsely with a sharp knife.

7 Add the apples, cranberries and walnuts to the batter and stir lightly to blend.

8 Three-quarters fill the cups. Bake for 25–30 minutes, until golden. Leave to stand for 5 minutes before transferring to a wire rack to cool. Dust with icing sugar before serving. Store in an airtight container for up to 3 days.

Per portion Energy 149kcal/624kJ; Protein 2.5g; Carbohydrate 20.4g, of which sugars 10.8g; Fat 6.9g, of which saturates 2.6g; Cholesterol 25mg; Calcium 30mg; Fibre 0.9g; Sodium 34mg.

Apple and cinnamon cake

Moist and spicy, this is perfect for packed lunches or afternoon tea.

Makes a 20cm/8in square cake
115g/4oz/½ cup low-fat spread
200g/7oz/1¼ cups dried, stoned dates
1–2 tart eating apples or 1 cooking apple, about 225g/8oz, peeled and grated
7.5ml/1½ tsp mixed (apple pie) spice
5ml/1 tsp ground cinnamon
2.5ml/½ tsp salt
75g/3oz/½ cup raisins
2 eggs, beaten
150g/5oz/1¼ cups wholemeal (wholewheat) flour, sifted
115g/4oz/generous 1 cup gram flour, sifted with 10ml/2 tsp baking powder
175ml/6fl oz/¾ cup unsweetened coconut milk

1 Preheat the oven to 180°C/350°F/ Gas 4. Grease a deep 20cm/8in square baking tin (pan) and line the base. Blend the spread and the dates. Add the apple, mixed spice, cinnamon and salt. Process until blended.

2 Scrape the apple and date mixture into a bowl and fold in the raisins and beaten eggs alternately with the flours, baking powder and coconut milk. Transfer to the prepared tin.

3 Bake for 30–40 minutes until dark golden and firm to the touch. Cool the cake in the tin for 15 minutes before turning out on a wire rack to cool completely.

Per cake: Energy 2036kcal/8588kJ; Carbohydrate 300g; sugar total150g; Fat, total 72g; saturated fat 4.5g; polyunsaturated fat 18.5g; monounsaturated fat 28g; starch 147g; Fibre 34.4g; Sodium 2412mg.

Apple and sour cream crumble muffins

One-third of the cooking apples in this recipe are sliced and coated in a sweet almond crumble, which makes a delicious crunchy texture for the muffin top.

Makes 8
3 cooking apples, peeled and cored
115g/4oz/generous ½ cup caster (superfine) sugar, plus 10ml/2 tsp for coating
5ml/1 tsp ground cinnamon
250g/9oz/2¼ cups plain (all-purpose) flour
15ml/1 tbsp baking powder
75g/3oz/6 tbsp butter, melted
2 eggs, beaten
30ml/2 tbsp sour cream

For the cinnamon crumble
30ml/2 tbsp plain (all-purpose) flour
45ml/3 tbsp demerara (raw) sugar
30ml/2 tbsp ground almonds
a pinch of ground cinnamon

1 Preheat the oven to 190°C/375°F/ Gas 5. Line the cups of a muffin tin (pan) with paper cases.

2 To make the crumble, combine all of the crumble ingredients together in a mixing bowl.

3 Cut one apple into thin crescents, and toss in the crumble. Set aside.

4 Dice the remaining apples. Sift 10ml/2 tsp sugar and the cinnamon over the top. Set aside.

5 Sift the flour, baking powder and sugar into a bowl. Stir in the melted butter, eggs and sour cream. Add the apple chunks and lightly fold them into the mixture.

6 Fill the cases with the mixture, then arrange the crumble-coated apple on top. Bake for 25 minutes until risen and golden. Cool on a wire rack. Store for up to three days.

Per portion Energy 272kcal/1144kJ; Protein 4.8g; Carbohydrate 42.8g, of which sugars 19g; Fat 10.2g, of which saturates 6g; Cholesterol 71mg; Calcium 65mg; Fibre 1.6g; Sodium 92mg.

Spicy apple cake

This moist and spicy apple cake comes from Germany where it can be found on the menu of coffee and tea houses.

Serves 12

115g/4oz/1 cup plain (all-purpose) flour
115g/4oz/1 cup wholemeal (whole-wheat) flour
10ml/2 tsp baking powder
5ml/1 tsp cinnamon
2.5ml/½ tsp mixed (apple pie) spice
225g/8oz cooking apple, cored, peeled and chopped
75g/3oz/6 tbsp butter
175g/6oz/generous ¾ cup soft light brown sugar
finely grated rind of 1 small orange
2 eggs, beaten
30ml/2 tbsp milk
whipped cream and cinnamon, to serve

For the topping

4 eating apples, cored and thinly sliced
juice of ½ orange
10ml/2 tsp caster sugar
45ml/3 tbsp apricot jam, warmed and sieved (strained)

1 Preheat the oven to 180°C/350°F/Gas 4.

2 Grease and line a 23cm/9in round loose-bottomed cake tin (pan). Sift the flours, baking powder and spices together in a bowl.

3 Toss the chopped cooking apple in 30ml/2 tbsp of the flour mixture.

Variation
Pears would also work well in this cake as they are moist and full of flavour.

4 In a separate bowl, cream together the butter, brown sugar and orange rind until light and fluffy. Gradually beat in the eggs, and then fold in the flour mixture, the chopped apple and the milk.

5 Spoon the mixture into the cake tin and level the surface.

6 For the topping, toss the apple slices in the orange juice and set them in overlapping circles on top of the cake mixture, pressing down lightly.

7 Sprinkle the caster sugar over the top and bake for 1–1¼ hours, or until risen and firm. Cover with foil if the apples brown too much.

8 Cool in the tin for 10 minutes, then remove to a wire rack. Glaze the apples with the sieved jam. Serve with whipped cream, sprinkled with cinnamon.

Per portion Energy 587kcal/2471kJ; Protein 5.5g; Carbohydrate 92g, of which sugars 69.7g; Fat 24.5g, of which saturates 10.6g; Cholesterol 40mg; Calcium 95mg; Fibre 2.5g; Sodium 129mg.

Apple cake with vanilla cream

Dessert apples are used in this recipe as they are naturally very sweet and therefore ideally suited to this sublime cake. It can be served while still warm yet tastes just as good when cold.

Serves 6–8
115g/4½oz/½ cup plus 15g/½oz/1 tbsp
   unsalted butter
7 eating apples
30ml/2 tbsp caster
   (superfine) sugar
10ml/2 tsp ground cinnamon
200g/7oz/1 cup sugar
2 egg yolks and 3 egg whites
100g/4oz/1 cup ground almonds
grated rind and juice of ½ lemon

For the vanilla cream
250ml/8fl oz/1 cup milk
250ml/8fl oz/1 cup double
   (heavy) cream
15ml/1 tbsp sugar
1 vanilla pod (bean), split
4 egg yolks, beaten

1 Preheat the oven to 180°C/350°F/Gas 4. Butter a 20cm/8in flan tin (pan) using 15g/½oz/1 tbsp of the butter. Peel, core and thinly slice the apples and put the slices in a bowl. Add the caster sugar and cinnamon and mix them together. Put the mixture in the prepared tin.

2 Put the remaining butter and sugar in a bowl and whisk them together until they are light and fluffy. Beat in the egg yolks, then add the ground almonds and lemon rind and juice to the mixture.

3 Whisk the egg whites until stiff then fold into the mixture. Pour the mixture over the apples in the flan tin. Bake in the oven for approximately 40 minutes until golden brown and the apples are tender.

4 Meanwhile, make the vanilla cream. Put the milk, cream, sugar and vanilla pod in a pan and heat gently. Add a little of the warm milk mixture to the egg yolks then slowly add the egg mixture to the pan and continue to heat gently, stirring all the time, until the mixture thickens. Do not allow the mixture to boil or it will curdle.

5 Remove the vanilla pod and serve the vanilla cream warm or cold, with the apple cake.

Per portion Energy 541kcal/2254kJ; Protein 7.6g; Carbohydrate 39.7g, of which sugars 39.3g; Fat 40.3g, of which saturates 20g; Cholesterol 227mg; Calcium 122mg; Fibre 2.1g; Sodium 135mg.

Potato and apple cake

Both sweet and savoury versions of this delicious Irish potato apple cake exist. The sweet one, here, was the high point of many a traditional farmhouse high tea, especially when using home-grown apples in autumn.

Makes 2 farls; serves 4–6
450g/1lb freshly boiled potatoes in their skins, preferably still warm
a pinch of salt
25g/1oz/2 tbsp butter, melted
about 115g/4oz/1 cup plain (all-purpose) flour

For the filling
3 large or 4 small cooking apples, such as Bramley's Seedling
a little lemon juice (optional)
about 50g/2oz/¼ cup butter in thin slices
50–115g/2–4oz/¼ – generous ½ cup caster (superfine) sugar, or to taste

1 Preheat the oven to 200°C/400°F/ Gas 6. Peel the potatoes and mash them in a large heavy pan until very smooth. Season to taste with the salt, and drizzle the melted butter over.

2 Knead in as much plain flour as necessary to make a pliable dough (waxy potatoes will need more flour than naturally floury ones, such as Kerr's Pink). The dough should be elastic enough to roll out, but do not knead more than necessary.

3 Roll the potato mixture out into a large circle and cut into four farls (triangular pieces).

4 To make the filling, peel, core and slice the apples and pile the slices of the raw apple on to two of the farls. Sprinkle with a little lemon juice, if you like. Dampen the edges of the farls, place the other two on top, and nip with your fingers around the edges to seal them together.

5 Cook in the preheated oven for about 15–20 minutes (when the cake is nicely browned, the apples should be cooked).

6 Slit each cake around the side and turn the top back. Lay thin slices of butter over the apples, until they are almost covered, and then sweeten with sugar. Replace the top and return to the oven for 2 minutes until the butter and sugar have melted to make a sauce.

7 Cut each farl into pieces and serve, pouring a little of the sugary butter sauce on the side.

Per farl Energy 786kcal/3307kJ; Protein 9.5g; Carbohydrate 121.9g, of which sugars 40.5g; Fat 32.4g, of which saturates 19.9g; Cholesterol 80mg; Calcium 117mg; Fibre 6.1g; Sodium 253mg.

Caramelized apple tart

The beauty of this sweet, caramelized apple tart is that it is made and baked in one pan. Although prepared upside down, when ready to serve, the pastry sits on the bottom with the caramel-coated apples on the top. This tart is delicious served with either cream or custard.

Serves 4
200g/7oz/scant 1 cup butter
200g/7oz/1 cup caster (superfine) sugar
6 large eating apples

For the sweet pastry
150g/5oz/10 tbsp butter
50g/2oz/¼ cup caster (superfine) sugar
225g/8oz/2 cups plain (all-purpose) flour
1 egg

1 Make the sweet pastry. Cream the butter with the caster sugar together in a food processor. Add the plain flour and egg. Mix until just combined, being careful not to overprocess. Cover and leave in a cool place for an hour before use.

2 Preheat the oven to 200°C/400°F/Gas 6. For the filling, cut the butter into small pieces. Using a shallow, 30cm/12in ovenproof frying pan, heat the sugar and butter and allow to caramelize over a low heat, stirring continuously for about 10 minutes.

3 Meanwhile peel and core the apples then cut them into eighths. When the butter and sugar are caramelized, place the apples in the pan in a circular fan, one layer around the outside then one in the centre. The pan should be full. Reduce the heat and cook for 5 minutes, then remove from the heat.

4 Roll out the pastry to a circle big enough to fit the pan completely with generous edgings. Spread the pastry over the fruit and tuck in the edges. Bake in the oven for about 30 minutes, or until the pastry is browned and set. Remove from the oven and leave to rest.

5 When ready to serve, gently reheat the tart on the stove for a few minutes then invert on to a warmed serving plate, so the pastry forms the base.

Per portion Energy 904kcal/3774kJ; Protein 4.6g; Carbohydrate 95.2g, of which sugars 66.5g; Fat 58.8g, of which saturates 31.5g; Cholesterol 116mg; Calcium 95mg; Fibre 3.6g; Sodium 559mg.

Deep-dish apple pie

This all-time classic favourite is made with rich shortcrust pastry. Inside, sugar, spices and flour create a deliciously thick and syrupy sauce with the apple juices.

Serves 6

115g/4oz/generous ½ cup caster
   (superfine) sugar
45ml/3 tbsp plain (all-purpose) flour
2.5ml/½ tsp ground cinnamon
finely grated rind of 1 orange
900g/2lb tart cooking apples
1 egg white, lightly beaten
30ml/2 tbsp golden granulated sugar
whipped cream, to serve

For the pastry

350g/12oz/3 cups plain
   (all-purpose) flour
a pinch of salt
175g/6oz/¾ cup butter, diced

1 To make the pastry, sift the flour and salt into a mixing bowl and rub or cut in the butter until the mixture resembles fine breadcrumbs.

2 Sprinkle over the water and mix to a dough. Knead lightly for a few seconds until smooth. Wrap the dough in clear film (plastic wrap) and chill for 30 minutes.

3 Combine the caster sugar, flour, cinnamon and orange rind in a bowl. Peel, core and thinly slice the apples. Add to the sugar mixture, then toss gently until they are all evenly coated.

4 Put a baking sheet in the oven and preheat to 200°C/400°F/Gas 6. Roll out just over half the pastry and use to line a 23cm/9in pie dish that is 4cm/1½in deep, allowing the pastry to overhang the edges slightly.

5 Spoon in the filling, doming the apple slices in the centre.

6 Roll out the remaining pastry to form the lid. Lightly brush the edges of the pastry case with a little water, then carefully place the lid over the apple filling.

7 Trim the pastry with a sharp knife. Gently press the edges together to seal, then knock up the edge. Re-roll the pastry trimmings and cut out apple and leaf shapes. Brush the top of the pie with egg white. Arrange the pastry apples and leaves on top.

8 Brush again with egg white, then sprinkle with golden granulated sugar. Make two small slits in the top of the pie to allow steam to escape.

9 Bake for 30 minutes, then lower the oven temperature to 180°C/350°F/Gas 4 and bake for a further 15 minutes until the pastry is golden and the apples are soft – check by inserting a small sharp knife or skewer through one of the slits in the top of the pie. Serve hot, with whipped cream.

Per portion Energy 591kcal/2488kJ; Protein 7.4g; Carbohydrate 89.9g, of which sugars 39.8g; Fat 25g, of which saturates 15.3g; Cholesterol 62mg; Calcium 117mg; Fibre 4.4g; Sodium 193mg.

Blueberry and apple pie

The traditional wild harvest of blueberries (also known as bilberries, whinberries or whortleberries) has always been gathered with great excitement. These berries are popular pie fillings and a good accompaniment to apples.

Serves 6
2 cooking apples, total weight
   about 400g/14oz
10ml/2 tsp cornflour (cornstarch)
350g/12oz/3 cups whinberries
40–50g/3–4 tbsp caster (superfine)
   sugar, plus extra for sprinkling
milk, for brushing

For the pastry
250g/9oz/2¼ cups plain
   (all-purpose) flour
25g/1oz/2 tbsp caster
   (superfine) sugar
150g/5oz/10 tbsp butter, chilled
   and cut into small cubes
1 egg

Cook's tip
Whinberries give out a lot of juice, so avoid using a loose-bottomed tin (pan) in case it leaks out on to the oven floor.

---

1 Sift the flour into a bowl and stir in the sugar. Add the butter and rub into the flour until the mixture resembles fine crumbs.

2 Stir in the egg and enough cold water until the mixture forms clumps, then gather it together to make a smooth dough. Wrap the pastry in clear film (plastic wrap) and place in the refrigerator for 20–30 minutes.

3 Preheat the oven to 190°C/375°F/ Gas 5.

4 On a lightly floured surface, roll out half the dough to make a circle large enough to line a deep 23cm/9in ovenproof dish or tart tin (pan). Gently press the pastry into the corners of the dish and ensure that the pastry hangs over the sides slightly.

5 Roll out the remaining pastry to a circle large enough to make a lid and check it for size.

6 Peel the apples, remove their cores and chop them into small pieces. Toss the apple pieces with the cornflour until evenly coated and arrange them in the bottom of the pastry case. Scatter the whinberries on top and sprinkle the sugar over. Lightly brush the edges of the pastry with water.

7 Lay the pastry lid over the fruit filling. Trim off the excess pastry and pinch the edges together to seal them well. Make a small slit in the centre to allow the steam to escape, then brush the top with milk and sprinkle with a little sugar.

8 Put the pie into the hot oven and cook for approximately 30–40 minutes until the pastry is crisp and golden brown and the filling is cooked through. While the pie is still hot, sprinkle with more caster sugar and serve with a dollop of ice cream or piping hot custard.

Per portion Energy 403kcal/1688kJ; Protein 5.76g; Carbohydrate 51.4g, of which sugars 18.15g; Fat 20.8g, of which saturates 12.5g; Cholesterol 81.5mg; Calcium 98.6mg; Fibre 3,5g; Sodium 157.5mg.

Crunchy apple and almond flan

Do not be tempted to put any sugar with the apples, as this makes them produce too much liquid. All of the sweetness is in the pastry and the crunchy topping.

Serves 8
115g/4oz/1 cup plain (all-purpose) flour
1.5ml/¼ tsp mixed (apple pie) spice
50g/2oz/¼ cup butter, diced
50g/2oz/¼ cup demerara (raw) sugar
50g/2oz/½ cup flaked (sliced) almonds
675g/1½lb cooking apples
25g/1oz/3 tbsp raisins
icing (confectioners') sugar, for dusting

For the pastry
175g/6oz/1½ cups plain
  (all-purpose) flour
75g/3oz/6 tbsp butter, diced
25g/1oz/¼ cup ground almonds
25g/1oz/2 tbsp caster (superfine) sugar
1 egg yolk
15ml/1 tbsp cold water
1.5ml/¼ tsp almond extract

2 Meanwhile, make the topping. Sift the flour and mixed spice into a mixing bowl and rub in the butter with your fingertips. Stir in the demerara sugar and flaked almonds.

3 Roll out the pastry on a lightly floured work surface and use to line a 23cm/9in loose-based flan tin (quiche pan), taking care to press the pastry neatly into the edges and to make a lip around the top edge. Use a rolling pin to trim off the excess pastry and give a neat edge. Chill the pastry flan for 15 minutes.

4 Place a baking sheet in the oven and preheat to 190°C/375°F/Gas 5.

5 Peel, core and thinly slice the cooking apples. Arrange the slices in the pastry case in overlapping, concentric circles, creating a dome of apples in the centre. Sprinkle over the raisins.

6 Cover the apples with the crunchy topping mixture, pressing it on lightly. Place the flan on the hot baking sheet and bake for 25–30 minutes, or until the top is golden brown and the apples are tender (you can test them with a fine skewer). Leave the flan to cool in the tin for 10 minutes. Serve warm or cold, with a generous dusting of sifted icing sugar.

Per portion Energy 358kcal/1499kJ; Protein 6.2g; Carbohydrate 42.5g, of which sugars 14.6g; Fat 19.3g, of which saturates 8.8g; Cholesterol 59mg; Calcium 86mg; Fibre 3.2g; Sodium 102mg.

1 For the pastry, place the flour in a food processor or mixing bowl and rub in the butter until the mixture resembles fine breadcrumbs. Stir in the ground almonds and sugar. Whisk the egg yolk, water and almond extract together and mix into the dry ingredients to form a dough. Knead until smooth, wrap in clear film (plastic wrap) and leave in a cool place for 20 minutes.

Cook's tip
Don't worry if the pie seems too full after adding the apple slices; as the apples cook the filling will drop slightly.

Apple turnovers

These fruity pastry parcels are always popular, and since they are baked in the oven, are a slightly healthier option than fritters fried in oil.

Makes 12

250g/9oz/2¼ cups plain (all-purpose)
    flour, plus extra for dusting
2.5ml/½ tsp salt
90g/3½oz/scant ½ cup cold butter
5ml/1 tsp white wine vinegar
500g/1¼lb tart apples, such as
    Goudrenet or Granny Smith
45ml/3 tbsp soft brown sugar
5ml/1 tsp ground cinnamon
2.5ml/½ tsp crushed fennel seeds
beaten egg, to glaze
icing (confectioner's) sugar,
    for sprinkling

1 Sift the flour and salt into a bowl, coarsely grate in the butter and rub in with your fingertips. Using the blade of a knife, gradually stir in 100ml/3½fl oz/scant ½ cup water and the vinegar. Gather the dough together and shape into a ball.

2 Roll out the dough on a lightly floured surface, then fold the top edge down to the centre and the bottom edge up to the centre and roll out again to a rectangle.

3 Fold in three again, cover with clear film (plastic wrap) and leave to rest in the refrigerator.

4 Peel the apples and grate coarsely into a bowl. Stir in the sugar, cinnamon and fennel seeds.

5 Preheat the oven to 200°C/400°F/Gas 6. Line a 30 × 40cm/12 × 16in baking sheet with baking parchment.

6 Roll out the dough on a lightly floured surface to 36 × 48cm/14¼ × 19in rectangle, then cut into 12 squares. Cover the centre of each with some grated apple and fold over into a triangle. Press the edges together.

7 Transfer to the prepared baking sheet and brush with beaten egg. Prick the tops several times with a fork. Bake for about 35 minutes, until golden. Remove from the oven and leave to cool, then sprinkle with icing sugar.

Per item Energy 156kcal/658kJ; Protein 2.2g; Carbohydrate 23.9g, of which sugars 8g; Fat 6.5g, of which saturates 4g; Cholesterol 16mg; Calcium 34mg; Fibre 1.3g; Sodium 47mg.

Apple strudel

This classic recipe is usually made with strudel dough, but filo pastry makes a good shortcut.

Serves 4–6

75g/3oz/¾ cup hazelnuts, chopped
  and roasted
30ml/2 tbsp nibbed almonds, roasted
50g/2oz/4 tbsp demerara (raw) sugar
2.5ml/½ tsp ground cinnamon
grated rind and juice of ½ lemon
2 large cooking apples, peeled,
  cored and chopped
50g/2oz/⅓ cup sultanas (golden raisins)
4 large sheets filo pastry, thawed
  if frozen
50g/2oz/4 tbsp unsalted butter, melted
icing (confectioners') sugar,
  for dredging

1 Preheat the oven to 190°C/375°F/ Gas 5. In a bowl mix together the hazelnuts, almonds, sugar, cinnamon, lemon rind and juice, apples and sultanas. Set aside.

2 Lay one sheet of filo pastry on a floured surface and brush with melted butter. Lay a second sheet on top and brush again with melted butter. Repeat with the remaining two sheets.

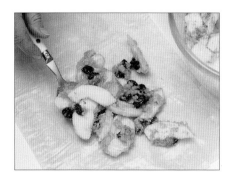

3 Put the apple filling on the pastry, with a 2.5cm/1in border all around.

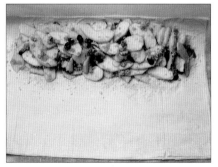

4 Fold in the two shorter sides to enclose the filling, then roll up like a Swiss (jelly) roll. Place on a lightly buttered baking sheet seam side down.

Cook's tip
Keep the filo sheets covered with a damp dish towel as you work.

5 Brush the pastry with the remaining butter. Bake for 30–40 minutes or until golden brown. Leave to cool before dusting generously with icing sugar. Serve the strudel warm or cold in thick diagonal slices.

Per portion Energy 287kcal/1199kJ; Protein 4.4g; Carbohydrate 29.1g, of which sugars 19.2g; Fat 17.8g, of which saturates 5.2g; Cholesterol 18mg; Calcium 60mg; Fibre 2.4g; Sodium 55mg.

PRESERVES

Preserving seasonal fruits and vegetables was once essential for survival and is one of the oldest of culinary arts. From tart to sweet, the range of apple flavours makes them a perfect addition to preserves such as jams, jellies, marmalades, sauces and chutneys, even spiced 'butter' and mincemeat.

Blackberry and apple cheese

This rich, dark preserve has an incredibly intense flavour.

Makes about 900g/2lb
900g/2lb/8 cups blackberries
450g/1lb tart cooking apples, cut
   into chunks, with skins and
   cores included
grated rind and juice of 1 lemon
800g/1¾lb/4 cups sugar, warmed

1 Put the blackberries, apples and lemon rind and juice in a pan and pour in enough water to come halfway up the fruit. Bring to the boil, then simmer uncovered for 15–20 minutes.

2 Leave the fruit to cool slightly, then turn into a sieve (strainer) and press into a bowl, using the back of a spoon. Measure the purée into a large, heavy pan, adding 400g/14oz/ 2 cups warmed sugar for every 600ml/1 pint/2½ cups purée.

3 Gently heat the purée, stirring, until the sugar dissolves. Increase the heat slightly and cook for 40–50 minutes, stirring frequently, until very thick.

4 Spoon the cheese into warmed, sterilized straight-sided jars or oiled moulds. Seal and label the jars or moulds. Store them in a cool, dark place for 2–3 months to dry out slightly.

> ### Cook's tip
> When the cheese is ready, you should be able to see the base of the pan when a wooden spoon is drawn through the mixture. Spoon a small amount of the mixture on to a chilled plate; it should form a firm jelly.

Per 900g/2lb Energy 3534kcal/15064kJ; Protein 13.5g; Carbohydrate 921.9g, of which sugars 921.9g; Fat 2.3g, of which saturates 0g; Cholesterol 0mg; Calcium 811mg; Fibre 35.1g; Sodium 75mg.

Apple sauce

Really more of a condiment than a sauce, this tart purée is usually served cold or warm, rather than hot. It is traditional with roast pork or duck, but it is also good with sausages, burgers, cold meats, pork pies, hot or cold meatloaf or cheese.

Serves 6
225g/8oz cooking apples
30ml/2 tbsp water
a thin strip of lemon rind
15g/½ oz/1 tbsp butter
15–30ml/1–2 tbsp sugar

1 Peel the apples, cut into quarters and remove the cores. Dice or thinly slice the apple quarters.

2 Place the apples in a pan with the water and lemon rind. Cook, uncovered, over a low heat until very soft, stirring occasionally.

3 Remove the lemon rind from the pan and discard. Beat the apples to a pulp with a spoon.

4 Stir in the butter, then add sugar to taste. Transfer to a serving dish, cover and leave to cool before serving.

Per portion Energy 60kcal/251kJ; Protein 0.2g; Carbohydrate 6g, of which sugars 6g; Fat 4.1g, of which saturates 2.7g; Cholesterol 11mg; Calcium 4mg; Fibre 0.6g; Sodium 35mg.

Rowan and crab apple jelly

This astringent jelly is made from the orange fruit of mountain ash trees. It is a traditional accompaniment to game, especially venison.

Makes about 2.25kg/5lb
1.3kg/3lb/12 cups rowan berries
450g/1lb crab apples, or windfall
    cooking apples
450g/1lb/2¼ cups sugar per 600ml/
    1 pint/2½ cups juice, warmed

1 Cut the rowan berries off their stalks, rinse them in a colander and put them into a preserving pan.

2 Remove any badly damaged parts from the apples before weighing them, then cut them up roughly without peeling or coring. Add the apples to the pan, with 1.2 litres/2 pints/5 cups water, which should just cover the fruit.

3 Bring to the boil and simmer for about 45 minutes, until the fruit is soft, stirring occasionally and crushing the fruit with a wooden spoon to help extract the pectin. Strain the fruit through a scalded jelly bag or a fine sieve into a bowl overnight.

4 Measure the juice and allow 450g/1lb/2¼ cups sugar per 600ml/ 1 pint/2½ cups juice. Return the juice to the rinsed preserving pan and add the measured amount of sugar.

5 Stir over a low heat until the sugar has dissolved, and then bring to the boil and boil hard for about 10 minutes until setting point is reached. To test, put a spoonful of jam on to a cold saucer.

6 Allow to cool slightly, and then push the surface of the jam with your finger. Setting point has been reached if a skin has formed. If not, boil a little longer and keep testing until it sets.

7 Skim, if necessary, and pour into warmed, sterilized jars. Cover, seal and store in a cool, dark place until needed. The jelly will store well for 6 months.

Per 2.25kg/5lb Energy 2340kcal/9993kJ; Protein 15.8g; Carbohydrate 606.4g, of which sugars 606.4g; Fat 0.5g, of which saturates 0g; Cholesterol 0mg; Calcium 1.03g; Fibre 54g; Sodium 80mg.

Rosehip and apple jelly

This economical jelly is made with windfall apples and wild rosehips. It is rich in vitamin C and full of flavour.

Makes about 2kg/4½lb
1kg/2¼lb windfall cooking apples,
    peeled, trimmed and quartered
450g/1lb firm, ripe rosehips
about 1.3kg/3lb/6½ cups sugar, warmed

1 Place the quartered apples in a large pan with just enough water to cover, plus 300ml/½ pint/1¼ cups of extra water. Bring the mixture to the boil and cook gently until the apples soften and turn to a pulp.

2 Chop the rosehips coarsely. Add them to the pan with the apple and simmer for a further 10 minutes.

3 Remove from the heat and leave to stand for 10 minutes. Pour the mixture into a scalded jelly bag suspended over a non-metallic bowl. Leave to drain overnight.

4 Measure the juice into a preserving pan and bring to the boil. Add 400g/14oz/2 cups warmed sugar for each 600ml/1 pint/2½ cups of liquid. Stir until the sugar has completely dissolved. Boil, without stirring, for 10 minutes, or until the jelly reaches setting point (105°C/220°F).

5 Pour the jelly into warmed, sterilized jars and seal. Label and store when completely cold.

Per 2kg/4½lb Energy 5684kcal/24,259kJ; Protein 8.4g; Carbohydrate 1505.7g, of which sugars 1505.7g; Fat 0.5g, of which saturates 0g; Cholesterol 0mg; Calcium 761mg; Fibre 7.7g; Sodium 94mg.

Spiced cider and apple jelly

This wonderful spicy jelly has a rich, warming flavour, making it ideal to serve during the cold winter months. Serve as a spread or use it to sweeten apple pies and desserts.

Makes about 1.3kg/3lb

900g/2lb tart cooking apples, coarsely chopped with skins and cores included

900ml/1¼ pints/3¾ cups sweet (hard) cider

juice and pips (seeds) of 2 oranges

1 cinnamon stick

6 whole cloves

150ml/½ pint/⅔ cup water

about 900g/2lb/4½ cups sugar, warmed

1 Put the apples, cider, juice and pips, cinnamon, cloves and water in a large pan. Bring to the boil, cover and simmer for about 1 hour.

2 Leave to cool slightly, then pour the fruit into a scalded jelly bag suspended over a non-metallic bowl and leave to drain overnight.

Cook's tip

There is no need to remove all the peel from the apples: simply cut out any bruised, damaged or bad areas.

3 Measure the strained juice into a preserving pan. Add 450g/1lb/2¼ cups warmed sugar for every 600ml/1 pint/2½ cups juice.

4 Heat, stirring, over a low heat until the sugar has dissolved. Increase the heat and boil, without stirring, for 10 minutes, or until the jelly reaches setting point (105°C/220°F).

5 Remove from the heat and skim off any scum. Ladle into warmed sterilized jars. Cover, seal and label.

Per 1.3kg/3lb Energy 3975kcal/16,950kJ; Protein 5.4g; Carbohydrate 990.6g, of which sugars 990.6g; Fat 0.3g, of which saturates 0g; Cholesterol 0mg; Calcium 561mg; Fibre 4.8g; Sodium 123mg.

Apple and cinnamon butter

Fans of apple pies and crumbles will love this luscious apple butter.

Makes about 1.8kg/4lb
475ml/16fl oz/2 cups dry (hard) cider
450g/1lb tart cooking apples, peeled, cored and sliced
450g/1lb eating apples, peeled, cored and sliced
grated rind and juice of 1 lemon
675g/1½lb/scant 3½ cups sugar, warmed
5ml/1 tsp ground cinnamon

1 Pour the cider into a large pan and bring to the boil. Boil hard until the volume is reduced by half, then add the apples and lemon rind and juice. Cover the pan. Cook for 10 minutes. Uncover and cook for 20–30 minutes.

2 Leave the mixture to cool slightly, then blend to a purée. Press through a fine sieve (strainer) into a bowl.

3 Measure the purée into a large, heavy pan, adding 275g/10oz/1⅓ cups warmed sugar for every 600ml/1 pint/2½ cups of purée. Add the ground cinnamon and stir well to combine.

4 Gently heat the mixture, stirring continuously, until the sugar dissolves. Increase the heat and boil steadily for 20 minutes, stirring frequently, until it forms a thick purée. Spoon the butter into warmed sterilized jars. Seal and label, then store in a cool, dark place for 2 days.

Per 1.8kg/4lb Energy 3145kcal/13,428kJ; Protein 6.1g; Carbohydrate 797.8g, of which sugars 797.8g; Fat 0.9g, of which saturates 0g; Cholesterol 0mg; Calcium 432mg; Fibre 14.4g; Sodium 92mg.

Spiced apple mincemeat

This fruity mincemeat is traditionally used to fill little pies at Christmas but it is great at any time. Try it as a filling for large tarts finished with a lattice top and served with custard. To make a lighter mincemeat, add some extra grated apple just before using.

Makes about 1.8kg/4lb
500g/1¼lb tart cooking apples, peeled, cored and finely diced
115g/4oz/½ cup ready-to-eat dried apricots, coarsely chopped
900g/2lb/5⅓ cups luxury dried mixed fruit
115g/4oz/1 cup whole blanched almonds, chopped
175g/6oz/1 cup shredded beef or vegetarian suet (chilled, grated shortening)
225g/8oz/1 cup dark muscovado (molasses) sugar
grated rind and juice of 1 orange
grated rind and juice of 1 lemon
5ml/1 tsp ground cinnamon
2.5ml/½ tsp freshly grated nutmeg
2.5ml/½ tsp ground ginger
120ml/4fl oz/½ cup brandy

1 Put the apples, apricots, dried fruit, almonds, suet and sugar in a large non-metallic bowl and stir together until thoroughly combined.

2 Add the orange and lemon rind and juice, cinnamon, nutmeg, ginger and brandy and mix well.

3 Cover the bowl with a clean dish towel and leave to stand in a cool place for 2 days, stirring occasionally.

4 Spoon the mincemeat into cool sterilized jars, pressing down well, and being very careful not to trap any air bubbles. Cover and seal.

5 Store the jars in a cool, dark place for at least 4 weeks before using.

6 Once opened, store in the refrigerator and use within 4 weeks. Unopened, the mincemeat will keep for 1 year.

Per 1.8kg/4lb Energy 6071kcal/25,579kJ; Protein 52.2g; Carbohydrate 963.6g, of which sugars 939.7g; Fat 227.3g, of which saturates 92.4g; Cholesterol 144mg; Calcium 1156mg; Fibre 44.4g; Sodium 488mg.

Apple and tomato chutney

This mellow, golden, spicy chutney makes the most of fresh autumn produce. Any type of organic tomatoes can be used successfully in this recipe.

Makes about 1.8kg/4lb

1.3kg/3lb cooking apples
1.3kg/3lb tomatoes
2 large onions
2 garlic cloves
250g/9oz/1¾ cups pitted dates
2 red (bell) peppers
3 dried red chillies
15ml/1 tbsp black peppercorns
4 cardamom pods
15ml/1 tbsp coriander seeds
10ml/2 tsp cumin seeds
10ml/2 tsp ground turmeric
5ml/1 tsp salt
600ml/1 pint/2½ cups distilled
    malt vinegar
1kg/2¼lb/5¼ cups unrefined sugar
    or rapadura

1 Peel and chop the apples. Peel and chop the tomatoes, onions and garlic. Quarter the dates. Core and seed the peppers, then cut into chunky pieces. Put all the prepared ingredients, except the red peppers, into a preserving pan.

2 Slit the chillies. Put the peppercorns and remaining spices into a mortar and roughly crush with a pestle. Add the chillies, spices and salt to the pan.

3 Pour in the vinegar and sugar, bring to the boil and simmer for 30 minutes, stirring occasionally. Add the red pepper and cook for a further 30 minutes, stirring more frequently as the chutney becomes thick and pulpy.

4 Spoon the chutney into warm, dry, sterilized jars. Seal each jar, label and leave to cool. Store in a cool, dry place.

Per 1.8kg/4lb Energy 5583kcal/23818kJ; Protein 35.7g; Carbohydrate 1432.9g, of which sugars 1420.3g; Fat 8.1g, of which saturates 1.9g; Cholesterol 0mg; Calcium 940mg; Fibre 56.4g; Sodium 6152mg.

Apple and red onion marmalade

This marmalade chutney is good enough to eat on its own. Serve it with good pork sausages for thoroughly modern hot dogs or in a ham sandwich instead of mustard.

Makes 450g/1lb

60ml/4 tbsp extra virgin olive oil
900g/2lb red onions, thinly sliced
75g/3oz/scant ½ cup demerara (raw)
    sugar
2 Cox's Orange Pippin apples
90ml/6 tbsp cider vinegar

1 Heat the oil in a large, heavy pan. Add the onions. Stir in the sugar and cook, uncovered, over a medium heat for 40 minutes, stirring occasionally, or until the onions have softened and become a rich golden colour.

2 Peel, core and grate the apples. Add them to the pan with the vinegar and continue to cook for 20 minutes until the chutney is thick and sticky. Spoon into a sterilized jar and cover.

3 When cool, label and store in the refrigerator for up to 1 month.

Per 450g/1lb Energy 1271kcal/5298kJ; Protein 13g; Carbohydrate 173g, of which sugars 152g; Fat 62g, of which saturates 8.6g; Cholesterol 0mg; Calcium 257mg; Fibre 16.6g; Sodium 41mg.

Kashmir chutney

In the true tradition of the Kashmiri country store, this is a typical family recipe passed down from generation to generation. It is wonderful served with plain or spicy grilled sausages.

Makes about 2.75kg/6lb
1kg/2¼lb green eating apples
15g/½oz garlic cloves
1 litre/1¾ pints/4 cups malt vinegar
450g/1lb pitted dates
115g/4oz preserved stem ginger
450g/1lb/3 cups raisins
450g/1lb/2 cups soft light brown sugar
2.5ml/½ tsp cayenne pepper
30ml/2 tbsp salt

1 Quarter the apples, remove the cores and chop coarsely, then peel and chop the garlic.

2 Place the apples and garlic in a pan with enough vinegar to cover. Bring to the boil and boil for 10 minutes.

3 Chop the dates and ginger and add them to the pan, together with the rest of the ingredients. Cook gently for 45 minutes.

4 Spoon the mixture into warmed sterilized jars and seal immediately.

> **Cook's tip**
> This sweet, chunky, spicy chutney is perfect served with cold meats for an informal buffet lunch.

Per 2.75kg/6lb Energy 3920kcal/16,737kJ; Protein 22.6g; Carbohydrate 1014.4g, of which sugars 1012.2g; Fat 3.3g, of which saturates 0g; Cholesterol 0mg; Calcium 599mg; Fibre 33.7g; Sodium 12139mg.

Apple and sultana chutney

The chutney is perfect served with farmhouse cheese and freshly made soda bread.

Makes about 900g/2lb
350g/12oz cooking apples
115g/4oz/⅔ cup sultanas (golden raisins)
50g/2oz onion
25g/1oz/¼ cup almonds, blanched
5ml/1 tsp white peppercorns
2.5ml/½ tsp coriander seeds
175g/6oz/scant 1 cup sugar
10ml/2 tsp salt
5ml/1 tsp ground ginger
450ml/¾ pint/scant 2 cups cider vinegar
1.5ml/¼ tsp cayenne pepper
red chillies (optional)

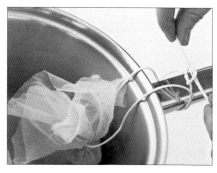

1 Peel, core and chop the apples. Chop the sultanas, onion and almonds. Tie the peppercorns and coriander seeds in muslin (cheesecloth), using a long piece of string, and then tie to the handle of a preserving pan or stainless steel pan.

2 Put the sugar, salt, ground ginger and cider vinegar into the pan, with the cayenne pepper to taste. Heat gently, stirring, until the sugar has completely dissolved.

3 Add the chopped apples, sultanas, onion and almonds. Bring to the boil and simmer for 1½–2 hours, or until most of the liquid has evaporated.

4 Spoon into warmed, sterilized jars and place one chilli in each jar, if using. Leave until cold, then cover, seal and label.

5 Store in a cool dark place. The chutney is best left for a month to mature before use and will keep for at least 6 months, if correctly stored.

Per 900g/2lb Energy 1299kcal/5525kJ; Protein 10.9g; Carbohydrate 299.5g, of which sugars 297.7g; Fat 14.9g, of which saturates 1.1g; Cholesterol 0mg; Calcium 254mg; Fibre 10.4g; Sodium 3.97g.

DRINKS

Apples can be used to make a wide selection of refreshing drinks, both of the alcoholic and the non-alcoholic varieties. For a hot summer's day choose a zingy Apple and Cranberry Spritzer or for a winter warmer a Mulled Cider. For a more substantial refreshment, how about an Apple and Barley Flummery?

Apple and cranberry spritzer

This colourful, zingy cooler combines tangy cranberries with fresh juicy apples and a fragrant hint of vanilla. Top up with sparkling mineral water for a truly refreshing spritzer.

Serves 6–8
6 red eating apples
375g/13oz/3½ cups fresh or frozen
   cranberries, plus extra to decorate
45ml/3 tbsp vanilla syrup
ice cubes
sparkling mineral water

1 Quarter and core the apples then cut the flesh into pieces small enough to fit through a juicer. Push the cranberries and apple chunks through the juicer. Add the vanilla syrup to the juice, cover with clear film (plastic wrap) and chill until ready to serve.

2 Pour the juice into glasses and add one or two ice cubes to each. Top up with sparkling mineral water and decorate with extra cranberries, threaded on to cocktail sticks (toothpicks). Serve immediately.

Per portion Energy 59kcal/255kJ; Protein 0.4g; Carbohydrate 15.3g, of which sugars 15.3g; Fat 0.1g, of which saturates 0g; Cholesterol 0mg; Calcium 6mg; Fibre 2g; Sodium 18mg.

Sweet, sharp shock

The combination of sweet red grape and tart apple is quite delicious. For a longer drink add sparkling water.

Serves 1
150g/5oz/1¼ cups red grapes
1 red eating apple
1 small cooking apple
crushed ice

1 Slice some grapes and a sliver or two of apple for the decoration. Roughly chop the remaining apples. Push through a juicer with the grapes.

2 Pour over crushed ice, decorate with the sliced fruit and serve immediately.

> **Cook's tip**
> Sugary grapes together with tart apples is one of those perfect flavour combinations that cannot be beaten.

Per portion Energy 156kcal/666kj; Protein 1.2g; Carbohydrate 39.7g, of which sugars 39.7g; Fat 0.3g, of which saturates 0g; Cholesterol 0g; Calcium 25g; Fibre 5.2g; Sodium 7g.

Strawberry apple slush

Sweet, juicy strawberries make a delicately fragrant juice. The addition of fresh apple juice and just a hint of vanilla creates a tantalizing treat that's perfect for sipping on a long, lazy summer's afternoon.

Serves 2

300g/11oz/2¾ cups ripe strawberries
2 small, crisp eating apples
10ml/2 tsp vanilla syrup
crushed ice

1 Put aside a couple of the strawberries and hull the remaining ones. Roughly chop the apples. Push all the fruits through a juicer and then stir in the vanilla syrup.

2 Half-fill two tall glasses with crushed ice. Pour over the juice, decorate with the reserved strawberries (slicing them if you like) and serve immediately.

Per portion Energy 95kcal/400kJ; Protein 2g; Carbohydrate 23g, of which sugars 23g; Fat 0g, of which saturates 0g; Cholesterol 0mg; Calcium 28mg; Fibre 3.5g; Sodium 100mg.

Apple-spiced beer

Lager takes on a whole new dimension in this fun and fruity cooler. Diluted with freshly squeezed apple juice and flavoured with ginger and star anise, it's a great drink for anyone who wants to pace themselves through a party. The spiced apple juice can be made several hours in advance and chilled in a serving jug (pitcher), ready for topping up at the last minute.

Serves 8–10

8 eating apples
25g/1oz fresh root ginger
6 whole star anise
800ml/1⅓ pints/3½ cups lager
crushed ice

1 Quarter and core the apples and, using a small, sharp knife, cut the flesh into pieces small enough to fit through a juicer. Roughly chop the ginger. Push half the apples through the juicer, then juice the ginger and the remaining apples.

2 Put 105ml/7 tbsp of the juice in a small pan with the star anise and heat gently until almost boiling. Add to the remaining juice in a large jug (pitcher) and chill for at least 1 hour.

3 Add the lager to the juice and stir gently to help disperse the froth. Pour over crushed ice in tall glasses and serve immediately.

Per portion Energy 42kcal/178kJ; Protein 0.4g; Carbohydrate 4.8g, of which sugars 4.8g; Fat 0.1g, of which saturates 0g; Cholesterol 0mg; Calcium 6mg; Fibre 0.9g; Sodium 7mg.

Apple and barley flummery

The Celtic countries share this old recipe, which is usually a cooked cold sweet based on oatmeal. This Irish variation is based on barley and also includes apples; sago or tapioca could replace the barley.

Serves 4–6
90ml/6 tbsp pearl barley
675g/1½lb cooking apples, such as
  Bramley's Seedling
50g/2oz/¼ cup caster (superfine) sugar
juice of 1 lemon
45–60ml/3–4 tbsp double (heavy) cream

1 Put 1 litre/1¾ pints/4 cups of water into a pan. Add the barley and bring gently to the boil.

2 Peel, core and slice the apples. Add them to the pan and continue cooking gently until the barley is soft and the apples are cooked.

3 Liquidize the mixture, or press through a sieve (strainer), and return to the rinsed pan. Add the sugar and lemon juice and bring back to the boil.

4 Remove from the heat and allow to cool. Pour into individual glasses, and chill until required. Stir in the cream and serve cold.

Per portion Energy 245kcal/1040kJ; Protein 2.5g; Carbohydrate 47.1g, of which sugars 28.3g; Fat 6.6g, of which saturates 3.8g; Cholesterol 15mg; Calcium 24mg; Fibre 2.7g; Sodium 7mg.

Cranberry and apple punch

This fruit punch is prepared in a slow cooker which extracts maximum flavour from the ginger and lime peel.

Serves 6
1 lime
5cm/2in piece of fresh root ginger,
  peeled and thinly sliced
50g/2oz/¼ cup caster (superfine) sugar
200ml/7fl oz/scant 1 cup near-boiling
  water
475ml/16fl oz/2 cups cranberry juice
475ml/16fl oz/2 cups clear apple juice
ice and chilled sparkling mineral water
  or soda water, to serve (optional)

1 Pare the rind off the lime and place in the slow cooker pot with the ginger and sugar. Pour over the water and stir until the sugar dissolves. Cover and heat on high or auto for 1 hour, then reduce the temperature to low or leave on auto and heat for a further 2 hours. Switch off the slow cooker and leave the syrup to cool completely.

2 Strain the syrup through a fine sieve (strainer) into a punch bowl and discard the ginger and lime rind. Squeeze the juice from the lime and strain through a sieve into the syrup. Stir in the cranberry and apple juices. Cover and chill in the refrigerator for 3 hours.

3 Ladle the punch over ice in tall glasses and top up with water if using.

Per portion: Energy 111kcal/475kJ; Protein 0.1g; Carbohydrate 27.9g, of which sugars 16.5g; Fat 0.1g, of which saturates 0g; Cholesterol 0mg; Calcium 8mg; Fibre 0g; Sodium 2mg.

Drivers' special

For best results when making this bubbly non-alcoholic cocktail always try to use the cloudy natural pressed varieties of apple juice.

Serves 10
1.2 litres/2 pints/5 cups unsweetened apple juice
juice of 1 lemon
4 small red eating apples
1.2 litres/2 pints/5 cups ginger beer
ice cubes, to serve
lemon slices or mint sprigs, to decorate

1 Mix the apple juice and lemon juice in a large glass jug (pitcher).

2 Wash and core the apples, but do not peel them. Slice thinly and add the slices to the jug. Stir well and, to prevent browning, check that all the slices are immersed.

3 Cover and set aside in the refrigerator to chill until required.

4 Shortly before serving, add some ice cubes and the ginger beer to the jug, and decorate with lemon slices, or sprigs of mint. Serve in tall glasses.

Per portion Energy 82kcal/352kJ; Protein 0.2g; Carbohydrate 21.4g, of which sugars 21.4g; Fat 0.2g, of which saturates 0g; Cholesterol 0mg; Calcium 15mg; Fibre 0.4g; Sodium 11mg.

Mulled cider

This hot cider cup is easy to make and traditional at Halloween, but it makes a good and inexpensive warming brew for any winter gathering.

Serves 20
2 lemons
1 litre/1¾ pints/4 cups apple juice
2 litres/3½ pints/9 cups medium sweet (hard) cider
3 small cinnamon sticks
4–6 whole cloves
slices of lemon, to serve (optional)

1 Wash the lemons and pare the rinds with a vegetable peeler. Blend all the ingredients together in a large stainless steel pan.

2 Set over a low heat and heat the mixture through to infuse (steep) for 15 minutes; do not allow it to boil.

3 Strain the liquid and serve with extra slices of lemon, if you like.

Per portion Energy 61kcal/258kJ; Protein 0.1g; Carbohydrate 9.3g, of which sugars 9.3g; Fat 0.1g, of which saturates 0g; Cholesterol 0mg; Calcium 12mg; Fibre 0g; Sodium 8mg.

GLOSSARY

The following is a glossary of terms used in this book. Words in definitions in *italics* have their own entry.

Anther The part of a flower's *stamen* that produces *pollen*.

Bare-root Describes a field-grown plant that is dug up for sale during the dormant period. *See also* container-grown.

Biennial bearing The tendency of a tree to produce a crop in alternate years, sometimes caused by lack of nutrients at critical times or incorrect pruning. Some varieties are more prone to biennial bearing than others.

Blossom end The base of a fruit, opposite the *stalk*.

Bordeaux mixture A copper-based fungicide widely used to control disease.

Bud A growing point on a plant's stem from which new growth will emerge; also, a flower bud.

Bud-grafting A method of *grafting*.

Bush A bushy tree grown with a trunk of 75–90cm (2.5–3ft).

Cambium A layer of tissue beneath the bark of woody plants, capable of producing new cells to increase the girth of stems and roots.

Central leader tree A tree that is allowed to develop its natural size and habit on a single, upright trunk.

Chilling requirement The need for a period below a certain temperature during the *dormancy* phase for flowering to be initiated.

Chip-budding A method of *grafting*.

Compatible Used to describe apple varieties that are capable of pollinating each other. For successful fruit set, the flowers of each must be open at the same time.

Container-grown A plant that has been

Below: Beauty of Bath

cultivated in a container. Such plants, generally available year-round, are always more expensive than *bare-root* plants.

Cordon A vigorous, upright stem that has usually been trained to grow at an angle. Short, stubby side shoots bear the fruit. Cordons must be trained in to a system of horizontal wires.

Crab A wild apple (or hybrid of one of these), grown mainly for the ornamental value of its spring blossom and small autumn fruits (inedible raw, these can be used to make preserves and jellies). Crab apples also make useful *pollinators*.

Cross-pollination The transfer of pollen from the anther of one flower to the stigma of one on another. Cross-pollination is often necessary for reliable fruiting.

Crown The top-growth of a tree.

Cultivar A selected form of a species that has arisen in cultivation, e.g. *Malus domestica* 'Golden Delicious'.

Deciduous Of a tree, losing its leaves in autumn and producing new ones the following spring.

Derris An organic pesticide, formerly widely used. Owing to its extreme toxicity, its use is not universally considered ecologically sound.

Diploid A variety of apple that carries 34 chromosomes, 17 from each parent. Diploid apples need the presence of a single compatible *cultivar* to set fruit. Most apples are diploids. *See also* triploid.

Dormancy The period when a plant is not in active growth. Usually the term is applied to plants during the winter resting period, though they can also experience dormancy during hot, dry periods in summer.

Espalier An apple grown as a series of evenly spaced branches trained strictly to the horizontal on a system of wires.

Ethylene A gaseous organic compound that is given off by fruits in storage.

Family tree A tree that comprises two or more separate varieties grafted on to a single *rootstock*.

Fan A method of growing whereby stems are trained in a fan arrangement, usually on a system of horizontal wires against a wall.

Fertilization The fusion of *pollen* with an ovule to produce fertile seed. *See also* cross-pollination.

Fertilizer An organic or inorganic product containing concentrated nutrients, added to

Above: Malus evereste *crab apple blossom.*

the soil) or sometimes sprayed on foliage).

Filament Stalk that bears the anther at its tip, together forming a stamen.

Fleece *See* horticultural fleece.

Fruit thinning Reducing the number of fruits carried by a tree to improve the quality of the ones remaining.

Fungicide A product that kills fungal spores (and usually also bacteria). Fungicide can be applied as a powder or solution.

Gall A tumour on a plant, usually a symptom of a disease spread by an insect vector. Some galls are benign.

Germination The emergence of the embryo plant from a seed.

Graft union The point at which the *scion* and *rootstock* are united.

Grafting The technique by which a stem cutting (the *scion*) from one plant is united with the roots (*rootstock*) of another so that they develop as a single plant.

Half standard A tree allowed to develop with a clear trunk of 1.35m (4ft).

Hardy A term applied to plants that are able to withstand frost.

Heirloom plant A cultivar that was once commonly grown but which is not now grown comercially. Heirloom plants are becoming more popular with gardeners in North America and Europe.

Hermaphrodite Having both male and female sex cells within the same flower.

Horticultural fleece A lightweight synthetic fabric used to protect blossom from overnight frosts (and also the roots of plants in containers). Fleece also offers some protection from flying insect pests.

Hybrid A plant that has been produced by crossing two distinct species.

Hybridization The process of crossing distinct species (or their hybrids) to produce new plants. Back-crossing with one of the parents can consolidate certain desirable characteristics.

Insecticide A product that kills insects.

June drop A natural phenomenon whereby trees shed excess fruits during late spring to early summer.

Lateral Describing the main side branches of a woody plant, usually showing a tendency to grow outwards.

Leader The main stem of a tree or shrub, which usually has a strong tendency to grow straight upwards.

Leaf mould A soil improver comprising the decomposed leaves of *deciduous* trees.

Lorette system A method of pruning trained trees in summer.

Maiden whip A young grafted tree without *laterals*.

Mulch Any material, but usually of organic origin, spread around the base of a plant directly on the soil to suppress weeds, keep roots cool and moist, and, if organic, feed the plant and improve soil structure as it breaks down.

Organic Of animal or plant origin.

Organic matter Decomposed plant remains and animal waste.

Partial tip-bearing Used to refer to a *variety* that bears its fruits on *spurs* but also at the tips of branches. *See also* spur-bearing *and* tip-bearing.

Perlite Small granules of expanded volcanic rock, usually added to *potting compost* to improve drainage.

pH A measure of the acidity or alkalinity of soil. A pH of 7 indicates that the soil is neutral, lower than 7 is acid, higher is alkaline.

Pheromone A secreted or excreted chemical factor that triggers a social response in members of the same species.

Pheromone traps Traps containing synthetic pheromones, used to indicate the presence of codling moth or other flying insect pests in apple trees.

Below: Ripe apples ready to harvest.

Pollen The male sex cells of a flower, which are formed in the *anther*.

Pollination The process by which pollen is transferred from the male reproductive organs (*anther*) to the female reproductive organs (*stigma*) to form seeds. Pollination can be effected by the wind or by insects.

Polypoidy The presence of a larger than usual number of chromosomes.

Pot-bound Describes a container-grown plant, with roots tightly filling the container. Pot-bound plants usually fail to establish and can show signs of die-back.

Potting compost A proprietary, sterile planting mixture, suitable for growing plants in containers.

Potting on The process of transplanting a plant into a container of the next size up.

Protected Geographical Status (PGS) A legal framework defined in European Union law to protect the names of regional foods, including certain apple varieties.

Pyramid A conical tree grown with a strong central *leader*.

Rind grafting A method of *grafting* often used to produce a *family tree*.

Rootball The roots and the soil or compost that clings to them when a plant is lifted from the ground or from a container.

Rootstock A plant that is used to provide the root system for a grafted plant. Rootstocks can confer certain desirable characteristics on the plants, e.g. vigour, a dwarf habit, resistance to disease and tolerance of certain soil types, etc.

Russeting A rough, dull marking, usually beige or brown, on the skin of an apple. Some varieties show more russeting than others, but many have no russeting at all.

Sap A general term for the fluid contained in the system of a plant.

Scion A shoot cut from one plant for *grafting* on to a rootstock.

Self-fertile An apple variety that bears fruit without the need of a pollinator nearby.

Self-sterile Used of an apple variety that cannot pollinate itself.

Side shoot A shoot that emerges from a main stem or branch, often at right angles.

Spur A short, stubby branch, arising from a *lateral* (sometimes from a *leader* or *sub-lateral*), bearing flowers and, later, fruits.

Spur-bearing Refers to a variety that produces its fruits on short, knobbly *spurs* that grow out of the length of the shoot. *See also* partial tip-bearing *and* tip-bearing.

Stalk The small slender stem that bears first the flower then the fruit. Apples are normally harvested with their stalks intact.

Stamen The male floral organ, bearing

an anther, generally on a *filament*, and producing *pollen*.

Standard A tree allowed to develop with a clear trunk of 2–2.1m (6–6.9ft).

Stepover A method of training whereby horizontal branches are pulled down low to the ground, so the entire plant is low-growing.

Stigma The female part of a flower that receives the *pollen*, leading to *fertilization*.

Stratification The process of chilling a fertile seed to break its dormancy and speed up the *germination* process.

Sub-lateral A stem, usually pointing upwards, arising from a *lateral*.

Temperate A term relating to climate zones between the subtropics and the polar regions, which experience four distinct seasons.

Tip-bearing Used to refer to a *variety* that produces its fruits at or near the ends of shoots. *See also* spur-bearing *and* partial tip-bearing.

Train To guide the stems of a plant, often contrary to its natural habit of growth.

Top-growth The parts of a plant that are above ground level.

Tree guard A collar placed around the base of the trunk of a young tree to protect the bark from rabbits and other pests.

Triploid A variety of apple with 51 chromosomes, 17 from the male parent and a double set of 34 from the female. For successful fruiting on a triploid variety, two other *pollinators* are required.

Trunk The principal central woody stem of a tree.

Variety An alternative term for *cultivar*.

Vector An insect or other invertebrate pest that introduces viruses or other diseases into plants as it feeds.

Vermiculite A lightweight, mica-like material added to *potting compost* to improve the drainage.

Whip *See* maiden whip.

Whip-and-tongue grafting A method of *grafting*.

Below: Captain Kidd.

INDEX

Below: May Queen.

Above: Opalescent.

Above: Pitmaston Pineapple.

Below: Winston.

Above: Delgollune.

Below: Golden Russet.

Above: Woolbrook Pippin.

Below: Jonagored.

Above: Rossie Pippin.

Below: Present van Holland.

Above: Annurca.

Below: Fukinishiki.